Keys to School Leadership

Phil Ridden &
John De Nobile

Text copyright © Phil Ridden and John De Nobile 2024

Third edition, 2024
Edwest Publishing,
Connolly, Western Australia, Australia.
www.edwestpublishing.biz

First published as paperback 2012 by ACER Press, an imprint of
Australian Council *for* Educational Research Ltd,
Camberwell, Victoria, Australia

This book is copyright. All rights reserved. Except under the conditions described in the *Copyright Act* 1968 of Australia and subsequent amendments, and any exceptions permitted under the current statutory licence scheme administered by Copyright Agency (www.copyright com.au), no part of this publication may be reproduced, stored in a retrieval system, transmitted, broadcast or communicated in any form or by any means, optical, digital, electronic, mechanical, photocopying, recording or otherwise, without the written permission of the authors.

ISBN: 9780645754643 (Paperback)
ISBN: 9780645754650 (E-book)

National Library of Australia Cataloguing-in-Publication entry:
Keys to School Leadership by Phil Ridden and John De Nobile.
Includes bibliographical references.

CONTENTS

Acknowledgements iii
The authors iv
INTRODUCTION 1
ADMINISTRATION, LEADERSHIP AND INFLUENCE 5
From administration to leadership 5
Beyond leadership to influence 15
TASKS, GOALS AND ACHIEVEMENT 24
From tasks to goals 24
Beyond goals to achievement 36
MAINTENANCE, IMPROVEMENT AND ALIGNMENT ... 49
From maintenance to improvement 49
Beyond improvement to alignment 62
INDIVIDUALS, TEAMS AND PARTNERSHIPS 74
From individual to team 74
Beyond team to partnership 84
DELEGATION, NEGOTIATION AND COLLABORATION 92
From delegation to negotiation 92
Beyond negotiation to collaboration 101
THE CLASSROOM, THE SCHOOL AND THE WORLD ... 114
From the classroom to the school 114
Beyond the school to the world 121

DEPENDENCY, EMPOWERMENT AND SUCCESSION .. 133
From dependency to empowerment... 133
Beyond empowerment to succession 142
ROLES, RELATIONSHIPS AND COMMUNITY 150
From role to relationship 150
Beyond relationship to community... 158
CERTAINTY, UNCERTAINTY AND COHERENCE 168
From certainty to uncertainty 168
Beyond uncertainty to coherence 176
THE TOP, THE CENTRE AND THE HEART AND SOUL. 186
From the top to the centre... 186
Beyond the centre to the heart and soul 193
THE CRITICALLY REFLECTIVE LEADER............................ 202
REFERENCES.. 210

ACKNOWLEDGEMENTS

As always, this book is dedicated to Kylie.

It is also dedicated to the many leaders who have been part of my life, and who have influenced my thinking and practice of leadership.

With special thanks to John, who shared this writing journey with me.
Phil Ridden

I dedicate this book to my ever patient wife, Antonette.

This book is also dedicated to all the leaders I have worked with and otherwise known in schools, and other places, over the years. You have inspired me and influenced me.

A special thanks to Phil, who has been wonderful to work with, bounce ideas off, be motivated by and have a few laughs with.
John De Nobile

The Authors

Dr Phil Ridden writes from has a broad field of experience and a strong passion for teaching and learning, developed over many years as a primary and secondary teacher, curriculum writer and consultant, professional development consultant, deputy principal and principal, school board member and parent in government and independent schools. He is an experienced school leader, who has received several leadership awards and honours.

Dr Ridden is the author of a number of books and innumerable articles in professional journals, magazines and e-zines, and has presented numerous keynote addresses, courses and workshops.

Now in semi-retirement, he continues to write and consult with schools from time to time.

Dr John De Nobile is an Associate Professor and Director of Postgraduate Coursework Studies in the School of Education at Macquarie University in Sydney. His work in schools has included roles as a teacher, school leader, adult educator, and educational auditor, where he developed expertise in school organisation, leadership teams, staff development and supervision, quality pedagogy, curriculum development, behaviour management and wider educational issues. His research interests include organisational psychology and teacher morale, school development processes and leadership. His current research projects concern organisational communication and middle leadership in schools.

Dr De Nobile has conducted research into educational leadership across all school sectors in Australia and overseas and authored more than 70 scholarly books, journal articles and conference papers based on his research.

Introduction

It's a simple task to make things complex, but a complex task to make them simple (Dettmer, 1997, p.88).

There is no shortage of books on leadership. Even school leadership is well represented in libraries. So why another one?

A little more than 30 years ago, Phil Ridden wrote *School Management: A Team Approach* (Ridden, 1992). It described the evolving meaning of school leadership, promoting the notion of team leadership and exploring the implications for practice. Although something of a 'skinny' (to use the language of today), it was pivotal in shaping the leadership of many principals, in Australia and beyond. In 2012, in partnership with John De Nobile, the book was updated as *Keys to School Leadership.* Some sections of that earlier text were quoted in this work, while other ideas were elaborated or reconceptualised. However, all of those ideas have evolved into new leadership concepts. These are the focus of this book. While there are many ephemeral ideas promulgated by those who are keen to promote their latest research, we have sought to identify concepts which we believe have some depth and self-sustaining power.

Times have changed. We all know that many of the demands and expectations with which we entered the profession no longer fit. Many school leaders find that the thinking and actions which earned them leadership no longer serve them adequately. Put simply, the knowledge and skills which got them there won't keep them there.

This book cannot change the world. What it can do is to change the thinking of those who are, or aspire to be, school leaders. We seek to do that by shifting the focus of school leaders in a number of key areas. If you keep focusing on the same ideas, you will see and respond in the same ways; but if you shift your focus to new areas, you see new possibilities, gain new insights and respond with new thoughts and actions. This book seeks to help school leaders to explore and understand concepts that are relevant to leading schools into the future.

Chapter 1 explores notions of leadership and the many roles that school leaders play. We then move beyond leadership to the concept of influence and its implications for leadership actions.

There are plenty of tasks to keep principals and other school leaders busy — but tasks have no meaning except as they contribute to goals.

Chapter 2 examines the shift for leaders from doing tasks for their own sake to focusing on goals. Goals, however, are not enough, so we then shift the focus from goals to achievement, and we explore the notion that achievement is better defined as growth than immutable targets.

Chapter 3 looks at how leaders have moved from maintenance, or 'keeping things steady', to improvement. However, real improvement in a school occurs when 'all the ducks line up', so we discuss the notion of alignment.

We live in a time of partnerships, when people from many perspectives work together constructively for a common purpose. While school leaders have moved to a team approach, creating many teams within the school, the notion of a contained team is no longer adequate, so we refocus on partnership — not just with staff, but with all those who have an interest in the school. Chapter 4 explores this shift.

Chapter 5 explores ways of sharing responsibilities with others. In the past, principals were considered successful if children's work standards in the basic subjects were high and the school ran efficiently. Now they are expected to involve the entire school community in making decisions about the school's goals and the use and development of its resources, facilitate the process of change to achieve those goals, support teachers and others involved in the school for their individual and corporate wellbeing, and provide leadership that allows everyone to feel satisfied with the outcomes.

In the past, too, it was enough for a principal to know what was happening in their school. Now they are expected to engage with the local community and the global education community and to understand the ramifications of events overseas on the politics of local education. Chapter 6 argues that while the business of schools takes place in the classroom, leaders need to see this in the context of school issues, and then to widen that perspective to the world beyond the school.

Chapter 7 shifts the thinking about accountability from dependence and compliance to empowerment, with leaders having the confidence and skills to involve others in setting, achieving and evaluating corporate goals, and, beyond that, to plan for succession.

Confidence and commitment are essential for leaders. Simply turning up at work to fill a role is not enough; connection with others matters. Even more, members of the school community desire to belong, to buy into their work and the life of the school. Chapter 8 charts the shift to relational leadership, and beyond relationship to the meaning and creation of community.

The confidence with which we anticipated the future and planned for it, including in all aspects of education, has been replaced by uncertainty. This will not diminish, but will be further complicated by paradoxes, in which we find ourselves choosing between seemingly equal options. Chapter 9 explores the shift from certainty to uncertainty, and the need to deal with paradox through the coherent articulation and application of values.

The view of leaders at the top has been replaced by an image of leaders at the centre of the networks and thinking of the school. Beyond that is the place which recognises the school's heart and soul, which leaders express and draw others into. Chapter 10 views leadership from the top, the centre and the heart and soul.

Over the course of the book we have sought to challenge leaders to reflect on their understanding and practice of leadership. Therefore, Chapter 11 explores the notion of critical reflection on that leadership.

This book brings together the perceptions of a practitioner with academic credentials, and an academic with practical experience. It is designed to be accessible to busy school leaders who want to quickly glean the key ideas. The key ideas are returned to and repeated throughout the book, to enable the reader to dip into the book and read sections or chapters as needed. Some readers, including those using this book for research, may also wish to explore some of the ideas in more detail. To assist with this we have expanded on some of the ideas as a prompt for further investigation.

School leadership is a complex task. By exploring emerging directions for school leadership, this book hopes to offer some clarity and challenge to leaders, in the hope of making their work more effective and rewarding.

1
Administration, leadership and influence

From administration to leadership

He who thinks he leads and has no-one following him is only taking a walk (Proverb, cited in Maxwell, 2007).

REFLECT

- What is a leader? What is leadership?
- How would you describe the role of a school leader, in less than 25 words?
- What have you done in the past week that could be defined as leadership?
- In which type of leadership activity do you spend most of your time?

SHIFT THE FOCUS

School leaders have, at various times and in a variety of places, been called administrators and managers, but school principals and others in positions of responsibility are now viewed as leaders. The change in terminology reflects a shift in the perception of the role. Leaders see their role and their purpose differently from administrators or managers, and this is seen in their thinking and behaviour.

There has also been a shift in our understanding of education and schooling. Past generations assumed that schools alone provided 'formal' education, with the home providing early education and ongoing 'life' education supported by religious and community groups. Increasingly, the distinction between what is learnt at home and at school is blurring, with the influence of computer-based access to information and learning programs. It is not clear how the role and impact of schools will evolve in the coming decades.

However, while the roles, structures and operations of schools may change — some would argue, *must* change — we believe that schools will continue. We also believe that school leaders will continue to play a key role in ensuring that schooling is relevant, supportive and influential in the lives of students. Schooling continues to matter, but must be seen in the context of learning anywhere, anytime, and at any age.

A context for change

Schools in Australia have been involved in several decades of accelerating change. This change has reflected social and cultural shifts in local communities and nations, global integration and international mobility, the swing in economic power from the Western nations to Asia, the development of information and communication technologies, the breakdown of boundaries and borders, and other environmental, social and economic pressures.

The changes in education also reflect educational research, especially changes in our understanding of successful schools and effective leaders. The impact has been felt in all sectors of schooling and across many nations. What will future education look like? Gurr (2010) quoted a number of writers who anticipated the following future changes in education at that time:

- a transition from teaching to learning, and from consumers to producers of knowledge
- exponential growth in information
- an age of hyper-individuality
- an expanding gulf between the literate and the super-literate
- the decline in traditional educational providers as touch points interfacing with the community
- the rapid development of online coursework and textbooks
- the personalisation of education, ensuring that every child's education is tailored to their needs, so as to support higher levels of student engagement.

These changes have occurred during a time of unprecedented measurement, development and accountability of students, teachers and schools. Much of this is part of the normal teaching and learning program, helping to facilitate personalised approaches to learning; but much is for teacher and school accountability and improvement purposes.

Reid (2019) summarised recent changes in education through two contradictory movements. The global education reform movement (GERM), was characterised by school choice and competition between schools, public accountability via publication of results of national testing, and consequent narrowing of curriculum and pedagogical choices, which together acted as a standardising force on schools. The 21st century learning movement, on the other hand, promoted new approaches to education designed to meet the needs of the future workforce, including working with artificial intelligence (AI), and problem solving approaches that may help society deal with existential challenges such as climate change.

This thinking pulls school leaders towards what Hardy (2021) called 'authentic accountabilities', in which teachers teach, assess and consider practice according to student needs and capabilities, rather than standardised curricula and testing. Such a shift is not only desirable, but necessary, according to Ridden (2018), who expressed the concern that 'governments and systems have commandeered assessment as a tool of accountability and change. There is a need to reclaim assessment for and by teachers. School leaders must have the knowledge and courage to lead this process' (p.49).

Evolving technological and social changes, including those precipitated or hastened by the coronavirus pandemic, are changing education: away from a prescribed and linear curriculum to a negotiated and flexible curriculum; away from building-confined schooling to anywhere schooling; away from prescribed methodologies to creative methodologies; and away from inherited and sustained management structures to flexible and needs-oriented structures.

Setting the scene for school leadership

Over the years, school leaders have been expected to play a range of roles. As managers and administrators, school leaders direct or control the affairs of the school, maintaining oversight of everyone and everything in it. Their focus is on maintaining the efficiency of the school's structures and processes, allocating and using physical and human resources to achieve the school's goals, and monitor their effectiveness.

As *line managers*, they are responsible for the performance of a group of staff who are formally accountable to them. This is a model much favoured in the public service, where hierarchies dominate, and where there are clear 'chains of command' and 'lines of accountability'. Line managers delegate to those immediately beneath them tasks and responsibilities, and accountability for them. In return, the manager provides resources, direction, feedback, coaching and training. The model, however, has limitations for schools, because schools are bureaucratically flat. In most schools everyone — even students and parents — has direct access to executive staff. In addition, the principal is the only employee legally accountable in the school. Line management in schools led to an overemphasis on decisions being made by the accountable officer (the principal); and to executive staff having a vast range of responsibilities — financial management, human resource management and development, program management, public relations and community liaison, marketing, central office liaison, client interaction, resource management, organisation (school) development, curriculum management, student management, day to day administration, and more — roles which in many organisations are each handled by designated people, or even departments.

As *team leaders*, school leaders share the knowledge and responsibilities of leading the school, make use of the skills and experience of staff, and, in return, support the growth and development of those who aspire to leadership.

As *instructional leaders*, they focus the attention and energies of teachers on student learning, seeking to remove impediments and distractions.

The list of titles could continue. You may recognise some of these terms and may have others of your own to add. This book will describe a number of other leadership roles, and elaborate on their context and purpose. A number of observations should be made about these classifications:

- There are many roles implicit in leading a school.
- The definitions used above are imprecise and overlap.
- It is difficult to argue that one role as more important than another, because each role is important at some times and in some situations. The various roles sometimes compete for priority, in particular circumstances and at particular times.
- People may also prioritise roles which match their personalities. For example, if you value tidiness, structure and organisation, you are likely to emphasise a different role from someone who values creativity, possibilities and open-endedness.

Towards leadership

The shift from a focus on management or administration to a focus on leadership results in different emphases. However, while it may be helpful to identify the different orientations of leaders and managers, leadership and management are complementary. The point is not to consider whether those who lead our schools are managers or leaders, but to emphasise two points.

The first is that school leaders must look for leadership opportunities rather than spend all their energies on administration. This may well involve what Caldwell (2023) described as 'risk taking'. We summarise this concept as leaders running with an idea and implementing it in collaboration with the school community. These are not off the cuff 'inspirations', but rather 'visions' informed by research or observed good practice that are likely to benefit students.

The second is that how you view leadership will affect how you exercise leadership. People tend to act in ways which reflect their beliefs about how things work best. For example, a particular principal might act on their view of leadership as supervising subordinates and gaining compliance by micromanaging staff members. An assistant principal from the same school, viewing leadership as primarily about development and promoting professional growth, might encourage experimentation with pedagogy or champion some deviation from the established school curriculum.

Because of this, it is important to be aware of the potential for conflict among various leaders within a school, each of whom might define leadership differently, or prioritise leadership roles differently. This can lead to frustration and dissatisfaction. However, insightful and confident leaders view the different perceptions as a strength, allowing each leader to exercise their abilities and interests. It is not possible for a leader to have skills — or even an interest — in every aspect of their role, but it is possible for the staff to have these skills and interests among them. It is also important for leaders to be aware of the need to assume particular roles at particular times, including roles with which they may feel uncomfortable. For example, a leader who is consultative and encourages independent thinking will sometimes need to make clear decisions, including unpopular decisions; a leader who is obsessed with order may sometimes need to allow a little 'mess' in order to encourage innovation.

The case study later in this chapter illustrates how management and leadership can occur in the same action: Ensuring the efficient recording of disciplinary incidents is management; creating a new system and implementing it in a way which integrates it into the school culture is leadership.

Understanding leadership

Some comments about leadership may help our understanding:

- Leaders possess many skills and capabilities, which are not allocated to an elite few. Any person with the desire to lead, and a degree of commitment and purpose demanded by the situation, can acquire and exercise successful leadership behaviour. No checklist of institutional manuals can make a person a leader.
- Leadership is a process, not a position nor a title. There are many people with leadership titles who do not lead, and many who lead without a title.
- Leadership is a relational process. It is the interplay of complex interactions between a leader, their followers and the situation. Because of this, there is no single model of leadership, no single way to exercise leadership, although there are some general principles that can be explored.
- Leading is a process of thinking and relating, not a set of actions.
- Leaders have impact on the way people behave and the way the school functions. They are intentionally inspirational, helping others to find their voice and purpose.
- Leaders seek and find new opportunities, start new projects and help others see the positive side of changes or innovations. Leadership is found in places of not knowing, of change, of new learning, of growth and of new directions.
- Everyone can be a leader in an appropriate context. Those who lead successfully with one group of people in one context may struggle as a leader in another context with other people.
- Leadership is not an end in itself. It is a role which is focused on a purpose.

Caldwell & Harris (2008) argued for a shift in the focus of school governance (all those charged with leading the school) from roles, authorities, responsibilities and accountabilities to the process of building the intellectual, social, financial and spiritual capital of the school, and aligning these to achieve goals. The writers define these terms as follows:

> Intellectual capital refers to the knowledge and skill of those who work in or for the school. Social capital refers to

the strength of formal and informal partnerships and networks involving the school and all individuals, agencies, organisations and institutions that have the potential to support and be supported by the school. Spiritual capital refers to the strength of moral purpose and the degree of coherence among values, beliefs and attitudes about life and learning … Financial capital refers to the money available to support the school (p.10).

While we may seek to highlight particular approaches and emphases in school leadership, separating and dissecting them to aid understanding, the power of leadership is in aligning and growing the school's capital — in every sense of that word described above.

Gadman & Cooper (2009) wrote of open-source leadership, which they described as similar in spirit to the recent phenomenon of open-source software development in information technology — a process that is collaborative, participative and evolutionary. Open-source leaders enable staff, students and parents to form networks in order to access information and other resources, to share ideas and to work together to achieve school goals. They see neighbouring schools and institutions as collaborators and resources rather than as 'the competition'.

Open-source leaders push for change, but do so collaboratively and with the needs of the organisation balanced by the needs of individuals. They are open and transparent leaders who encourage input from outside the organisation as well as from within it. They recognise that change is messy and that their visions for the organisation can change as the world changes. Indeed, constant adaption of vision and innovation are key aspects of life. In times when 'school choice' and 'competition' have the potential to encourage fickleness in parents and movements of students from one school system to another, the need for principals to initiate change and do it quickly and effectively is paramount. Open-source leadership provides some possible ways to make it happen.

Gadman & Cooper comment that open-source leadership is done with people and not to them; that it relies on the power of communities and not solely the person at the top; and that the visions and belief systems of open-source leaders change as they are influenced by changes around them and input from others.

CASE STUDY: THE LEADERSHIP—MANAGEMENT NEXUS

Jacqui, the deputy principal at Normanville High School, was having problems keeping track of behaviour issues in the school. The records being kept, mostly in the form of incident reports, had adequate information, but there was no way to quickly retrieve student records or, worse still, no way to quickly and easily see trends in the behaviour of individuals or groups over time. Jacqui thought this unacceptable because, as students would be referred to her, she felt that she needed to be both consistent and progressive in her dealings with them.

She designed an electronic record of discipline matters using a basic spreadsheet program, devising a coding system for behaviours and disciplinary actions. On this record, one could view individual student records of behaviour and disciplinary actions taken over time as well as trends in behaviour problems and how effectively certain disciplinary actions were. In order to help this work, she also designed new incident report slips that reflected the structure of the database.

At a staff meeting, Jacqui introduced her new system as a trial and encouraged staff to use the new incident report slips. The new system has been running for six months now and all staff members have adopted it. If they need to check on how a student is doing, just two minutes in Jacqui's office is all that is needed, as opposed to swimming through a sea of incident reports and other paperwork. Those responsible for administration appreciate this efficiency too. Jacqui is already starting to see which disciplinary actions are least and most effective as well as patterns in the behaviour of some students.

MAKE IT PERSONAL

The challenge for school executive staff is to move beyond the demands of administration and management to demonstrate leadership.

Ask yourself, to what degree do I:
- function effectively in managerial roles?
- demonstrate leadership? In what ways do I do this?
- balance the 'maintenance' aspects of management with the 'change' aspects of leadership?

FURTHER INVESTIGATION

Australian education in context

As anyone who has worked in education can appreciate, throughout the world there are various levels of schooling to meet the needs of students. Typically, the levels can be categorised as early childhood or early years education, primary or elementary schooling, and secondary schooling. However, there are many variations, with some schools catering only for the early years, middle years, or senior years; many catering for Kindergarten to Year 12; some catering for pre-Kindergarten. Tertiary education caters for university and further academic education and technical or vocational training, although the boundaries between these may be blurred.

In Australia, around 65% of students attend government schools, 20% systemic Catholic schools, and 15% independent schools, operated by religious or community groups, based on particular values, beliefs or philosophies of education. Federal and state governments provide funding, to differing degrees, for all schools in Australia. (ABS, 2022).

School leadership structures and roles vary between countries, levels of schooling, and providers of schooling. School leadership structures, titles and responsibilities vary between states, systems and schools. However, this does not tell the whole story in relation to levels of responsibility.

In addition to the principal, 'senior leadership' positions may include deputy principals, assistant principals, vice principals, deans or directors of curriculum. Leaders may be designated responsibility for specific areas, such as administration, student wellbeing, teaching and learning, information and communication technology, innovation, school development, and others. These positions carry responsibilities for the core business of the school and its effective operation. 'Middle leadership' positions may include some of the above titles, plus heads of learning areas or year levels, curriculum leaders and others. Responsibilities of these leaders are more narrow or focused. In some schools there are also 'junior' leadership positions, such as coordinators, assistants, senior teachers and so on, and these staff support leaders who have extensive responsibilities, or support their teacher colleagues. In addition, there may be a number of other leadership roles within the school occupied by non-education staff, with responsibilities for supporting education by sustaining the organisational machinery of the school.

An awareness of the history of education of a country is helpful for understanding contemporary educational structures and processes. Barcan (1995) and Marginson (1997) describe the political and socioeconomic developments that shaped schooling in Australia to the 1990s. Symes & Gulson (2008) cover the period to the 2010s. Recent commentaries on developments in Australian education can be found in Reid (2019) and Rodwell (2020).

Similarly, theoretical knowledge of leadership structures beyond education can help to inspire or refine educational practice. The discussion of open-source leadership in this chapter is based on the writing of Gadman & Cooper (2009), but these and related concepts are viewed differently by other writers, including Peshawaria (2017), Owens & Valesky (2022), Schermerhorn et al (2020), and Cole (2019). It is interesting to note that many school leaders are completing courses such as Master of Business Administration (MBA) and Graduate of the Australian Institute of Company Directors (GAICD), which provide insights into leadership beyond schools.

Beyond leadership to influence

Who shall set a limit to the influence of a human being? (Emerson, 1860, p.45).

REFLECT

- How do you evaluate the success of your leadership?
- What strategies seem to be most effective in achieving those successes?
- What evidence do you have that you have made a positive difference to the school and to individuals within it?

SHIFT THE FOCUS

'The true measure of leadership is influence, nothing more, nothing less.' This succinct statement from Maxwell (2007, p.13) encapsulates the power of leadership. It is reinforced by Barker (2002), who says, 'Leaders exist in organisations to make things happen that would otherwise not happen in their absence. No mystery should be attached to leadership, as it involves nothing more than the exercise of a power to influence people towards the achievement of desirable outcomes' (p.49).

School leaders must be bold to lead, always seeking better ways of achieving better outcomes, rather than managing in order to maintain the status quo. In doing this, leaders are sometimes caught in the issues of power and authority, seeking to achieve change in individuals, and, through them, in the school, but not wanting to appear autocratic. There is a need to shift the focus to the real power of leadership — the ability to influence.

Sources of influence

There are several sources of influence that a school leader may choose to use, such as the following.

Positional authority assumes that formal leadership positions usually command some respect, because they reflect the leader's knowledge, experience and ability and have the backing of the employing authority. However, position is influential only as long as the people in these positions continue to earn respect through their actions. Their positions merely buy them time to establish this.

Expertise, or a perception of expertise, may be derived from qualifications, experience, or acquired knowledge. In schools, experienced teachers may influence less experienced teachers. The 'expert' must be seen to have both knowledge and credibility, which may be linked to their personal qualities. Hence, a very experienced or highly qualified teacher may not be influential because they are seen to be arrogant or excessively critical of others.

Charisma is a compelling strength and attraction in a person's personality, which can exert influence on others and even inspire their devotion. Some people may be universally liked and respected simply because they have attractive personalities and communicate in ways which connect effectively with people. Our emotions provoke strong responses in us, often overriding our intellect. So, for example, we may be influenced to do what someone suggests because they empathise with us, and consequently we believe they understand us and have our best interests at heart. Similarly, we may be influenced to act in ways suggested by someone whose words or actions inspire us. The inspiration motivates us to do things which we might normally feel more inhibited about.

Role models or heroes influence us by the example they set us, and which we attempt to emulate. Their influence may be helpful or unhelpful. We may be influenced to support someone who is helping the needy, because we are impressed by their selflessness and compassion; we may also be influenced to drink alcohol to excess, because we want to emulate a 'hero' who does this.

Reward and punishment are external pressures which influence our actions. People tend to repeat the actions which are rewarded, whether the reward is psychological, such as affirmation, or material, such as money. Most people tend to avoid repeating actions for which they are punished, unless they are gaining some other longer-term or unseen reward. Linked to punishment are coercion and manipulation, strategies which influence people in compelling ways.

There are other forms of influence, such as manipulation, ambition, desire and love.

However, Patterson et al (2008) describe an alternative framework. They argue that the forces that impact human behaviour connect with just two mental maps. People ask simply 'Can I do what's required?' (ability) and 'Will it be worth it?' (motivation). The authors then link these two factors to personal, social and structural sources, to identify six sources of influence which they believe make change inevitable:

- Personal motivation: Make the undesirable desirable by connecting to people's values.

- Personal ability: Surpass your limits by acquiring new skills and behaviours.
- Social motivation: Harness peer pressure by enlisting leaders, partnering with opinion leaders, and becoming an opinion leader yourself.
- Social ability: Find strength in numbers through 'just-in-time' teamwork. Structural motivation: Design rewards and demand accountability, modestly rewarding early success and punishing only when necessary.
- Structural ability: Change the environment, and harness its power to support new behaviour.

This analysis gives a broader context within which to locate the sources of influence cited earlier in this chapter.

Power and responsibility

Some of the sources of influence mentioned above can be seen as the exercise of power or authority. Power is often taken to mean 'a coercive force — either overtly to compel, or covertly to manipulate'. Power is supported by authority, 'a sanction bestowed to legitimate the use of power' (Greenleaf, 1977, p.167). Students' required attendance at school is a consequence of the use of such power and authority, as are their class groupings, the nature of the curriculum, the choice of teacher, the nature of the learning process, the behaviours expected, and more.

In a school context there can be an uneven distribution of power. Adults are responsible for the welfare and education of minors; some leaders direct aspects of the work of colleagues and are responsible for ensuring that expectations are met and procedures followed. However, there is a blurring of meaning here between *power and authority* and *responsibility*. Responsibility may imply an imbalance of power, but not the complete removal of power from one person by another. To do so is to create an environment with the potential for abuse. No-one should be powerless.

Perhaps the distinction is better understood in terms of the following classification:

- 'Power over' is a relationship in which one person has the power over the welfare and rights of another. Clearly there are elements of 'power over' in a parent-child or teacher-student relationship, but this is not abusive as long as the adult's clear purpose and driving motivation are the welfare of the child.

- 'Power with' is a relationship within which each uses their particular sources of power for a common goal. In a school context, one person may use their influential power with another's knowledge power, another's personal power and another's positional power to lead the staff through a process of change. This is a powerful process in schools.
- 'Power through' is a relationship in which power is exercised through another person. For example, a school leader may work with an influential colleague to achieve change in the school. Principals use power through teachers to achieve student learning.

Contemporary discourse often distinguishes between *power*, which resides within institutions, and *agency*, the power to make a difference that lies within individuals. Each of us has agency in certain contexts. Hence Hunjan & Keophilavong (2010) explain that 'we do not see power as being held solely by the few, but rather as something dynamic that can be found in the hands of many, and can manifest itself in both positive and negative forms' (p.2).

Spheres of influence

Most teachers and schools have a conscious, often documented, system of rewards and punishments. However, they may be less conscious or deliberate in identifying and using other forms of influence.

An analysis of the strategies by which the leadership group or the teachers in your school influence students would be enlightening. Some strategies would be overt and intentional. However, staff may be unaware of some influences they exercise, especially those which may influence students in ways which are counter to their intentions. It would therefore be additionally interesting to classify the strategies, to identify whether the teachers, leaders and students are aware of each source of influence, and its impact.

A useful exercise is to draw two concentric circles on a piece of paper. In the inner circle, list all the people or contexts over which you have significant influence. You might list here your partner, family, friends, particular colleagues, certain aspects of school life. In the outer circle, list those people or contexts over which you would like to have more influence. In this section you might list a particular family member or friend, a particular colleague, an aspect of the school's life. This exercise may make us more aware of the influence we have on some people and situations. It may also help us to identify the areas of our personal and professional aspirations.

A second step is to identify the source of influence which is associated with each of the items in the inner circle of your chart, and the sources of influence most likely to assist you to achieve greater influence over the things in the outer circle. As Duignan (2010) explains:

> School staff members bring a complex combination of unique mental, emotional, physical, and spiritual endowments to their relationships and work environment. Often it may not be their roles or positions … that, primarily, determine their individual and group's capacity to influence and make a difference; rather it is their purposeful and mutually supportive relationships and fields of influence that create morally uplifting and inspiring learning environments that motivate group members … towards realising the vision, mission and core values of their organisation, as well as their own potential as human beings (p.1–2).

Using influence

Influence for its own sake is simply an ego trip. Leaders must be very clear about whom they are trying to influence and for what purpose. For a school leader, the purpose of influence is to achieve change in individuals and in the school.

Leaders are not always aware of their influence on individuals. Have people quoted to you things you said years earlier, which you had forgotten, but which struck a chord in them, or cited actions which influenced them in positive ways? Leaders must be aware — as much as is reasonable — of the power of their influence, because, as Morgan (2006) reminds us, influence involves 'an ability to define the reality of others … and hence the way they act' (p.183–184). Such influence also carries a moral responsibility, to influence people to change in ways which bring them greater fulfilment, and enable them to influence communities, such as the school, in positive ways.

Leaders also use their influence to achieve change in the school, change which shifts the school closer to the vision which the leader has in mind. That change may be about culture, learning, teaching, curriculum, relationships or other aspects of school life. Changing a school essentially means changing enough individuals that the culture of the school changes. That is, there is a shift in the accepted values, priorities, expectations and practices of the school. Re-culturing a school is a complex task, because it involves changing, not just practices and procedures, but the thoughts and values, and even the purposes, of (ultimately) all the individual members of the school.

There are a number of factors key to achieving sufficient influence to change the culture:

- Trust: Fullan (2010) suggests that the two key dimensions of trust are integrity (sincerity, reliability, honesty) and competence (skill, effectiveness) (p.66). That is, people need to know that you will meet their expectations in getting things done, that you will behave in ways which are reliable and consistent, and that you will deal with people and issues honestly and sincerely.
- Articulation and communication: The expectations and goals must be consistently and frequently articulated in every possible forum. Gradually, people will come to understand, accept and then endorse what is being said.
- Salesmanship: Sometimes, basic persuasion or 'salesmanship' is necessary to help people to see the value of a particular way of thinking or acting, and to embed it in their thinking.
- Momentum: Culture is shaped by individuals acting in concert. Some ideas may begin with a handful of people. Gradually, as the ideas gain acceptance, they gather momentum, pervading the thoughts and actions of people and shaping their thinking. The more people who buy into the idea, the greater is the momentum, until the idea becomes so irresistible that it is simply accepted as part of the culture.

At the heart of this is influence. While coercion may achieve adherence to new procedures, changing the culture requires changes to ways of thinking by the members. Such leadership is transformational.

In his influential writing, Bass (1990) explains that transformational leadership 'occurs when leaders broaden and elevate the interests of their employees, when they generate awareness and acceptance of the purposes and mission of the group, and when they stir employees to look beyond their own self- interest for the good of the group' (p.21).

Transformational leaders raise the consciousness of followers by appealing to their higher ideas and values, transforming the school's goals into personal goals for the members. They don't force people to follow, but motivate them, so that they feel uplifted and empowered.

Transformational leadership has four components:

- Idealised influence involves charismatic vision and behaviour that inspires others to follow.
- Inspirational motivation is the capacity to motivate not just individuals, but the entire organisation, to commit to the vision.

- Intellectual stimulation encourages followers to be aware of problems, question assumptions, and to be innovative and creative.
- Individualised consideration involves coaching followers in line with their specific needs to reach high levels of achievement.

These four dimensions are interdependent. The transformational leader formulates desired goals into a vision that shows a future worth striving for; shares this vision with employees; sustains long term commitment by employees by including their contributions; and provides guidance and support to ensure success (Jensen et al, 2019; Stone et al, 2003).

Leithwood & Jantzi (2006) identify three key strategies which transformational leaders use: setting directions, developing people and redesigning the organization (p.205).

- Setting directions results in staff developing shared understandings of a vision for the school. It requires leaders to communicate their vision of how the school could be and how achievable it is. Leaders should display optimism and confidence that inspires staff to consider working towards this shared vision of school. They act in congruence with the vision and thereby become role models. They develop goals and priorities; promote teamwork and the development of shared vision; establish high expectations of performance and achievement; and exhibit consistently high standards of moral and ethical conduct.
- To develop people leaders identify the strengths and needs of staff members and work to improve their knowledge and skills. This component requires leaders to be good listeners and be able to recognise areas of strength and weakness. Actions include taking time to get to know the individual strengths and needs of staff members; recognising and appreciating differences in abilities and needs among staff; mentoring staff members toward acquisition of new knowledge and skills; creating opportunities for learning to occur; promoting a climate supportive of change and professional growth; and challenging staff to think of new possibilities; and acting in ways that reflect values, beliefs and a sense of mission.
- Redesigning the organisation is necessary for leaders to build a school culture that values participation, collaboration and constructive relationships. The aim is to have a school that, in outlook, could be described as a 'learning organisation'. Actions include encouraging participation in decision-making; developing teams and committees; fostering positive and constructive working relationships among staff and between the school and parents as well as outside bodies.

In essence, transformational leaders do not achieve organisational goals by a system of rewards and penalties, but by enlisting people to the cause, so that their goals become aligned to the organisation's goals. Jensen et al (2019) sum it up by asserting, 'the distinctive theoretical aspect of transformational leadership is the leader's intent to activate employees' higher order needs' (p.8).

CASE STUDY: PARENT INVOLVEMENT AT FELLSTEAD SECONDARY SCHOOL

James, a young teacher at Fellstead Secondary School, felt that the students and their parents had an overly relaxed attitude to attendance. Parents withdrew students regularly during term time to go on holidays. They used school days for shopping expeditions. Students were often seen congregating in the local shopping centre in school time, but parents sent absentee notes to school with stories about sickness and other excuses. James felt that learning was undervalued, and that his best efforts to assist students to learn were impeded by a lack of continuity.

He decided to try to change things. To achieve this, he felt he needed to influence the attitudes of both students and parents. He also needed to gain the support of the principal. First, he explained his concerns and his strategy to the principal, who was impressed, provided some helpful feedback, and offered his support. Then James obtained details of student attendance during the year, and negotiated a deal with a local fast food outlet to provide vouchers. He selected the best attending students, and sent them a personal letter of congratulations on their attendance and an invitation to meet him to receive a surprise in the canteen before school one morning, when he congratulated each of them again, and gave them a voucher as a reward for their attendance.

He then invited students and their parents to an evening meeting. At the meeting, he introduced each student, highlighting their particular strengths and qualities, and showing a sample of each student's best work. Students and their parents were moved, but even more so when he congratulated parents for the children they had raised.

Something in the attitudes of the students and the parents changed that night.

MAKE IT PERSONAL

The challenge for school leaders is to understand the power of influence — who they influence and how — and use this influence purposefully.

Ask yourself:

- Who significantly influences me? What is the source of their influence? Was I consciously aware of it before now?
- Who are the most influential members of staff? Who do they influence? How?
- In what ways, and with whom, have I been influential? How do I know? How did it make a difference to them or the school?

FURTHER INVESTIGATION

Leadership frameworks

A number of leadership frameworks and standards seek to describe the behaviours and qualities of effective leadership. Increasingly, they are used to guide the development of leadership capacity in schools.

The Australian Council for Educational Leaders has produced a Leadership Capability Framework (ACEL, 2023). It is structured around three foci: leading oneself for learning; leading others for learning; and leading the organisation for learning. Within each area, a number of dimensions or capabilities are identified. The framework suggests resources that individuals can use to develop a particular capability, identified either through personal reflection or use of a diagnostic assessment tool.

The Australian Institute for Teaching and School Leadership has facilitated the development of a National Professional Standard for Principals (AITSL, 2014), which was endorsed by the Ministerial Council for Education, Early Childhood Development and Youth Affairs. The standard sets out what principals are expected to know and to do. It expects leaders to develop vision and values, knowledge and understanding, and social and interpersonal skills, and identifies key professional practices, including leading teaching and learning; developing self and others; leading improvement, innovation and change; leading the management of the school; and engaging and working with the community.

2

Tasks, goals and achievement

From tasks to goals

Where you're headed is more important than how fast you get there (Covey, Merrill & Merrill, 1997, p.1).

REFLECT

- How busy has the past week been?
- How have you spent your time?
- How has it made a difference to student learning and wellbeing?

SHIFT THE FOCUS

How do you describe your work? Perhaps you focus on one of the following:
- your tasks, such as supervising teachers, monitoring student outcomes, organising events, interviewing parents, disciplining students
- your areas of responsibility, such as human resource management, facilities management, public relations, student achievement
- your accountabilities, including who you are accountable to, and who is accountable to you
- your goals, such as ensuring the school's performance targets are met.

At various times and in various situations, each of these perspectives is appropriate. However, schools are very busy places. Without a goal orientation, it is easy for school leaders to become exhausted while achieving very little.

School leaders need to shift their focus from tasks to goals. Some of the tasks in a typical day will be practical (organising, writing, planning, recording, teaching), producing something to show for the effort. However, many will be thinking tasks, either alone or with colleagues (reading, reflecting, reviewing, conceptualising, evaluating), which may not produce any immediately observable 'product'. Whatever the nature of the activity, its measure should not be in terms of visible product, but in terms of supporting the achievement of goals.

Review the school's goals

Your school will have defined goals. Some will be located in the school's documentation; some will be located in the culture and apparent in the way things are done at the school. Consider the following questions:

Are the goals articulated?

Are the school's goals clearly documented, published in a form which all may read, frequently mentioned and reflected in practice? Schools exist for certain reasons identified by the government, and the school authority or the community it serves — but each school has its individual goals and priorities because of its unique context and the needs of the students.

If there is limited knowledge of the school's goals, or if the school's goals are not considered very important, then they need to be reviewed, and articulated or promoted more effectively. Perhaps they are dated and no longer reflect the school's priorities; perhaps they were created by an individual principal and reflect that person's goals rather than the school community's goals; perhaps energy went into creating the goals as an intellectual activity, but they were never really built into the school culture; perhaps staff turnover has been high, and the induction of new staff has failed to ensure an understanding of the goals. Whatever the reason, if the goals are poorly known and accepted, they need to be promoted or revised.

If the goals are not clear, involve the school community in identifying them. The process needs to involve all stakeholders: parents, who probably have the strongest commitment and longest time investment in the school; students, including primary students, many of whom have clear views on the purpose of schooling in general and on the goals of 'their' school in particular; and all staff, not just academic staff, and not just the leadership group.

It is better if final agreement and acceptance is achieved by consensus rather than majority voting. The chosen goals should be accepted, rather than 'won'. There will never be perfect agreement on the wording of all goals, but there needs to be an understanding that what is sought is a workable and acceptable set of goals.

Are the goals appropriate?

Does each goal refer to one specific issue that has meaning for everyone in your school? Is each worded in a way which everyone — not just teachers — can understand? Is the list balanced, reflecting the range of purposes identified and their relative emphases?

While there may be agreement about the general content of school goals, they should be redefined for the school community and local context, expressed in words that are appropriate to the community demography, attitudes, values, aspirations, issues, language and resources.

Are the goals assessable?

Are the ideas sufficiently clear that their achievement can be assessed and that people's work can be evaluated against them? That does not mean that each goal must be able to be quantified with a simple objective score. A goal related to academic performance may be assessed this way, but goals which relate to inclusion, sense of worth or values cannot be so simply scored. Nevertheless, each goal should be sufficiently clear that some agreement could be reached about how well it is being achieved.

When assessing the achievement of goals, consider quantitative data, which give a score or rating to demonstrate the levels or extent to which things are being achieved, as well as qualitative data, description-based surveys or checklists that provide information about achievements not easily counted, such as attitude changes over time or feelings about accomplishments, and which extend understanding of the quantitative data. Be sure to set timelines against which accomplishments or milestones can be recorded.

Are the goals achievable?

Are the goals realistic? Specifically, are they achievable with your:
- students: are all students capable of achieving each goal or only those of above-average ability?
- physical resources: are the necessary facilities, equipment and finance available or obtainable?
- staff: do teachers have, or could they acquire, the knowledge, skills and interests to enable the goals to be achieved?

- community: does the community support each goal or can community attitudes be changed so that they support the goals?
- time: will you be able to see evidence, in the short term and long term, that progress is being made towards the achievement of the goals?
- energy: do the staff and school community have the enthusiasm and drive to achieve those things that require extra effort?

Are the goals applied?

Are the goals reflected in the life of the school — in the school's dialogue, allocation of resources, staff development, curriculum, use of time and energy, practices and policies?

You might need to determine the goals in practice. One way is to consider each school goal, and invite staff to list evidence of its support — for example, physical resources are allocated to support the goal; and areas where it needs more support — for example, professional development needs to be directed towards the goal.

Leave these lists on display for a week, encouraging people to add to the lists as they go about their work. You might also invite parents and students to participate in a similar exercise. Then review the lists to set new action to support the achievement of the goals.

Review your role

School goals are related to the purposes of schools, which exist to serve students in particular ways. The school leader's goals represent their specific responsibilities in connection with the school's goals. This might include preparing school newsletters, because they inform parents and so gain their support for school activities and because they enable school expectations to be articulated and demonstrated; organising special events, because they promote excellence, focus on learning and enhance the self-esteem of students and staff; and interviewing parents, because the school and home need to collaborate to achieve optimum student outcomes and facilitate healthy growth in students.

For any school leader, there are enough things to do to fill the available hours many times over. For those who also have a significant teaching load, the responsibilities appear limitless. You need to be selective about what you do. When you have a clear and meaningful set of goals, there is a clear purpose for your work.

What is the essence of my role?

Most of us are familiar with mission statements. They summarise an organisation's focus and purpose, trimmed back to its basic essence. Try writing such a statement for your role, in one sentence.

The value in this exercise is in stripping the role down to its bones. Beyond all the tasks you do, beyond the expectations of others, beyond the cynicism and frustrations of the demands, why is it that you and your role are essential to the effective functioning of the school, which has at its heart student learning?

It may be an illuminating exercise to ask your colleagues to define the essence of your role, and to compare their understanding and observations with yours.

What are the essential elements of my role?

In an ideal world, what are the key elements of your role; that is, what things should you be spending your time on to achieve your purpose? Limit the list to 6–10 items. For example, your list might (or might not!) include:

- Managing teacher performance (observing classes, coaching teachers …)
- Communicating with staff, parents, students (writing newsletters, clarifying policies and procedures …)
- Challenging practice and improving outcomes (reviewing students' progress; and reading, attending conferences and meeting with innovative staff, to question what we are doing and how we might do better)
- Sharing and reporting, with leadership colleagues, school council, Parent meetings …
- Building community (assemblies, chatting with parents …)
- Etc.

Now, allocate to each item a percentage which indicates how much time you would ideally like to spend on each purpose. Remember that the total cannot exceed 100, but you might keep the total to 90, to allow for unexpected, but unavoidable, issues.

How am I using my time?

It need not be a difficult task to get a sense of where you time is going. For three to five days, record what you do with your time. You might try recording on a chart divided into 15 minutes slots. There is no need to be obsessive, because every day will be different, but be as disciplined as possible about recording.

Then link each task to a purpose on your list. You may need to add other areas of responsibility to the purposes, in order to classify some tasks.

Add the times, calculate the percentages and review the data. Fig. 2-1 provides a table which you might use or adapt. The review of the data should prompt questions such as these:

- How do I think I should be using my time?
- How am I using my time?
- Where are the greatest areas of mismatch?
- Why?
- Does it matter?
- How can I change the way I spend my time?
- Who might help me to review my role or my use of time?

The intention behind this activity is not to create a sense of guilt nor to increase frustration. The role of a leader is never perfectly predictable, especially in a school. There will be days when you work 'flat-out' all day, yet, at the end of the day, are unsure what you have achieved. The intention of the exercise is to consider ways to be more purposeful and focused. Below we suggest some ways you might do this.

What am I doing and why?

Be willing to constantly evaluate what you are doing and why. This will give your role meaning and purpose. Your purpose is to achieve things, not simply to do things. Consider your responsibilities and tasks in relation to your purposes. Do things, not for their own sake, but because they seem to be important in achieving the school's goals. It may be useful to create a list of the ways you believe your time could be most effectively spent, with a suggested time allocated to each, and then to compare this with a log of how you actually spend your time.

Each task must justify its worth against other activities in achieving the school's goals, and that may affect whether it is done at all.

There may be a task which you or your predecessors have historically done, but you decide is an inappropriate way to spend your time. Others may expect you to continue to do it, but that is not sufficient reason to continue with it. What does it achieve? Where does it fit into the scheme of things? What will happen if no-one does it? Are the consequences significant?

When a task is done with an eye on its purpose and not as an end in itself, it may change your thinking as to how it should be done. Be open and creative about new ways to do traditional tasks. Could the task be incorporated into another function or task, so that it no longer has a life of its own? Could it be done less often? Could it be done in a different way, at a different time or place, or using a different format? A brainstorm session with colleagues may reveal a number of potential alternatives.

Expectations of others can be changed, especially when there's a clear purpose against which to assess the worth of a task. You might:

- Ask others to explain how the task is important in achieving goals.
- Explain the benefits for staff in your new priorities. Better still, demonstrate the benefits in terms of better outcomes, better support from parents, and better support for them.
- Stop doing the task and see what happens. If the school begins to fall apart, that task was worth doing. If little of significance changes, it can't have mattered much.
- Watch for improved outcomes, relationships and effectiveness in the implementation of your new priorities.

Encourage your colleagues, too, to evaluate the ways they spend their time, using the goals as criteria. Be willing to allow them to drop or do differently those tasks which are geared to procedures and tradition rather than goals, and to re-evaluate your own expectations of them.

Am I the best person to do it?

When considering what needs to be done to achieve the goals, ask what you should do that no-one else can do. There's a strange tradition in schools that anything that teachers can't do, gardeners don't have to do, cleaners refuse to do or that seems an imposition on clerical staff, is left to the principal or deputies! The anomaly is that well qualified, influential and higher paid staff perform many of the least skilled tasks.

Don't do things which no-one else will; do things which no-one else can. Do things which no-one else has the perception, knowledge, skills, influence or authority to do.

When faced with a task, ask whether people could do it for themselves. Could support staff do it? Could students or parents be given responsibility for it? Is it worth employing someone else, perhaps just at peak times, to attend to it? Will someone else volunteer to do it, and what incentive could be offered? And are there others who might actually do it better than you? There are many new responsibilities for leaders, which cannot simply be added to existing responsibilities. They require leaders to be brutally objective and critical in deciding what is worth doing, creative and explorative in finding alternative ways of doing things, and analytical and assertive in restructuring responsibilities of others. A focus on goals and purposes enables sound and defensible decisions to be made.

How might I do it better?

Australian research identified six keys to professional improvement of teachers:

- building a learning culture, where people are continually engaged in learning
- coaching and mentoring, by staff colleagues or external consultants
- collegiality and collaborative approaches to planning and learning
- feedback
- classroom observation
- professional learning (Nexus Strategic Solutions, 2009, p.16–17).

The principles apply to school leaders also, with 'classroom observation' replaced by observations by colleagues or work shadowing.

The structured and cyclical review of performance in schools has been something that has developed slowly but steadily since the early 1990s. This requires teachers, school leaders and other staff to account for their performance to a nominated superior. The process leads to the establishment of personal goals and action plans. These goals can be related to wider school strategic goals, personal work issues, or, most commonly, a combination of both.

While this activity has become widespread in Australia, it is not yet practised by all schools and school systems. Furthermore, in some educational systems it is mandated only for school leaders, while in others all staff members are required to undertake it. It is variously known as performance review, management, appraisal, development, and other terms.

Some processes encourage '360-degree feedback'. This involves seeking feedback on a person's performance from someone to whom they are accountable, from a peer, and from someone who is accountable to them — from people 'above, beside and below'. A principal should seek feedback from their director or board chairperson, or other to whom they are accountable; from a range of colleagues (teachers, clerical staff, technicians, gardeners); and from parents and students. Often this process is restricted to a minimal number of people. There is logic in seeking feedback from as many people as possible because the more people who are asked, the wider is the range of perspectives obtained; the relative importance of matters identified can be seen; the unique issues of individuals (for example, a parent with particular grudge) are balanced; and the feedback will not simply duplicate the feedback obtained regularly from selected close or supportive colleagues, but may offer more surprising and challenging insights. The principles can be extended to reviews of other school leaders.

Whatever the mandated or localised processes might be in your school, explore the use of performance reviews to enhance your own and others' performance. Seek feedback from a range of sources. Encourage challenging feedback, and not simply affirmations.

CASE STUDY: PERFORMANCE GOALS AT ST WILFRED'S SCHOOL

> Since being appointed as a coordinator at St Wilfred's School Paula has had many responsibilities. Most of these have had to do with curriculum development, but this year her responsibilities will include supervision. She has been made the Stage 2 (Grades 3 and 4) supervisor, which means she will oversee teaching programs of and provide guidance to four teachers. This is a daunting enough task for her, but things are set to get especially challenging. Recent national testing results have shown that students at St Wilfred's are particularly weak in some mathematical concepts and the principal wants each stage supervisor to ensure that teachers 'lift their game' in the given areas. The principal wants to see improved results in next year's tests.
>
> Paula has rarely been in positions where she has had to influence colleagues. Mario, another stage supervisor and a coordinator like her, has told her not to be too 'freaked out' by the challenge. It's easy for him to say (she thinks to herself); he's been doing it for years. Paula knows this task will require her to extend herself and learn new skills so, the following week, at her performance management interview with Bernadette, the deputy principal and her immediate supervisor, the issue and her concerns are discussed. They both agree that one of Paula's performance goals for the current year will be to 'Initiate observable changes in the mathematics teaching of Stage 2 teachers.'
>
> They agree that key strategies to help her achieve the goal must include some professional development in the area of leadership communication and conflict management. Bernadette also suggests Paula team up with Hector, another stage supervisor with limited experience in this area, so that they might learn and reflect on practice together and avoid the pitfalls of working in isolation.

MAKE IT PERSONAL

The challenge for school executive staff is to change from doing what no-one else wants to do to what no-one else can or should do, and from a focus on tasks to a focus on goals and purposes.

Ask yourself, in the past week, to what degree was my work:
- focused: was I actually trying to achieve something or just filling in time?
- Purpose-oriented or goal-orientated: was I doing tasks for their own sake, or did I have a clear perception of why I was doing things?
- relevant: were my actions directly related to what I was trying to achieve?
- proactive: did I plan things that I saw as important and do them?
- effective: did my achievements make a difference?
- rewarding?

FURTHER INVESTIGATION

Review of the school goals

If you were appointed to another school, what criteria would you use to review the school's goals? The literature provides many sets of criteria against which goals may be reviewed. For example, the United States-based Center for Comprehensive School Reform and Improvement (2009) presents a clear set of areas for investigation in relation to goals, including curriculum, instruction, school culture, leadership effectiveness and parental involvement.

In the Australian context, state jurisdictions have general guidelines about aspects of schooling that may be the focus of goals. These are easily accessed on school system websites. There are some common principles, but also some interesting variations. Exploring these may provide valuable insights into the development or enhancement of a process for your school, or even a unique process for you. The Victorian Department of Education (2020) in particular provides examples of relevant goals and scaffolds for goal setting and examination.

In relation to the role of school leader there are many performance review processes in use in schools, and much written on the subject. More than two decades ago, when school self-review was still a developing field, Cranston (2000) provided an action research based system framework that could be adapted for use by school leadership teams. Later, the Dare to Lead project, managed by the Australian Principals Associations Professional Development Council (APAPDC, 2007), published a comprehensive school review checklist in relation to indigenous education that helps school leaders to review what is happening in their schools. It provides a model from which leaders can structure their own roles and priorities. Areas of review include partnerships, expectation setting, strategic planning and health and wellbeing.

Organisational citizenship

Organ (2018) described organisational citizenship behaviour as individual behaviour that promotes the work and goals of the organisation, including, 'stellar attendance, helping a colleague resolve a work problem, maintaining a neat and organized workplace, going the extra mile to help a customer, and providing encouragement to new hires.' (p.296). This extra effort or alternative, discretionary, effort which employees provide beyond their prescribed role is a great bonus to the organisation. However, this effort is not always supportive of the organisation's goals (Bowler, 2006). It may be helpful to identify organisational citizenship behaviour in your school, and to determine the degree to which behaviours are supportive of, or opposed to, the school's goals and priorities.

Fig. 2-1. Review of leadership role and use of time

In the table, list your key purposes, as you see them or as they are defined. Next to each indicate the relative importance of each in terms of the % of your time each should (ideally) receive. Record how much time you actually spent on each during the observed times. Convert to a % and compare. (Make your own assessment as to what constitutes a fair and reasonable working day for a school leader. If you have teaching responsibilities as well, just consider the time available for leadership activities.)

My mission:			
My key purposes as a leader	% of time which should be spent (ideally!)	Amount of time I spent on this last week	% of time I spent on this.

Beyond goals to achievement

Even if you're on the right track, you'll get run over if you just sit there (Rogers, 2011).

REFLECT

- How well are the roles and energies of staff directed towards the school's goals? What evidence do you have to endorse or refute your opinion?
- Who have you affirmed this week? For what? Was it related to the achievement of the school's goals?
- When you praise people — students, staff or parents — do you connect your words of praise to school goals?

SHIFT THE FOCUS

Doing tasks to keep busy is unacceptable; focusing on goals is desirable; ensuring achievement of these goals is essential. Leaders need to move from being busy, encouraging and rewarding activity, to evaluating the worth of what they and others are doing, and focusing it towards purposes and goals.

But it is no longer enough for the processes and the focus to be right; leaders need to review what they, their colleagues and their students are achieving. There is a need to shift the focus from articulating the goals and directing activity towards them, to ensuring achievement of the goals, or, at least, identifying progress towards their achievement.

There is a role for data collection and analysis in this process. However, data alone will reveal little, and may even be misleading, unless the process is carefully thought through.

Review what matters

Before embarking on a data gathering or analysis exercise, consider what matters. What is important in the school? Presumably the answer to this question has some correlation with the identified goals. What is it you want to know? Word this as a series of precise and delimited questions. For example, rather than wanting to know 'how students are doing', it would be more helpful to ask questions such as these:

- How are students performing academically compared with national norms?
- How well should they be performing, given their innate abilities?
- What progress have they made since the last measure?
- Is this as we would expect, better or worse?
- Are the answers the same if we focus just on boys, or girls, or Indigenous students, or some other sub-group?
- Are the answers the same for each learning area or subject?
- Are there particular areas of knowledge where progress is cause for celebration or cause for concern?

Clearly these are only sample questions, and should be familiar. You need to decide your questions, with 'big' questions broken down into more specific questions. The questions you ask will determine who or what is 'measured', the data you choose to collect, the tools you use to collect it, the way you go about it, and the way the data are analysed.

Yet the process is complex of gathering information is complex. Ridden & Heldsinger (2014) provide several principles:

- Effective assessment is an integral part of teaching and learning. The 'high stakes testing' by governments and systems sits outside the day to day work of the classroom.
- Effective assessment is comprehensive. It does more than ascribe a numerical value to a student's academic progress.
- Effective assessment provides worthwhile and credible information, which leads to improved student learning.
- Effective assessment and evaluation provide answers to questions.
- Effective assessment facilitates informative reporting.
- Effective assessment informs school-wide evaluation processes.

They argue that 'Teachers must be assessment literate and understand how to use information to support learning and inform teaching, as well as being able to ensure that the communication processes of the school enable honest and professional discussion of data without defensive or accusative posturing' (p.107). So school leaders must consider carefully what questions they are seeking to answer; what is reviewed; how and when it is reviewed; how the information gathered is manipulated and interpreted; what conclusions are drawn from it; and what action results.

Explore measuring instruments

This does not need to be a task for the principal alone. Small ad hoc groups of staff may be each allocated one goal and asked to suggest ways to measure its achievement. The suggestions can then be reviewed by a member of the school executive or by staff as a group, and a process put in place to measure the achievement of each goal.

Some will be easy to measure using measuring instruments provided to the school. Compulsory national tests, tertiary entrance or end-of-school tests are examples. It would be a shame to ignore the data these provide at no additional effort from the school. However, tests are designed for particular purposes, and it is important to remember this when the data are reviewed. Caution is needed in using tests designed for particular purposes to provide information for other purposes. (An example is the use by the media of tertiary entrance scores, designed to rank individual students for entrance to university, to rank the quality of schools.)

It is important that, where possible, historical data, as well as current data, is accessed. The main variable in achievement data in a school is usually the particular cohort being measured. As any teacher knows, the student cohorts in two successive years, taught the same material by the same teachers, can achieve widely differing results. The variable is the students themselves. Data gathered over several years can identify trends.

Ensure before commencing that the instruments you choose will give you, or enable you to infer, valid and reliable answers to the questions you ask. In simple terms:

- *Validity* refers to whether the instrument measures what it claims to measure. That is not always as obvious as it may seem. A mathematics test which focuses on problem solving strategies and presents each problem in a complex paragraph may be measuring the student's reading ability as much as their mathematical ability. We get a feeling for validity if the results given by the instrument are similar to the results we expect to see (given all the inherent problems of a one-off test).
- *Reliability* refers to the degree to which the results are consistent. That is, if we use a particular mathematics test each year, and each student's results or ranking fluctuate wildly from year to year, then we cannot rely on the data provided by the test.

If there are certain tests which you regularly use with students, review these to ensure that staff members have confidence in them. Where possible, use more than one set of data to answer important questions.

Some important goals may be more difficult to measure. They may refer to relationships or personal qualities of students. That is not to say these things cannot be assessed. Surveys and checklists can give useful data about these goals. External consultants, such as university staff, may also be willing to assist in measuring goals in your school.

It may be necessary to gather data from staff and parents as well as students. For example, if you have goals which reflect qualities such as independence, initiative, self-management or effort, these cannot simply be inferred from academic achievement. While teachers might like to think that all students who work hard do well, while those who do not apply effort fail, this is not so. There are many factors that determine students' academic achievement or academic performance (which are not the same thing). To identify the qualities, you might need to ask parents to report on their children's homework practices or self-management strategies. You might also need to ask teachers, or the students themselves.

Teacher performance may be an important measure. There are many schools where students complete a survey, often online, about their teacher's performance: their apparent preparation, the clarity of their instructions or explanations, the learning strategies they use, the way they relate to students, whether the teacher cares about them and their learning, and so on. These data are exceedingly valuable. It matters little if a couple of students have used the opportunity to 'get at' a teacher. It will be apparent where the responses are clustered if a scale is used, and the clustering of ideas if open- ended questions are used.

In our experience, most information gathered in this way is overwhelmingly affirming of teachers, and specific in what students appreciate about the teacher and what they would like to see the teacher do differently. What is more, it can be used with children as young as eight years old. (Children under this age tend to think their teacher is perfect in every way, except for not giving them enough chocolate or building them a swimming pool!)

Depending on the questions asked, it may also be necessary to measure the behaviour or performance of the school's leadership group. Again, this may involve questioning staff and parents, and using a variety of measuring instruments.

The purpose is to find ways to gather data which will tell you, or from which you can infer, the answers to your questions, which in turn reflect the school's goals, purposes and emphases.

The difficulties of measuring student progress

During their time in school, students will grow. Some of that growth will be natural, such as their physical and neurological growth; some will be due to their parents' influence, such as their moral or spiritual growth; and some will be due to their interaction with peers and others, such as their social and emotional growth. And some growth will be due to the influence of the school — their academic learning, in particular. The school may also contribute to the student's social, emotional and moral growth, or particular aspects of their physical growth. The contribution that the school makes to the student's growth is the 'value added' by the school. The difficulty here, of course, is in isolating the impact of the school.

Student achievement can be adjusted for family background. National testing does this by comparing the performance of students at one school to those of statistically similar schools. However, these data do not show the progress of an individual student, but simply provide a mean score for all students, and ignore a range of other student population factors that may have an impact on the aggregate of student achievement.

Alternatively, the student's achievement can be shown as progress from an earlier achievement level, compared with all other students in the school cohort or compared with the mean progress for all students tested. This ignores the innate ability of each student, so it is difficult to know whether a particular student should be expected to progress at an average rate, or a greater or lesser rate; and whether your school should show average progress, greater or less.

Merging these two ideas, a statistical model is sometimes used which compares progress made by each student to progress made by other students with the same initial level of attainment, with an adjustment for background factors.

It is unreasonable to suggest that a student could spend their days in a school and the school have no impact on them. Even a disengaged student is likely to absorb some aspects of the curriculum. The value added by a particular school can therefore be considered as the value added to the student's growth by attendance at this particular school, in excess of the growth one would assume would occur because of their attendance at any school. The difficulty with these notions of value-adding is that it is impossible to isolate the effect of a school on a student's growth. We cannot attribute all of a student's learning, even all academic learning, to the school.

While it is difficult to measure a student's many diverse dimensions at the start and end of their schooling and claim the changes are all due to the school, it is still important that assessments of student achievement, and of the value of the school's actions directed towards this achievement, are informed by data.

Observe and infer

There is no point in testing for the sake of testing. There is also no point in gathering data and keeping it secret. Place the data before those staff affected by it, or who have influenced it.

Ask staff to make observations. Before trying to explain the data, be clear about what the data show. Sometimes we are so keen to use data to prove a point that we overlook worthwhile observations, so take time to collate observations. Then try to explain your observations.

Some people look at data, observe a trend or an anomaly and offer an emphatic explanation. The problem here is that such explanations are inferences, and they need to be offered tentatively. For example, staff may observe that science test results are noticeably better this year than last year. Because the school put a lot of resources into improving the teaching of science, we might infer that this is the reason for the improvement. However, it may be that this year's cohort is simply far better at science than last year's cohort; or that this year's test happened to focus on a section of the course which our teachers always teach well; or the teachers happened to predict accurately the content of the test this year; or the construction taking place in the next building has finished, and students are able to hear and concentrate better! It may even be that, while the results look good on paper, the improvement is not actually statistically significant within the limitations of the test, which is a matter for a statistician to decide.

The real significance of the improvement is usually evident only in trends over several years, or from a large number of students. Inferred explanations are important, but always a little tentative. Sometimes inferences can be tested. If we think the improvement is the result of a certain approach, we can continue that approach and see if the improvement continues. We can also crosscheck our inference with other data, such as asking students whether they think the new approach is helpful. While their affirmation alone would not necessarily convince us, coupled with improved results we might decide that the new approach is succeeding.

Maintain healthy scepticism about data

It is important to place this argument in context. Some people speak of 'data-driven' practice. It is preferable to think of 'data-informed' action, because some cautions are in order:

- The data reflect what is measured. The high-stakes national testing conducted in some countries focuses on selected learning outcomes, and overlooks many others.
- The data depend on the focus of the measurement and manner of measurement. This is best explained with an example. There are many tests of reading, developed by highly credible researchers, comprehensively trialled and normed against specified populations, and generally well reputed by educators. Yet if administered to the same students at the same time, the correlation between the results may not be strong. This does not mean that any particular test is faulty; rather, each test emphasises a different reading skill (such as word recognition, word decoding, vocabulary, or comprehension), and requires a particular type of test skill (such as multiple choice, cloze, or essay answers).
- Test data are typically acquired from a single test on a single occasion. In some schools, this testing is done at stressful times, such as when students first arrive at the school, or even on an orientation day.
- The strongest data are acquired from a range of methods over a period of time. Hence, the most reliable and comprehensive data about a student's learning are the accumulated test results and observations of the student by a teacher over a period of time. Some teachers would prefer to base their information on a single test administered themselves, than on a year or more of accumulated data from a predecessor. This shows disrespect for colleagues, and arrogance about one's own judgements. If experience has shown that the judgements of a particular colleague cannot be trusted, we ought to hold that colleague accountable, challenging them in a spirit of openness to justify their evaluation, rather than assume that all earlier assessments of a student are faulty.

Therefore, while data should be used to inform our actions, remember that there are many sources of data. One-off tests have limitations in terms of student performance and statistical analysis, so results should be cross-referenced with other data about the student. Information gathered should go beyond students' academic performance to include other outcomes.

Not everything worthwhile can be measured, nor is everything that can be measured worth measuring. In the accountability era, we have been obsessed with statistics; yet teachers know that much of the highly valued work which they and their students do cannot be scored with a number. We need to be more accepting of descriptors, and to get cleverer about descriptors which have meaning and value.

Fullan (2010) suggested three rules concerning data:
- Set up a robust, accessible data system based around a few high standards.
- Don't take any one year's results too literally. Think of three-year windows in terms of moving up, down or flatlined.
- Make it crystal clear that by far the primary role of the data is for improvement — this means that the first response to underperformance is to invest in capacity building and not to take punitive action (p.61).

Take action

The data may be used for celebration among staff and students, if this seems appropriate. It may also be used for some self-criticism. However, the most effective use of the data is to make changes.

The observations gleaned from the data, and the inferences proposed, should be used to influence action. There is little point exploring the data, then simply putting it in the filing cabinet. Invite staff to suggest actions which reflect the data.

There are many factors which impact on student performance. These include the quality of teaching, the classroom learning environment, the expectations of teachers, the time on task and degree of student engagement with the learning, and the school's learning culture, for example. Therefore, in seeking to improve performance, it is important to consider all related factors, and take action to influence any of these things which appear relevant.

Enhance the quality of teaching

Teachers may be more comfortable suggesting that improvement requires better resources or more technology than suggesting that their own teaching skills should improve. School leaders need to lead professional dialogue which challenges teachers to consider all the factors which influence student learning, including taking a close look at themselves — how they teach, their understanding of how students learn and their application of these ideas, how they relate to students, their expectations of students, their ability to engage students, the quality of feedback they provide, and so on. It is here that the most potent difference can be made. It is better that a student is taught in a quarry by an excellent teacher than in the finest classroom by an average teacher.

Clear time for learning

So much time in a school day and a school year is time lost to academic learning. Of course, there is an important place within school life for ceremonies, rituals, celebrations, and even certain administrative impositions. However, there may be a way to structure the daily timetable or the year's planner to make better use of priority learning times, and to provide a better flow of time for learning. For example, the periodic structure of the day which is typical of most secondary schools may not be the best structure for learning.

Promote engagement

Within classrooms, teaching methods do not always focus student attention on learning. Students sitting with hands up, or waiting in line for assistance at the teacher's table, are not learning. Observe teachers to see how often students are, or are not, on task.

Similarly, being in class, listening to a teacher, does not mean students are engaged in learning. Observe teachers to see the degree to which students are engaged. This will be evident in their attention to the task, their interest (even excitement!), their responses, their questions, and their thinking about and beyond the task.

Ensure differentiated learning is taking place in your classrooms. Students for whom the work is too easy or too difficult cannot engage with it, and are unlikely to be learning much. Within reasonable practical boundaries, teachers must attempt to target the learning to the understanding of each student.

Reward what matters. Some schools have systems that reward students for all sorts of things *except* academic achievement. Ensure that students are rewarded for behaviours that contribute to or reflect the school's goals.

Direct resources towards goals

Budget priorities do not always reflect key goals. For example, significant funds may be diverted to high-profile projects, administration, or buildings and facilities, which may have little impact on student learning; while classrooms, teaching-learning resources, professional learning or the availability of teachers and learning support are financially suffering.

Human resources should also be linked to goals. There is increasing flexibility, even in government and other systemic schools, for principals to determine how to allocate staff to positions of leadership, and the roles which they play. Leaders can include those who are not part of the formal promotional pathways. They may be appointed to short-term positions, and rewarded at the school level with a responsibility allowance or non-contact time. They can also include those who are exercising leadership initiative within the school.

So often in schools, it is assumed that school leaders know what is expected of them. It is assumed that they have seen others performing the same role, and therefore know what is required. However, their expectations of their responsibilities, and the expectations of others, may not be helpful in focusing the school's energies on what matters most. The responsibilities of leaders should be clarified, documented and published to staff, and clearly linked to the school's purposes or goals.

In the same way, the school's time and money for professional learning may need to be reviewed to ensure that teachers receive tuition in areas most likely to enhance the achievement of goals.

Reward what matters

People respond to praise and other affirmations. Some schools may appear to be excessive in their use of physical rewards (such as certificates, stickers or gifts), and the danger here is that students learn to expect, even require, rewards in order to perform. A word of affirmation in many schools is enough, and does not need to be rationed.

However, it is important that what is rewarded connects to what really matters. Sometimes the simplest things to observe are rewarded most often, yet may have little impact on student learning or other goals of the school. It may be interesting for staff to monitor the awards given to students, identify the reasons for which they are given and compare these with the school's core goals. It may also be interesting for teachers to observe peers, noting each time a student is affirmed and the reason for the affirmation.

Beyond goal achievement to growth

The point made in this chapter was that it's not enough to set goals; what matters is achieving them. But in our experience we might also wonder whether there is an issue with goal setting.

Goals can stretch us, but they can also limit us. They can motivate us, but they can also discourage us. For example, a school may set a goal of being in the top 10% of schools in NAPLAN for Writing. This is a goal which they may never achieve, and lead to eventual frustration. However, they are actually successful if they are continually improving their ranking or the percentage of students above the norm, or if there is consistent progress by a target group of students.

The key to goal-setting is that the goals must reflect growth. The challenge is to define that growth, and determine how it will be assessed.

CASE STUDY: THE ACTION PLAN

Julie and Theo are the Year 4 teachers at St Wilfred's, a Catholic school in an inner metropolitan suburb. They have just left their stage meeting rather concerned as Paula, their area supervisor, has given then something of a challenge. She has asked them both to consider engaging in professional development in the teaching of mathematics, with a particular focus on concepts relating to time and graphs and data, in the first half of the year and to develop an action plan for their curriculum and teaching in these areas in the second half of the year. Paula has requested that they include this when setting goals for their annual performance review this year. The idea is to use the new knowledge to improve teaching and learning in the area.

Both Julie and Theo would acknowledge that the writing was on the wall. At a staff meeting late last year the principal expressed some dissatisfaction about a trend in the national testing results over the last three years, which indicated Year 3 and Year 5 students at St Wilfred's were far below the state mean in these areas in particular. At that time it was announced that improvements to aspects of numeracy would be one of the school's strategic goals in the longer term. However, they did not realise at the time what a crucial role they would need to play and how it would impact on their own work in the coming year.

With Paula's assistance and support, Julie and Theo have worked out a plan to develop their teaching of mathematics, beginning with the teaching of time. They have drafted the following action plan to guide their work:

- Assess their students on the concept of time using tasks they have designed as well as modified questions from the standardised tests.
- Participate in some professional development sessions on teaching time being offered through the Catholic Education Office. Use ideas and new learning to plan a unit of work on time.
- Design and teach the unit of work.
- Reassess students using similar tasks and compare results, looking for significant changes since the first assessment, as well as trends as identified in the national test result summary.

> Reflect on the success of the professional development and the action plan. Consider what strategies to apply to the teaching of graphs and data.

MAKE IT PERSONAL

The challenge for school leaders is to change from doing things because they are directed towards goals to doing things because they are achieving goals.

Ask yourself, to what degree do I:
- use data to inform my decisions?
- involve others in reviewing the school's achievements?
- critically explore ways to improve achievement (without making excuses for performance) and involve others in identifying strategies?

FURTHER INVESTIGATION

Informative assessment

Nationally mandated and commercially available tests provide a great deal of analytical data about individual student performance and the performance of student cohorts. This data can usually be mined for specific comparisons between genders and various other sub-groups, and for analysis of different strands of the curriculum. Few school teachers and leaders, however, have training in interpreting data. As a result, often very superficial use is made of the wealth of data provided by these tests. Valuable information is lost, and sometimes incorrect or misleading conclusions are drawn. In addition, many educators assume that such tests are the only way to gather information about student learning. This is highly misleading (albeit an understanding, we might argue, that governments and systems have been keen to promote in recent times). Yet, 'Much of what teachers and learners do in classrooms can be described as assessment' (ARG, 2002).

Educators are not always clear about the distinction between
- assessment for learning (formative assessment), as teachers constantly check students' understanding and adjust their teaching
- assessment of learning (summative assessment), often used to identify mastery of the curriculum or to rank students or schools
- assessment as learning, by making students aware of learning goals; and
- assessment for teachers, to evaluate their learning programs and strategies (Ridden & Heldsinger, 2014, p.3).

But Forster (2009), argues that, 'Informative assessment does not make a distinction between the contexts of assessment or their stated primary purposes. Rather, it focuses on how teachers and students make use of assessment information to both understand and improve learning' (p.5). Put simply, we cannot see what learning is taking place in a student's mind, nor the impact that any particular action by the teacher is having on that learning. The purpose of assessment is to make learning visible (Heldsinger, 2012; Hattie, 2009).

There are many resources that can help schools to be assessment literate, and to use assessment strategies and tools appropriately and effectively. Most systems have helpful documents and consultants.

3

Maintenance, improvement and alignment

From maintenance to improvement

Only mediocrity can be trusted to be always at its best (Beerbohm, 1954, p.350)

REFLECT
- In a review of your school, in what areas would the school be seen to be performing well?
- In what areas do you have difficulty defending the school's performance to parents?
- List three areas in which you would like to see improvement in the school.

SHIFT THE FOCUS
There are many leadership metaphors which have evolved over the years. The traditional mark of an efficient administrator was that they 'ran a tight ship' and 'kept things running smoothly'. For many people it remains the measure of effectiveness.

For executive staff in schools, it is often difficult to find time to do more than the most pressing things. The school has a life of its own, generating work necessary simply to keep it operating. It is not unusual for school leaders to reflect at the end of a very busy day and find it difficult to recall 'where the day went'. In this context, it is tempting to focus on maintenance functions, to ensure that the school operates without panic, conflict or stress. But when the focus is on goals and achievement, this is no longer an appropriate indicator of effectiveness. The structures, tasks and procedures have no value in themselves; they are simply ways to achieve the goals.

There is a need to shift the focus from maintenance to a constant search for improvement; and that will certainly mean 'rocking the boat' on occasions.

It means identifying what needs improving, and applying your knowledge of change processes to achieve that change.

What if it ain't broke?

Some will argue, 'If it ain't broke, why fix it?' There are several problems with this philosophy. If we spend all of our time in the ship's engine room, keeping the engines humming smoothly, we lose sight of what is happening around us and ahead. We lose direction, the sense of where we were sailing to and why, and how we are progressing. We become oblivious to the changing weather and other dangers and fail to see opportunities.

Handy (1995) described a pattern of progress and renewal followed by enterprises, from empires to businesses, to life itself: an initial struggle, followed by growth, a peak in performance, and then a decline of gradual deterioration. He plotted this pattern as a sigmoid curve, a sideways S-shape (Fig. 3-1). Handy argued that the secret of constant growth is to start a new sigmoid curve — that is, to begin a new enterprise (point A in the diagram) — before the first one starts to wane or peter out. If we wait until something is broken (point B), we will likely find that it is beyond fixing, or that the down time for fixing or replacing it will cripple us.

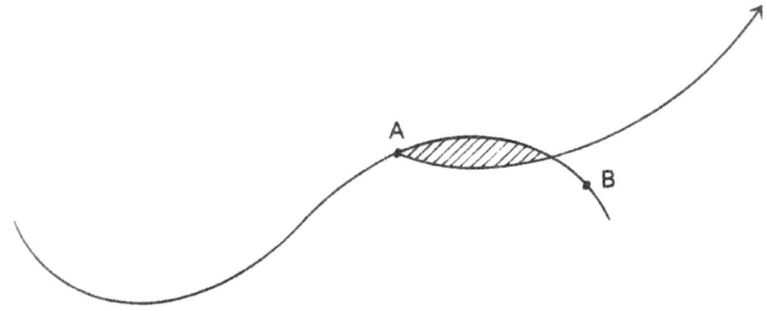

Fig. 3-1. The sigmoid to identify the time for change
Adapted from Handy, 1995, p.51

This idea seems simple enough: Start making changes — implement new pedagogical approaches or new technology, for example — before problems with the old way of doing things appear. However, leaders who are aware they are at a 'point A' may need to ask colleagues to see things that might not yet be obvious. This makes change challenging especially when things appear to be going well. Uncertainty can be felt and lead to resistance. Therefore, the shaded area between the two curves represents what Handy called "a time of great confusion" (p.52).

The message for schools is that maintenance is an inappropriate posture. The search for continual growth or improvement requires us to move from a position as a target of change to a centre of change. And we need to manage the shady periods with a combination of deftness and patience.

Senge (2006) also reminds us that too much focus on the maintenance functions of organisations may blind us to peril (p.7). School leaders can get bogged down in the mire of administrative, managerial tasks and, as a result, fail to look beyond that to see what trends are emerging or how those tasks relate (or not) to evolving circumstances. Leaders must ask questions and challenge the status quo, because such action creates an opportunity to look at our assumptions about 'the way we do things here', compare it to what is actually happening and, if needed, initiate change based on evidence.

This opens leaders and staff up to the views of others and the resulting discourse can eventually lead to some kind of shared vision of where the school needs to be in relation to the current situation. Discourse about school issues between leadership and other staff can be greatly enabled if openness of communication is a prominent feature of interactions within the school (De Nobile, 2021).

Successful learning organisations do this continuously. There is no 'end' to school improvement; it is a continuing process which school leaders must foster, and encourage the staff to work on cohesively for the benefit of the school.

Create a change-ready environment

For a school to be able to change effectively, it needs to be predisposed to change. To achieve this, develop a change mentality in the school community, so that change is accepted as a normal, manageable and enriching aspect of the school's life.

Foster an environment of trust, by giving teachers the confidence that they have some control over decisions which directly affect their work, that change is being promoted for educationally 'right' reasons, and that in implementing change, they will be supported by resources, feedback, the public backing of leaders, diminished pressures in other areas, and tolerance of short-term failure.

Develop communication networks through which problems can be shared and feedback obtained, and provide staff with the avenues to openly share views and make collaborative decisions.

Promote a collaborative climate, by evaluating and then improving the quality of working relationships among staff.

Model openness to change through your own behaviour, and have an innovation mind-set. Face each day with the intention to make the future better than the past, and actively seek ways to do that. By changing yourself, you let others see your willingness to evaluate and improve your own performance. Talk about courses you attend, new ideas you are trying to implement and problems you are having. Be open to suggestions from staff that impact on your work.

Explore emerging educational concepts, knowledge and practices, through professional reading, conferences and networks. Encourage discussion of educational issues, and be an educational expert, able to explain what ought to be and why. Use staff meeting time to initiate discussion about educational issues which are relevant to the school. Use influential staff members to lead discussions, in small groups or pairs, so that teachers are engaged in the issue. Encourage staff to identify topics for discussion and to initiate conversations with leaders about ways to improve learning. Challenge staff to argue how action in a particular area will achieve improvement. Allow them to similarly challenge you! (Avoid using staff meetings for staff or leadership 'gripes', or for information dissemination; discussion time is too scarce to waste.)

Encourage staff to question why things are done in the school, as well as how they are done. Let new ideas be heard and considered. Avoid dismissing ideas because of circumstances or history. When new ideas are proposed, talk about them positively, including new ideas initiated by the central authority. It's easy to concentrate on the problems implicit in new ideas, and to foster antagonism to them. Instead, look for the opportunities on offer to a school that wants to take charge of the idea and make it their own. Ask, 'What's in this for teachers and students?'

Encourage innovation. Progress is made when people are prepared to 'stick their neck out' and turn an idea into practice. So praise staff members who try new things; provide feedback; connect them with other innovators; offer support; and publicise their work to colleagues, the school community or the wider community. Recognise small changes as well as major innovations. If it represents change for a person, it is significant to them.

With that in mind, support even the most radical thinkers. Yes, they may strain relationships from time to time, and they may impede what you thought would be a simple decision-making process; but their constant questioning and challenging, if dealt with appropriately, will inspire creative thinking in others. Respect those who are 'cracked', because they let in the light. Respect those who are looking through a different window, because they will see things others don't.

Understand the politics of the school. Identify, gain the support of and satisfy the needs of the influential members, the resisters, the analysts, the lobbyists, the confident, the insecure, the leaders and the followers.

Promote the concept that change is growth. Highlight the improvements that result from change. From time to time, publicly trace the evolution of procedures, policies or practices in a way that demonstrates growth in understanding or maturity.

Encourage open communication

Creating a school climate which is open to change, and modelling that change is the norm requires a range of leadership attributes and processes, but among the most important are openness of communication and democratic forms of leadership.

The interactions between staff members in a school can be described in general terms from closed to open. Open communication is typified by honest, even candid, interactions between people. It implies trust between senders and receivers of information. Some typical characteristics of open communication in schools include:

- people exchanging ideas, including ideas which challenge existing culture, values and beliefs
- willingness to tell a colleague 'bad news' relating to themselves or an aspect of the school, and a willingness to receive 'bad news', especially if modelled by school leadership
- absence of 'shooting the messenger' or belittling others' opinions
- a perception that people can be trusted with sensitive information and that they will trust you
- a prevailing feeling that people are generally honest and trustworthy.

By contrast, closed communication promotes distrust, leading to a lack of meaningful and important information sharing. Some behaviours indicative of closed communication include:

- information being changed, omitted or otherwise distorted in order to make the sender 'look okay'
- reluctance by people to share their true feelings or opinions, because they perceive their feelings and opinions are not valued
- a perception that school leaders are not honest and tend to withhold information
- a lack of trust among staff and between school leadership and staff (Hoy & Miskel, 2013, p.200).

If open communication prevails in the school, information which people need to perform their work or make decisions is not restricted nor withheld. This applies to 'upward' and 'downward' communication; that is, information from staff to the school's leaders, and information from the school's leaders to the staff (De Nobile, 2023).

Open communication is important to team building, facilitating input into decision-making and promoting positive staff morale. It also, facilitates the free flow of school cultural information, collegial and managerial support and, of course, levels of trust necessary for school change and improvement (De Nobile, 2010).

Understand change processes

The assumption is often made that, if an idea is sound, then people will support it — or *should* support it.

However, we do not change organisations; we change people. Most people's primary response to change is emotional, not intellectual, so good ideas and persuasive logic alone will not bring about change. Ridden (2011) described the typical range of emotions experienced during exposure to an innovation (Fig. 3-1).

He argued that the emotions and concerns people experience are normal; that they are somewhat sequential, moving through the effect of the change on ourselves, our work, our students and our school; and that person must move through the stages at their own rate. The implications for school leadership is that the support needed by each person depends on the stage they are at (Ridden, 2011, p.14–16).

Fig. 3-2. Emotional responses to change.
Adapted from Ridden, 2011, p.15.

Identify areas where improvement is needed

There will be things to change in the school and in the performance of individual staff members. Identify roles, structures, procedures, actions and people impeding the achievement of the school's goals, or acting against the school's purposes. Be aware of:

- individuals: staff members who are having difficulties with students, colleagues, parents, policies or procedures, or with their own professional motivation, as well as staff members who have high self-esteem and competence
- interactions: tensions between staff, as well as ways in which staff are supporting each other
- issues: matters that are causing frustration or discontent, and those that are causing great satisfaction, including areas where the school is performing well and areas where it is not
- influences: things and people that are changing, whether in positive or negative ways, and the reasons for these changes
- implementation: practices and behaviours that don't support the school's purposes and ethos, and those that do, noting in particular those practices which are embedded in the school culture

- improvements: areas where improvements are sought, are being made, or are necessary
- innovation: people who are trialling new approaches, and exploring ways to improve, whether on behalf of the staff or individually.

Where appropriate, check your perceptions by discussions, with individuals, small groups or whole staff; focused observation; formal data gathering; and performance review processes.

It will become evident where improvement is necessary. Then focus activity where the need is most critical and where success is most likely, and intervene with individuals to enhance performance.

Make change liberating

The discussion thus far in this chapter has focused on the school's staff. And yet, most of what has been said applies to other members of the school also. Students and parents also need to understand the need to recognise when the time is right for change; to be change-ready, trusting the school's actions and motives; to enjoy open and honest communication with the school's leaders and other staff, and with the parent body; and to be able to share their perceptions of where change is needed.

Everyone is accountable for the way they help to achieve the school's goals. The whole school community should know what the school is trying to achieve, and be able to evaluate the actions that take place to achieve that standard. And all stakeholders have a role to play in achieving the goals — academic staff, support staff, students, parents, the school board or council, even volunteers.

To some, this will sound intimidating because everyone knows what's expected, and everyone can consider how well it's being achieved. Staff cannot take refuge in jargon, esoteric argument, fuzzy goals, or patronising educational gobbledygook. Nor can the school's leaders. However, it is also liberating, because the expectations are public. This means that teachers know what is expected and cannot be criticised for not achieving some secret purpose or private expectation. Members of the executive staff are able to see when staff members are not performing to expectations, and have an objective basis for discussing an individual's performance.

Consequently, people can argue for changes to structures, procedures, policies, programs and resource allocations against a declared standard, and can argue against demands on their time and energy, or the allocation of resources, which appear to be inconsistent with the goals. They can hold others, including executive staff, accountable against the same standards.

There is a clear basis for identifying where change is appropriate and for promoting it.

In addition, change should be liberating in the breadth of the expectations. Everyone should understand what will constitute success. Some leaders like to set specific targets, such as getting 20 per cent of the school's students in the top 10 per cent of the state in some specified state or national test. An alternative standard is a growth-oriented target, such as continual improvement year by year against a valid and worthwhile outcome. Handy (1995) puts it succinctly: 'We do not need to change the world. To nudge a little bit of it along will be enough' (p.264).

In education, of course, continual improvement is difficult. Each cohort of students embodies a range of variables which will affect their performance in whatever area we care to define and measure their progress. Maintain a balanced perspective, and seek trends. As Blanchard & Shula (1995) note, 'Success is not forever, and failure isn't fatal' (p.41). The notion of open-ended improvement is congruent with the Japanese management concept of *kaizen*, which emphasises continuous, day-to-day improvement of work processes driven by the insights of workers, and aims to increase productivity by improving workers' ownership of their own work. In schools, this means that continual improvement should make learning for students, and work for staff, a better experience than before. If the school demonstrates a culture that values change, openness, teamwork, empowerment and participation in decision-making, then change for the better is likely (Wellington, 2000).

School accountability

Increasingly, schools are being asked to give evidence of value-adding. More demanding accountabilities have led to more participatory and comprehensive review procedures.

Many schools are involved in a cycle of self-review. School self-reviews typically happen at regular intervals, may be audited by educators from outside the school, and should result in strategic development plans which describe how the school will improve or add value over a set period. From these development plans may come annual plans which break down the larger tasks into sub-tasks achievable within a year or in months or weeks. Achievements may be fed back to the school community via annual reports which schools publish to the wider community.

Individual performance reviews may relate to key goals in an annual plan and strategic plan, ensuring that individual performance and growth contributes to the achievement of school goals.

The school review process ascertains how a school has improved and how it adds value for students. Staff members are involved in the process and generally tend to feel more committed to achieving the goals that emanate from the process, and to personal growth because they can see how their work may contribute to student learning and other aspects of the school.

The process encourages critical reflection about current practice and the development of visions for future, more effective practice. It fosters productive relationships, collegiality, support and democracy that are so important to morale. It also enables school communities to develop the personal mastery, team mentality and shared vision typical of learning organisations which can help schools identify potential problems before they become difficult to manage.

CASE STUDY: IDENTIFYING AREAS FOR IMPROVEMENT AT ALDERSTONE HIGH SCHOOL

Alderstone High School is a medium-sized secondary school in the outer suburbs. The school has a good reputation for academic excellence. Every year the percentage of students offered university places is higher than average for the region, and the school has higher than average percentages of students in scoring the upper bands of achievement in mathematics, economics, geography and modern history in Year 12 exams.

Alan has been the principal at Alderstone for the last 12 months. He has spent that time getting to know the staff, the culture of the school and the school's curriculum-based and co-curricular programs. Several things have become clear to him about how the school 'ticks':

- Most staff members have an impression that Alderstone is a 'better' school than its immediate neighbours and they are proud to say they work there.
- While there have been recent professional development days in quality pedagogy, the majority of teachers favour more traditional methods of teaching, such as teacher input sessions, lessons closely linked to textbooks, and the use of computer technologies mainly for the preparation and presentation of student work.
- Some staff members, mostly department heads, view the pedagogical changes championed by the quality teaching 'push' (their term) as a threat to the quality of their programs and the achievements of their students.
- Parents are very supportive of the school's teachers and their teaching methods, and reacted defensively when Alan broached the topic of

quality teaching and the recent staff development days at a recent meeting of the parents and friends' association.
- Some students have confirmed Alan's concerns about teachers' uninspired pedagogy during casual chats on the grounds during lunch times.

While things look okay, Alan can see problems ahead. These problems will require the school to come to terms with the concepts associated with quality pedagogy, and soon. His key observations from available data are:

- While student results in English are high compared to other schools, there is a slight downward trend in results from national testing and Year 12 exams.
- The proportion of the school's students from non-English speaking backgrounds has increased significantly, without any change in relevant programs or teaching strategies.
- There has been increased incidence of disruptive students and inappropriate behaviour.

Alan's extensive professional reading and previous experience in other schools have led him to recognise that more effective pedagogy could help improve student behaviour and achievement. He also recognises the importance of English and technology to students moving into work or further study.

His task is clear: He has to get the school to change in this area to meet the coming challenges.

MAKE IT PERSONAL

The challenge for school leaders is to move from the comfort of maintaining what is, to the uncertainty of achieving what should be.

Ask yourself, to what degree do I:
- articulate expectations of staff and students?
- model a constant quest for improvement?
- encourage a change mentality in staff?
- encourage questioning of policies, programs and procedures?
- facilitate processes that make change possible?
- understand and manage change in the school?
- intervene to coach and support individual teachers who need to grow professionally?

FURTHER INVESTIGATION

Changing schools

A great deal of literature is available on the topic of changing schools. A search of the literature for names such as Michael Fullan, John P Kotter and Peter Senge will lead you to a reservoir of resources.

Understanding the concepts and principles of change is essential. However, change is idiosyncratic and influenced by a myriad of variables. A principal may introduce a sustained innovation with minimal effort in one school, yet fail disastrously to implement the same innovation in another school. The reasons are explained above.

There are many case studies of change in the literature, from carefully researched academic articles to anecdotal narratives in non-refereed journals for school leaders, such as *Leading and Managing*, *Australian Educational Leader,* and *Leadership in Focus*. An exploration of these in the light of your understanding of the process of change may be helpful in considering the effectiveness of change processes in your school.

Accountability

Past processes of review depended upon inspectors, who visited schools and reported on compliance, strengths and areas for improvement. While this process might have kept schools in step with the expectations of government and society, the potential for teachers and school leaders to be disconnected from it was high, because they were not involved in the process, other than preparing and collecting documentation. In more recent times, education systems in many countries have developed more sophisticated and participative methods of review for registration and accreditation. This has happened in tandem with increased pressure from governments and the wider community for schools to be accountable for what they do. While it is generally the case that schools come under the rules and regulations set down by various government acts, and are monitored by government appointed authorities, the responsibility for review and subsequent action is often delegated to school systems, where relevant, and to individual schools.

It is now common practice for schools to undergo self-review. This is typically done in accordance with frameworks or guidelines which reflect the requirements of governments and systems (Antoniou et al, 2016) or, in the case of independent schools, the school's governing body or target community (Gurr et al, 2022).

It may interest you to explore how government and non-government schools in your locality conduct self-reviews; to compare the processes designed by various education systems; and to consider how self-review processes integrate with system processes. You might also consider the degree to which self-reviews actually impact a school's goals, policies, procedures and outcomes.

Beyond improvement to alignment

It's what you learn after you know it all that counts (Wooden, 2010).

REFLECT

- How would you rate the quality of education your school provides? What criteria do you use? What evidence do you cite?
- How do you decide where to spend money, where to allocate staff?
- Where are the school's resources and energies directed, and how does this reflect the goals and values of the school?

SHIFT THE FOCUS

A shift from maintenance to improvement requires an understanding of change processes. Change must be directed towards improving teaching and learning, which is the school's core or 'moral' purpose. Dempster (2009) believes that school leaders should be driven by a clear moral purpose to improve students' lives through learning. 'To put it starkly, principals are not there to make students' lives worse; they are there to see that their schools concentrate on improving students' learning and ultimately their achievement' (p.2).

However, while the school might identify and implement a plethora of improvements, there is a need to consider the 'whole package', and to ensure that the school's resources and energies are all aligned towards this core purpose.

A model for alignment

Caldwell & Spinks (2008) illustrate the application of the concept of alignment by suggesting that:

> The design of state-of-the-art facilities must be consistent with the design of a relevant curriculum that must, in turn, be delivered through a range of pedagogical practices by professionals with the knowledge and skill to accomplish the task, with each of these consistent with the needs of society and the expectations of the community. Plans and budgets should enable this alignment (p.29).

They elaborate this notion in a 'model for alignment', arguing that to transform a school there is a need to align the intellectual, social, spiritual and financial capital of the school, and to align these with the interests of students and the goal of transformation. This requires, they argue, outstanding governance or leadership (p.32–33).

The idea is, in many ways, obvious, yet its implementation is complex. There are many facets to the life of a school which principals and other leaders must oversee; many competing demands for time, energy and resources; many priorities to be addressed; many voices who claim the right to be heard; many tensions to be resolved.

Those voices do not only come from within the school, but from system authorities and government bodies. The administrative and accountability expectations of regulatory authorities are often a distraction for the core business of the school. School leaders may chart an easy path, even unwittingly, but find themselves responding to persuasive or insistent demands and priorities. In that process, resources can be dispersed widely. It is a challenging task for school leaders to ensure that time, money and energy are directed to the school's focus.

Financial, spiritual and social capital is addressed in various other sections of this book. Intellectual capital refers to the level of knowledge and skill of those who work in the school. How can that be developed?

Instructional leadership

Effective school leaders are instructional leaders, committed to improving student outcomes. Such leaders are proactive and interactive, rather than reactive or inactive. Woolfolk Hoy & Hoy (2008) noted that principals and other leaders can demonstrate instructional leadership through:

- focusing on academic excellence by celebrating student achievements and espousing values of academic success and hard work
- focusing on instructional excellence through regular monitoring of achievements, school climate and support for improvement
- focusing on the importance of the teacher as a decision-maker regarding curriculum and pedagogy
- providing support, resources and other materials that will enable teacher success
- keeping up-to-date with developments in various aspects of teaching and learning, and sharing these with staff
- taking the lead role in celebrating student and teacher achievement and the school vision and culture.

In his synthesis of five major research projects on leadership for learning in schools, Dempster (2009) identified that leaders best affect student learning outcomes when they:

- have an agreed and shared moral purpose
- instigate 'disciplined dialogue' about learning in the school plan, monitor and take account using a strong evidence base
- are active professional learners with their teachers
- attend to enhancing the conditions for learning
- coordinate, manage and monitor the curriculum and teaching
- use distributive leadership as the norm
- understand the context of their work and connect with parent and wider community support for learning.

The work of Hallinger and his associates (Hallinger & Hosseingholizadeh, 2020) has been influential on school improvement efforts in Australia and worldwide. Their model identifies three prime roles for school leaders, especially principals:

- Define the school mission: set clear and measurable goals, ensure they are known to everyone and are worked towards
- Manage the instructional program: develop quality teaching and learning, by monitoring student progress, adjusting curriculum and pedagogy and using feedback to inform teacher practice.
- Develop a positive school learning climate: provide learning infrastructures (including time), model professional support, model high standards, and encourage good practice.

Some educators question the use of the term 'instructional leadership'. MacNeill et al (2003) argue that instruction is a limiting term that relates to one part of the teaching and learning cycle, and that it typically describes only principal behaviours and not those of other members of the school community. The authors argue instead for 'pedagogic leadership'. Others prefer the term 'leadership for learning' when describing the actions of leaders to influence best practice teaching in their schools (e.g., Marsh et al, 2016; Robinson et al, 2009).

However, it is not a question of which of these things a leader should do to enhance student learning; they are all important. The power is in their alignment, in ensuring that all actions are directed towards student learning.

Building students' trust

A key role for leaders is to create a learning culture. According to the media, there are many schools in which learning is frustrated by the actions of some students, where teachers spend more time dealing with disruptive students than teaching, and where the teaching process is constantly interrupted by inappropriate student behaviour.

In such schools there is a sense that staff and students are on opposing sides; that the role of students is to harass teachers as effectively as possible, and the role of staff is to respond by repressing students as much as possible. This is an adversarial 'I'll get you before you get me' attitude.

The challenge for leaders is to promote a culture in which students understand that all staff are on their side; that teachers' whole purpose for turning up each day is to help each student learn, and to enrich students' lives in whatever way they can; that staff and students are travelling the same path together. In such schools, staff and students are not adversarial, but collaborative, with students seeking to help staff in their efforts to help students.

Is this naïve? Certainly not. It is how all successful schools operate. It is the essence of schooling. The challenge for leaders in adversarial schools is to change the culture. How can this be achieved?

- Collaborate with students. Build conversations with student leaders and seek their support. This includes those who have formal leadership roles and those who are influential among their peers. Involve them in the enterprise of learning. Ask students to identify practices which inhibit learning.
- Deal with disruptive students. This may involve serious disciplinary action, or removing these students from classrooms. There are creative ways to accommodate these students in places where they do not disrupt the learning of others. However, it also means taking time to talk with students, to understand their issues, to develop rapport, to seek to change their attitudes to school.
- Collaborate with parents. Ensure they also understand the expectations and the focus. Confront those who seek to be adversarial with staff. Reinforce the message that all adults (parents and staff) are working for the student's wellbeing and progress.
- Address practices which impede learning, even if the school has 'always operated this way' or 'there is no other way to do it' or 'staff won't like it'.
- Articulate appropriate values. It is important that consistent, positive messages about learning are displayed, heard and reinforced regularly;

messages which espouse the value of academic success, recognition given to those who exhibit high standards or improvement, the role of hard work, the need for engagement with learning, and so on. Celebrate learning.

Committing to professional learning

A commitment to student learning implies a commitment to staff learning also. If learning is genuinely valued, it is valued for all. It pervades the life of the school community. The notion of lifelong learning should be given active expression among teachers.

In a school where learning matters to staff, teachers should be challenged by professional learning. Many teachers prefer courses which reinforce what they already know, but avoid courses which explore ideas which are new to them or about which they have limited knowledge. Ironically, when a briefing or course is offered, it is often the person who knows the most about the topic who is chosen to attend. Look at the courses your colleagues attend to see if this is so in your school. Such events may provide excellent opportunities for professional networking, and the development of focused expertise, but they should also challenge participants' current understandings, or provide new ways to apply the knowledge.

Professional learning should be focused on the school's priorities and needs. Clearly teachers need to be able to attend professional learning which is tailored to their individual needs. However, the school should also have identified areas of curriculum practice where there is a need for up-skilling or new thinking. If a particular learning experience involves a working group of staff within a school, the learning can be targeted to the specific needs of staff within the context of your school, the implementation and application of the learning can be planned, colleagues can support one another and challenge one another in applying the learning, and there is a common context and language for continuing dialogue on the topic.

School leaders should participate in professional learning with staff. When the staff learns together, school leaders can — should — also be involved. The content of the course may have no direct application to the principal's work; it may take them away from other priorities to which they would like to attend; but their presence has several key purposes:

- It emphasises that this matters.
- It emphasises shared responsibility. It says that 'we are in this together as a school, and we need to address this together as a school', rather than 'this is your problem; you fix it. I have my own issues.'

- It provides a common context and language for further dialogue with the principal during the application and implementation of the ideas.
- It enables the principal to take a lead in professional dialogue about learning.
- It enables the principal to share his or her experience and wisdom about learning.

Approaches to professional learning for staff should model good practice. Schools should be exemplars of quality learning not just for students, but also for staff — and even for parents. Successful professional learning is typically:

- learner-driven, grounded in participants' questions and issues
- differentiated to meet the needs of participants
- contextual, connecting with teachers' work and current contexts, and with sound research and expertise beyond the school
- timely, addressing teachers' needs at the time when they are ready
- experiential, engaging teachers in practical tasks, and providing opportunity for inquiry, experimentation and feedback
- interactive and collaborative, providing opportunity for sharing of knowledge and experience between participants, and encouraging teacher reflection, judgement, application and creativity
- sustained, supported by modelling, coaching and problem-solving, and providing ongoing feedback
- transformative, with the clear and public purpose of bringing about change in teachers' thinking and practice.

Learning methodologies are continually evolving in response to new knowledge about the neuroscience of learning, and new information and communication technologies. If these methodologies are used, where appropriate and helpful, to facilitate student learning, then they should also be used to facilitate professional learning experiences of teachers.

As part of the sustained professional learning of all staff, professional dialogue should be part of the culture of the school. Conversations about learning ought to be evident in many contexts within the school.

The school as a learning community

Where learning is acknowledged as the key purpose of the school, the school as a community also learns. Procedures are regularly reviewed and refined; policies are understood and applied or changed; relationships are nurtured; trust is sought; the modes and effectiveness of communication are continually assessed; shared understandings are articulated and clarified.

This is commonly referred to in the literature as organisational development, 'the practice of changing people and organisations for positive growth' (Richards, 2010). Senge (2006) reminds us that learning organisations are 'organisations where people continually expand their capacity to create the results they truly desire, where new and expansive patterns of thinking are nurtured, where collective aspiration is set free, and where people are continually learning to see the whole together' (p.3)

However, although aspects of organisational development can be applied to schools, organisational theory has failed to effectively describe schools. The school is far better described as community than organisation (Ridden, 2003a). Peck (1987) in describing community, includes contemplation as a characteristic. He explains that a community is contemplative in the sense that it is reflective, constantly examining itself; and aware, in that it knows itself, the world outside and the relationship between the two (p.66). The community of the school needs to be reflective, constantly seeking to learn about itself and how it can grow and improve.

In recent times the term 'professional learning community' (or PLC) has been used to describe how schools nurture the instructional capacity of teachers. One helpful description gleaned from recent research described PLCs as places where teachers share their practices, support one another and collaborate regularly to achieve common goals (Admiraal et al, 2021).

In the same way that individual learning stays with the individual, changing them forever, so learning by a school should also stay with the school beyond the tenure of any individual staff member (including the principal), changing the school forever. Implicit here is the notion of sustainable leadership, which embodies the principles and actions that lead to widespread, continuous and long-lasting school improvement.

Sustainable leadership is about continuity. It rejects the idea of charismatic leadership, as the ideas, vision and energy that are attached to such leaders tend to disappear after they move on. It promotes the idea of continuation and planning for succession. Hargreaves & Shirley (2009) suggested seven principles of sustainable leadership:

- depth of purpose
- breadth of purpose, as a shared responsibility
- endurance over time
- justice in attending to all students' learning
- resourcefulness in the use of resources
- conservation in connecting tradition with vision
- diversity of curriculum, pedagogy and ideas (p.97–98).

Hargreaves & Fink (2006) described sustainable leadership as 'a meal, not a menu' (p.251). All these principles taken together make sustainable leadership work.

Leadership learning

Leadership learning involves learning to think and act effectively as a leader. It applies to those who lead and those who aspire to do so. A school's intellectual capital is increased by enhancing the leadership capacity of the school; that is, the capability of those in positions of leadership, and others who exercise leadership or aspire to exercise leadership, or (sometimes overlooked) who might be encouraged to develop and use their leadership abilities.

Much leadership learning takes place beyond the context of a physical or virtual classroom. While ease of access and flexibility make online learning increasingly popular, effective learning is often focused on experiential and practical learning, integrating theory and practice. Strategies may include co-learning with other leaders in the school; developing a shared construction of meaning; validating personal knowledge and experience; developing a sense of community, care, connection and collegiality; exploring the 'big picture'; generating ideas and exploring possibilities and options; encouraging formal and informal leadership; internships; problem-based learning, through real and complex problems and dilemmas; project-based learning and action research; sharing authority for learning and collaborating around practical issues; coaching and mentoring; formalised faculty and team planning and evaluation; supervision of teaching and learning programs and classrooms; leading professional learning teams and other opportunities to lead for learning; and shared or modelled leadership (Anderson & Cawsey, 2008; Hallinger, 2011).

Some leaders enhance their own growth through partnering with a peer mentor. In describing this process, Loader (2003) described the need for professional development 'that makes principals look at themselves differently; that makes them examine their interactions with others and the effect that they have on people; and learn to do things differently and more effectively' (p.28).

In a similar way, many leaders are now seeking professional coaching. According to research by Robertson (2016), leadership coaching can become a transformative process that allows leaders to act with confidence and agency, able to reflect on their own experiences, and to develop their own colleagues. In doing these things leaders are more likely to enact the moral purpose of making a positive difference to teachers and students.

Health and wellbeing

While identifying areas to align to increase the intellectual capital of the school, it is also necessary to consider the place of student and staff health and wellbeing.

The moral purpose of schools is student learning and wellbeing. Students cannot learn effectively if they are not in a state of physical, mental and emotional wellbeing. Poor physical health, mental or emotional stress and social discomfort all impede a student's ability to focus, to integrate information and ideas, to 'think straight'.

In the long term, students' lives are likely to be impacted as much by the wellbeing as by their academic learning. Their wellbeing will affect their functioning in the workplace, and their happiness and safety in life.

Wellbeing has been conceptualised in many ways. From his classic research Seligman (2011) described five elements that contribute to wellbeing including positive emotions, positive relationships, engagement in things that are pleasurable, meaningful experiences and a sense of accomplishment or achievement. Hesketh and Cooper (2019) described two types of wellbeing: eudaimonic and hedonic. Eudaimonic wellbeing refers to having a positive view of life, while hedonic wellbeing concerns our feelings of happiness or pleasure.

Wellbeing requires the development of a sustainable positive mood and positive attitude, which is reflected in satisfaction with self, relationships and learning experiences at school, and a view of life characterised by hope, confidence, contentment and self-efficacy. Recent research (Cross, 2021; Hossein et al, 2023; Powell et al, 2018; O'Grady, 2010) suggests that the current emphasis on student wellbeing is driven by concerns about:

- a tendency towards increased anxiety and stress among youth (especially during and after the COVID-19 pandemic)
- pressures on young people to indulge in unhealthy activities, often as a result of inappropriate (but very visible) role models, family vulnerabilities and dysfunction, religious and cultural tensions, and violence and cyberbullying
- unhealthy patterns of sleep, nutrition, diet and exercise among children and young people
- unrealistic expectations of parents and governments concerning the roles of schools

- increasing legal compliance requirements of schools in terms of child protection, health, safety and wellbeing.

This concern about wellbeing, or 'wellness' as it is increasing called, extends beyond students. Staff wellbeing also matters, for reasons similar to those above, and because of the educational impact of a teacher's state of wellbeing, and the legal occupational health and safety requirements. And schools find themselves increasingly involved in the wellbeing of parents and families, because this impacts the wellbeing of students.

It is possible to speak of the wellbeing or health of a school also. This reflects the quality of relationships, the sense of purpose and efficacy of all members of the school community, the sense of community or belonging of the members, the sense of hope, the quality of communication, the ability to resolve conflict, and other qualities. The effectiveness of the review processes described earlier in this chapter depend upon the health or wellbeing of the relationships: the presence of trust, acceptance, effective communication, listening, decision-making processes, and so on.

The wellbeing of leaders also matters. A leader who has a sense of hope, a positive attitude, and a sense of satisfaction or contentment, will have a positive influence on the wellbeing of others within the school community.

CASE STUDY: THE WHOLE-SCHOOL STRATEGIC REVIEW

Alan is concerned about the way things are going at Alderstone High School. The school is performing well, but there is evidence of stagnation. The school is not due for strategic review until next year, but he decides to bring it forward a year after noting that many of the goals from the previous review are close to being achieved. After some discussion his executive team agree that the review at this time would be beneficial.

At the next staff meeting, the review is accepted after some cries of 'not again' and 'must we really?'. However, there is general acceptance that it should go ahead. It's early February, so his plan is to announce the review once a review team has been organised and a timetable for key activities is drafted, which should be first week of March. The outline of the review is:

- An eight-member review team, consisting mainly of teachers and school executive staff with a parent and a student representative, will be organised through a combination of volunteer members and appointed members. Alan has asked his deputy principal to head the team.

- The review will be announced via school newsletter, with the review team and a draft timeline listed.
- Focus groups will be facilitated by members of the relevant stakeholder groups, with the aim of identifying progress strengths and weaknesses in key areas such as curriculum, pedagogy, facilities and so on. Teacher sessions will be facilitated by teachers, parent sessions by trained parents, student sessions by trained students.
- The review team will analyse the data from focus groups to identify themes that may be the subject of further investigation in subsequent sessions.
- The review team will send surveys to all stakeholders to triangulate data from the focus groups as well as investigate the extent of issues that arose from them.
- The review team will interpret the data, identify themes and prepare an initial report, which will be circulated to stakeholders for comment.
- The review team will collect, organise and inspect key documentation for auditors from another school to report on curriculum compliance and evidence of quality teaching.
- The review team will collect data to appraise the school's financial situation and inspect the school site to assess the state of facilities.
- The review team will identify key areas for development that will guide subsequent strategic planning. The strategic plan, once finalised, will be published to the school community.

One of Alan's major goals in this review is to, over time, initiate change in teacher pedagogy. He anticipates, with some excitement, that staff will see how disconnected they are from student needs, interests and learning styles when the student focus groups are convened. He hopes that this will be the catalyst for long-term change, which should lead to better-motivated students and better results.

MAKE IT PERSONAL

The challenge for school leaders is to align the many aspects of school life so that they work in harmony and synergy.

Ask yourself, to what degree do I:
- focus the school's energies and resources on the school's moral purpose?
- ensure that the school's intellectual, social, spiritual and financial capital is aligned with the needs of students?
- question — and encourage others to question — practices which are not aligned with the school's purposes?

FURTHER INVESTIGATION

School review and improvement

Many of the concepts and strategies involved in school review and improvement relate to aspects of the process of program evaluation. In turn, program evaluation inevitably becomes part of the review process. There is a body of literature in the area, including the work of Owen (2006) in Australia, and Fitzpatrick et al (2011) in the United States.

It may be of interest to compare the theoretical work on this topic with the practical experiences of your own school and other schools, especially if compared across sectors and states.

4

INDIVIDUALS, TEAMS AND PARTNERSHIPS

From individual to team

We have no hope of solving our problems without harnessing the diversity, the energy, and the creativity of all our people (Wilkins, 2024)

REFLECT

- Do you use the word 'team' to describe work groups in your school, such as executive team, leadership team or science team? If so, in what ways do these groups act as teams?
- How well do the staff in your school work together, share ideas and resources, and support each other?
- What are the advantages of teams over other work structures or individuals?

SHIFT THE FOCUS

In the past executive staff and others in positions of responsibility were able to work alone. Each had a list of tasks, which they simply got on and did.

Schools are no longer like that. A principal alone is a limited resource trying to meet unlimited needs. Contemporary school leadership requires the skills and insights of multiple leaders to be acknowledged, respected and expressed. This requires a shift in focus from leaders and teachers as individuals working in the same building, with closed office and classroom doors, to a true culture of collaboration, support and shared purpose.

The notion of team

The word 'team' is used in this section, but a team is not just a group of people. Teams achieve results which exceed those achievable by individual team members. Effective team leaders are secure in themselves, willing to share responsibility, able to empower others and not intimidated by the abilities of others.

A team is a number of people with complementary skills who are committed to a common goal for which they hold themselves mutually accountable. There are a number of challenges in this. Teamwork requires:

- purposeful collaboration: it does not allow members to 'tag along'
- responsibility to act with others: it does not always allow members to choose when to collaborate nor with whom to collaborate
- the sharing of skills: it does not allow members to hold back insights and expertise
- mutual accountability: it does not allow members to avoid responsibility for the process and the outcomes.

Key groups within the school — the members of executive or leadership groups, for example — need to see themselves as teams. However, in many schools the word *team* is simply a euphemism for people who work in proximity to one another either with respect to their location or their role. We may call a group of teachers a 'professional learning team', because they are (at least in theory) focused towards a common goal and supporting one another in achieving it, but they may be no more a team than a group of people waiting at a supermarket checkout.

Teams succeed when the members put the team before their individual needs, when team goals supersede individual goals. Previously we described how professional learning communities work to achieve common goals. These often manifest as broader, more populous teams whose aim is to support professional capacity among everyone, although the ultimate goal is often oriented to student achievement.

Diversity

The team benefits from the different skills, knowledge and insights of its members. In a team, diversity is a strength. While we often assume this to refer to gender and ethnicity, and tend to focus on 'visible' diversity, it is important that the team also encompasses diverse experiences, skills, interests and ways of thinking.

In highly reputed research and subsequent conceptualisation, Belbin (2010) has written of roles people play in teams. (An instrument is available to identify each person's naturally preferred role.) Belbin posits that effective teams contain people with a range of roles, rather than like-minded and similarly oriented members.

Each member of the team is valued for their particular abilities, and is allocated a role according to those abilities. An effective team, therefore, knows and uses the strengths of the members.

How well do the executive staff (or members of the leadership team) in your school know one another? Who is the best person to prepare a report, organise an event, facilitate a decision-making session, gain support of an obstructive colleague, negotiate for support from a community member, deal with a tense parent, mediate staff conflict, write a newsletter, write a press release, research information, manage a process of change, offer creative ideas, or lead a strategic planning group? Do their roles match their skills?

Team members work in a cooperative and coordinated way, each aware of what the others are doing. They don't duplicate effort or blame others for not doing things, but plan things carefully, so that each knows what is expected of him or her.

At different times each member of an effective school executive team assumes a leadership role within the team, and a visible leadership role within the school. All members of the school executive team are willing and empowered to accept responsibility. Legal responsibility may rest with the principal, but functional responsibility is accepted by all executive members. That means that all members of the team are willing to be held accountable for the decisions they make and the actions they take.

If the school fails to achieve its purposes, the team shares the responsibility and concern for solutions. When things go right, they share the praise.

Purpose and values

Team members all understand and support the team purpose. While diversity in the abilities of the executive staff is a strength, diversity of purpose is not. It is essential that the team members are all pulling in the same direction, that they are clear about the school's mission and purpose, the school's goals and their priorities, and the values and key principles which influence decisions. All team members should articulate these consistently and frequently to colleagues within the school, and remind one another of them during discussions.

Decision-making

Team members are all involved in decision-making. That does not mean that every decision requires a meeting. In effective teams there is a shared sense of direction, trust is present, and individuals are competent and confident to make decisions without reference to others.

'Democratic leaders' actively promote participation in decision-making. Some decisions are made as a team, some discussed by the team, others reviewed by the team afterwards. There may be consultation on key decisions; invitations to identify key issues; invitations to staff members to lead investigations or decision-making processes; and majority or consensus decision-making on particular issues. At the heart of democratic leadership is the genuine opening up of school decision-making processes to all staff.

This is not the same as pseudo-participation, which may involve manipulating discussion agendas so that some issues are not discussed or placing conditions on participation. Pseudo-participation looks like participation on the surface, but is not sincere, because no action is taken relating to staff input (De Nobile, 2008).

Unity

It is important that the executive staff demonstrate unity, so that they are seen by others as a team. Staff members need to know that they cannot play one member off against another, and to have the confidence that members of the team are not making decisions to score points against one another. Executive leaders will disagree, as they question and challenge one another. But the outcome is presented to others as a united view. To demonstrate unity:

- Avoid disagreeing on every issue. If there is frequent disagreement, the team needs to spend more time together, developing common understandings.
- Avoid acrimony during disagreements. Keep discussions focused on issues not personalities, and demonstrate respect for colleagues.
- Don't signify agreement during private discussions, then disagree in the public forum later. Resolve the issue honestly within the team.

Support

By supporting one another personally, team members feel valued, and have their needs for consideration, encouragement, affirmation, reassurance, social engagement and empathy fulfilled. Team members also relate personally to one another: engaging with sincerity; listening empathetically; knowing, asking about, and listening to stories about people and things that are important to others; offering special assistance to colleagues during times of particular need; sharing colleagues' concerns and joys; and sharing humour (De Nobile, 2009).

Team members support and encourage one another's professional growth. This is demonstrated when team members:

- praise colleagues for their achievements, for jobs well done, creative or sound ideas, and pleasing outcomes
- commend and support one another in discussions with other members of the school community
- provide and accept feedback
- share ideas, offer assistance to one another and acknowledge the assistance of other team members
- show respect, consideration and patience
- express confidence and trust in the abilities of others
- share praise and positive feedback received from outside the team.

Individuals who contribute jointly to a task are sometimes jealous when one is singled out for commendation. They compete to be the person identified as the real force behind the success. But in a team, the members share the success, and are pleased for commendation received by the team leader or other individual, because the team members see this as a commendation of the team. They acknowledge the support and contribution of the team.

Identity

The will to work together is critical in effective teams, but it is not sufficient to make the group feel like a team. Members of a team share a common history — no matter how short this may be in time — and can look back on their growth as a team. People in effective teams are also likely to describe interdependence and common purpose as key elements of the relationship (Freedman & Somech, 2021). Teams typically go through a number of stages as they develop cohesion and common purpose (Tuckman, 1965; Vaida & Serban, 2021).

The essential factor to enable a team to develop a history and grow is time. However, one of the difficulties for many rural, remote and other small schools is the frequent turnover of executive staff. How can the executive team function in these schools?

- Document the school's mission, goals, principles and priorities clearly, so that incoming staff can understand them readily. Talk with the departing principal and with continuing staff in order to understand the nature and focus of the school as soon as possible.
- Develop quickly as a team. Spend significant time together before the start of the school year, and in the early weeks of the year.
- Articulate the reasons for your decisions, and expect others to do the same. Review together decisions and actions which others question. The discussions will enable everyone to understand the underlying values and expectations which each brings to their role.

Communication

Communication is the key to effective team performance. People cannot act in unison with different information, so team members do not conceal information as a tool of power. Team members share information, unless there are critical reasons for confidentiality. All members of an effective school executive team need to know about resources and budgets, staff changes, tensions and conflicts, and current issues and activities. They also need to know about issues that affect, or have the potential to affect, school relationships, outcomes and effectiveness; and to be aware of emerging issues, and how these might be handled, if it becomes necessary.

In a team, members do not jealously guard their ideas for their own kudos. If a team member has an idea which may help others, or benefit the school, they share it, and allow others to take the idea, develop it and implement it.

A lack of time is often cited as the main inhibitor of effective communication. Time is a scarce resource in a school, and it is often difficult to find time when a small group of people are available together. Executive staff will not get together regularly unless it is planned. To maximise the time available and the value of it, try timetabling executive staff meetings for at least a semester ahead, ideally at a regular time, perhaps for an hour per week. Have time for planned agenda items and for discussion of emerging issues. Make this appointment firm. Close the door. Be unavailable to the phone or visitors during this time. Train clerical staff to protect you.

Honest communication also requires assertive behaviours. Acknowledge the right of every member to have and express opinions and feelings. Encourage team members to explain how they feel if they are uncomfortable with the team dynamics. Resolve tensions. Maintain trust and goodwill.

Growth

Teams need to grow, as individual members, and as a group (Freedman & Somech, 2021). That requires conscious effort to improve the individual and team competencies. Ensure that you:

- Enrich the jobs of other team members. Allow them opportunities to lead, to innovate, to show initiative, to make decisions. Provide team members with new experiences.
- Direct colleagues to relevant professional learning, and participate in appropriate professional learning together.
- Encourage career opportunities in team members. Seek to improve their work conditions.
- Give team members your time. Build relationships.
- Respect the right of team members to an open and honest opinion, even if it disagrees with yours.
- Seek to use the most appropriate people for roles, but avoid unnecessary stereotyping of roles and abilities, by gender, tradition or any other classification.
- Provide individual feedback and coaching. When team members make a mistake, use it as an opportunity for training, not punishment nor 'point scoring'.
- Obtain feedback from people outside the team.
- Set improvement goals.
- Reflect on and celebrate achievements.

While it is obvious that every employee is accountable to a leader 'above' them in the organisational structure, leaders are in turn accountable for growth in those 'beneath' them. Every leader has a responsibility to coach staff for growth. This involves challenging their thinking, as well as challenging them to accept new responsibilities and attempt unfamiliar tasks.

This also involves connecting them with colleagues, within and beyond the school, professional learning opportunities and professional networks. Don't direct, connect.

Cranston & Ehrich (2009) describe a tool used to measure the micropolitics of senior leadership teams in order to inform a process of growth. The authors argue that the use of the tool requires readiness, which includes an acceptance that there will always be things which can be improved upon and that reflecting, reviewing and learning can lead to growth in improved team dynamics and practices, and a willingness by all team members to engage in the process by accepting and addressing issues identified. They point out that change will take time and may challenge existing dynamics, practices and relationships; and that an external facilitator may be needed during the process.

The executive or senior leadership team

Some people say, 'If you want a job done right, do it yourself'. In schools, doing it all yourself is not an option for principals. The increasing complexity of school management requires knowledge, skills, experience, perceptions and time, well beyond the capabilities of any one person. There is no longer a place for the 'one-man-band'. It has been replaced by the conductor, who brings together all the players, to work together harmoniously. Principals of effective schools make use of the experience, skills, knowledge and energies of all staff, and involve executive staff in a shared leadership role. The focus is on achieving goals, through the most effective use of the people available.

Team leadership enables each member of the executive team to develop a role which is personally and professionally rewarding; consistent with their skills; and critical for the organisation. The role needs to have impact on educational and organisational practices to improve achievement of the school's purposes and outcomes.

Principals, deputies and other senior leaders need to see themselves as co-managers in an exciting and demanding enterprise. Their experience, knowledge, skills and attitudes differ. That's not a weakness, but a strength. Their purpose and responsibility will be essentially the same: to see that the school functions in the best way possible to achieve its vision for the good of students and with the welfare of all members of the school community in mind.

The staff as a team

Staff members, also, need to develop a team orientation, working together and sharing skills and resources.

In large schools, staff members are often divided in their work and thinking, so encourage and facilitate interaction across boundaries within the school, such as different departments, year levels, or buildings. Find ways for staff to learn about the skills, experiences and interests of others, and provide opportunities for individuals' skills, experiences and interests to be developed and used. This might include encouraging staff to play leadership roles, irrespective of their formal position or status. Provide opportunities for permanent leadership roles, such as chairing standing committees, and ad hoc roles, related to specific activities or events.

CASE STUDY: THE LEADERSHIP TEAM AT DALE PARK HIGH

Dan is the principal at Dale Park High School, a medium sized school in the inner city. There are 700 students, 38 teachers and 15 non-teaching staff. The leadership group consists of Dan, his deputy principal, Mahta, and eight departmental heads. In the three years since Dan arrived at Dale Park, he has been trying to build a cohesive leadership team. His first step was simply to start using the language of teamwork, referring to the group as the school leadership 'team'. The next step was to facilitate the team's revisiting of the school vision, and identifying priorities for development in light of a recent school review and consultations with the whole staff. As a result, Dan now feels that the leaders have become a cohesive team whose members are aware of one another's roles and support one another. More importantly, they have become advocates for the school vision when other staff members complain about things or oppose initiatives.

While the heads were all very good at managing their various learning areas, there were jobs in the school that needed doing which Dan did not have time to manage, even though he had experience in them in his previous roles. Dan invited his team to look at the list of projects that needed attending to and invited each of them to take responsibility for one area. That was it: a simple invitation. By the end of that week all of the jobs were taken. The responsibilities of the school leadership team now look like this:

- Robert, head of mathematics, coordinator of the school notebook project
- Jo, head of English, coordinator of the school's 100th anniversary celebrations
- Hugh, head of studies of society and culture, student welfare manager
- Naveen, head of technology and applied studies, coordinator of the school landscaping project
- Sarah, head of science, coordinator of the national curriculum implementation
- Li, head of creative arts, coordinator of gifted and talented programs
- Dimitri, head of personal development, health and physical education, coordinator of the school library redevelopment
- Erica, head of languages, coordinator of school-community outreach projects.

When the team meets each fortnight, each person is expected to give updates on their additional areas of responsibility. There is action happening on all fronts and they have enlisted the help of other staff and even students in informal committees. Dan now feels the school will be able to meet the targets of its strategic development plan on time, and this would not have been possible if he and his deputy alone were managing all these programs. When Dan arrived at the school, he sensed that morale among the leadership team was declining. There was a culture among staff of 'I only look after my own area', which was preventing the school from addressing its other needs. The expansion of responsibilities of the leadership team has made the school more responsive to its own needs, and has developed a greater sense of unity and purpose among the leadership team that is impacting on the culture and climate of the school in a positive way.

MAKE IT PERSONAL

The challenge for school leaders is to think of themselves of part of a leadership team, and to encourage other staff to connect in high functioning teams.

Ask yourself, to what degree do I:
- work with other school leaders as a high functioning executive or leadership team?
- encourage staff to work as teams, using the synergy of teamwork to enhance achievement?
- promote understanding and growth of a team culture within the school?

FURTHER INVESTIGATION

The characteristics of teams

There is a huge library of resources describing the characteristics and operation of teams. It is interesting to compare the insights of the various writers. Begin with books by John Maxwell, Patrick Lencioni, Spencer Johnson and Ken Blanchard, but the list is long.

Review the members of school based teams of which you are a part, in the context of Belbin's (2010) work. Consider how well-balanced the team is, in terms of containing members who play a range of roles, and evaluate the effectiveness of the team. You may identify particular roles which are missing from the team and which impair it effectiveness.

Beyond team to partnership

The biggest sources of opportunity are collaboration and partnership. And today, with digital communication, there is more of that everywhere. We need to expose ourselves to that as a matter of doing business (Parker, 2024)

REFLECT

- Who do you consider a 'partner' in your work?
- What are the distinctive features of your relationship?
- Are there programs or initiatives that your school would like to develop or maintain, but for which you would benefit from increased resources or expertise from outside the school?

SHIFT THE FOCUS

While teams continue to be important in the functioning of schools, the challenge is to develop a range of partnerships with colleagues, parents, students, the wider community, other educational organisations and businesses.

Networks and partnerships are not new phenomena, but what is changing is their use among people or organisations who might previously have seen themselves as competitors. For example, failing schools are partnering with successful schools, and public schools are partnering with private schools in ways that enable teachers and leaders to share knowledge.

There are clearly many forms that formal and informal partnerships may take. The challenge for school leaders is to be creative in seeking partners, canny in partnering effectively and symbiotically, and focused in seeking better outcomes for students.

Understand partnerships

In a partnership, the partners are bound together purposefully, sometimes even legally. They are jointly responsible for the operation and achievements of the partnership. The partnership does not discriminate between the partners. Partners work *with* one another, never *against*, nor even *near*. Therefore:

- The partnership is an entity in itself. The partnership succeeds or fails, not the individual partners, even if one partner feels they have contributed more than another, or that another partner has blundered.
- The actions of the partners are intertwined and interdependent. If one partner operates in a way which does not complement the actions of others, the partnership will suffer.
- There must be more than gracious condescension in allowing members to perform particular roles. If the roles have been unwisely allocated, the partners must work together to review and retrieve the situation.
- In a partnership, there must be trust and synergy of ideas and actions.

In a partnership, there is an understanding that 'we're in this together', that 'we stand or fall together', and 'success will depend on each of us individually playing our part and all of us working together'. While there are clear similarities between teams and partnerships, there are two ways in which the notion of partnerships in schools goes beyond that of teams.

Firstly, partnerships extend beyond the staff, and even beyond the school. Most teams in schools involve staff only, but partnerships may involve staff, parents and students, and groups outside the school. Many teachers have observed that the evolving role of leadership requires that the principal spend a significant amount of time out of the school. One of the reasons for this is their involvement in networks and partnerships — meeting with local business groups, local government, parent groups, universities, principal networks and others. Partnerships are not only focused within the school, but also beyond it.

Secondly, partners are involved because they want to be. They are enlisted to the cause. Their work goes beyond the physical or intellectual, and connects with their emotions. Membership of a staff team is typically a consequence of a member's formal role (such as in the executive team or school leadership team), by invitation (by a leader or existing team member), or by voluntary action (for example, a teacher offering to assist with the graduation preparations). Teams can be built around cooperation, but partnerships require commitment.

How can such a notion apply to schools, where roles and authority structures are clearly defined? Schaps (2003) suggested three basic principles:

- Successful partnerships are based on reciprocity. This means that all those involved in the partnership have overlapping responsibilities for student learning.
- Developing effective partnerships is a democratic process. Partnerships should recognise different interests, races, religions and education of

participants, and resolve conflicts through mediation, negotiation and compromise.
- Effective partnerships provide a variety of opportunities. These might include parent education, family support, good communication, opportunities to participate in decision-making, and strategies that foster learning.

Caldwell (2006) adds a further insight by arguing for the term *synergy* rather than partnership:

> A word like 'partnership' does not capture the complexity of relationships that should be created and the benefits that should accrue to all parties. 'Synergy' best captures the intention. Derived from the Greek *synergos* — working together — Webster's Online Dictionary explains that synergy is 'the phenomenon of two or more discrete influences or agents acting in common to create an effect which is greater than the sum of the effects each is able to create independently' (p.40)

He also writes of *sagacity*, defined as 'the intelligent application of knowledge acquired from years of learning and experience'. This is most commonly expressed in networks, which provide a mechanism for the sharing and transfer of knowledge and wisdom between schools, and between schools and other companies and organisations.

These concepts are of particular application in networks and partnerships between staff or schools that might previously have seen themselves as competitors, such as teachers sharing pedagogy instead of closing the classroom door, or private schools sharing facilities with government schools.

Partner with staff

There is a notion in some schools that each teacher is responsible for a group of students, clerical and other support staff are responsible for their tasks, and the leaders are responsible for the overall performance of the school. That is a traditional organisational approach. It is not the way a team works, and is certainly not the way a partnership works.

Students' learning and wellbeing are the responsibility of all. Here are some ways to develop this understanding:
- Emphasise purpose. Ensure that *all* staff, no matter what their role, see their work as supporting student learning and wellbeing.

- Hold all staff responsible for students. Students are the responsibility of the school, not just those teachers who teach them during a normal week. Even clerical staff can accept a role in the development of students through any interactions they have with them.
- Hold all staff responsible for the school's performance, not just the leadership group.
- Encourage all staff to show leadership, sharing their insights and taking action to align the school's activities with student learning.

Partner with parents

School leaders and staff are also in partnership with parents. Much is written about 'parents as partners'. However, partnership with parents must be more than a cliché.

Teachers know about a child's *learning* and what is required to meet the expectations of the curriculum. Parents know their child's *abilities*. They know what their child finds easy and difficult, where they shine and where they struggle. They know the personal (life) skills which are never seen at school, but which are treasured within the family.

Teachers know about *child development*. They understand the physical, emotional, social and intellectual development of children and youth, especially in the year levels they teach. Teachers know about an individual child's behaviour and responses in a school context, and have a respectful and friendly relationship. They recognise areas in which a student's development exceeds expectations, and areas in which their development is cause for concern. They are able to justify their judgements because of their experience with numerous children, and their theoretical knowledge of child development. Good teachers use any opportunity to get to know students beyond the teacher-curriculum-student context, but the knowledge is still limited.

Parents know about *their* child's development. Parents know how their child responds within the family and with friends, and have an intimate authority relationship with their child. Parents know their child's emotional responses, how their child responds when corrected, praised, teased, harassed, angry, sad, unable to cope. They recognise when their child's smile hides embarrassment, when their aggression hides insecurity, when their 'mouth' is used to protect a fragile self-esteem. They know their child's interests and motivations, their dreams and hopes, the things they will work on for hours, the way they spend their time. They know their child's issues — struggles with family breakdown, unwell family members, parents who need continual care by their children, their child's own unpublicised health issues.

The list could go on. Teachers and parents must partner together because each has unique knowledge about the child. All of this knowledge is important for the child's growth. To some teachers, all that matters is the child's education. To the parent, school is, rightly, just one component of their child's life. What matters to them is their child's development and growth, not just academically, but in all areas of their life, personality and character.

Partner with students

Students are a key part of the school partnership structure. Students are not in the school to be 'done to', but are at the heart of the school's purpose.

Schools exist for student learning. The work of students is to learn. The work of staff is to facilitate that learning. This may sound simplistic. Of course, schools encourage many aspects of students' development. However, at the heart of it, staff are working for the welfare of students. The partnership of staff and students will show in:

- the quality of relationships between staff and students, within the classroom and outside it, which will reflect respect, care, trust, warmth and sincerity
- the attitude of students to their learning and the attitude of teachers to their teaching, which will reflect a commitment to learning and teaching, and a spirit of collaboration between staff and students.
- the teaching-learning environment in the classroom, which will reflect engagement with learning, genuine effort and recognition of achievement for every student by staff and students.

Levin (2010) reported on the effect of 20 minutes of supportive adult attention on moving a student from the wrong path to the right one. The time may be spent in one block or in a two-minute conversation on each of 10 consecutive days. The time is not spent in tutoring, but in simply getting to know the student, in developing a relationship. Not only does this give the teacher a deeper and more positive understanding of struggling or difficult students, but often dramatically changes the way the student engages with the class. This expression of care by the teacher is one way that a teacher- student partnership can be developed.

Partner beyond the school

Increasingly, schools are seeing value in forming partnerships beyond the school. Schools are being supported with funds, knowledge and skills from businesses, charitable groups and individuals. In return, those groups or individuals are achieving their goals, which may have a business or community focus, or simply be goals of altruism. Partnerships with universities give schools access to current research and expertise, in exchange for support in the education of pre-service teachers, and the provision of a research context and a pool of participants. Increasingly, schools are partnering with other schools, even those with whom they may be seen to be in competition for enrolments. There are times and contexts in which schools must compete, and those in which they must collaborate, and the skill of the leader is in knowing when to compete and when to collaborate.

This is implicit in what Ellyard (1998, p.34) called the trend towards communitarianism. He illustrated it with an example from Hampden-Turner & Trompenaars, who contrast the 'finite game' businesses play, aimed at defeating competitors and, if possible, eliminating them from the game, with the 'infinite game', aimed at continually improving the capabilities of organisations, including competitors, to be successful. Competitors actually share their knowledge so that everyone will compete more effectively, and so that losers are invited to learn from winners. This is certainly a model for schools, who are jointly committed to better education and care for *all* students, despite the constant efforts of media and some politicians to set schools, and school sectors, against one another.

The NAB Schools First awards program (2010) provided a range of examples of schools partnering with community groups:

Programs work most effectively where the partnership is functional, and not just financial. That is, the organisation or individual does not simply hand over money, then withdraw. Nor do they look over the school's shoulder to ensure they do things right. Rather, the organisation or individual continues to offer advice, expertise and ideas, shares in monitoring the value added by their contribution, and uses their networks or knowledge to help the school access further support.

In many programs, schools seek the support of other organisations within the community to enhance the education of students. However, schools are often key partners in programs designed to enhance local communities. These programs might be designed to enhance community belonging, engage youth in employment, or develop a sense of community responsibility, to diminish feelings of dependency and to build hope (Gross et al, 2015; Teo et al, 2022). Schools play a leading role in many of these community partnerships because schools help to define and unite neighbourhoods; provide basic education and transmit values from one generation to the next; and prepare young people for employment and civic responsibilities. Improving education is a goal which unites and energises parents and communities.

MAKE IT PERSONAL

The challenge for school leaders is to develop partnerships with other organisations, so that through the sharing of resources and expertise, all the partners involved achieve things they wouldn't have been able to do on their own.

Ask yourself:
- With whom do I truly partner? Is there real synergy?
- If we were a business partnership, how would we seek to improve our effectiveness as partners?
- As a school, with whom might we partner? What is my role in initiating these partnerships?

FURTHER INVESTIGATION

Partnerships

The notion of education partnerships is still developing, as schools and other entities work through issues related to competition and cooperation, giving and taking, withholding and sharing, and the ways in which seemingly unrelated enterprises can work together. An increasing number of authors is addressing this issue; see, for example, Hargreaves & Shirley (2009), Caldwell (2023), and Hora & Millar (2011).

Take the initiative in inviting principals of schools in your neighbourhood — government, Catholic, independent, and all levels (early years, primary, middle, secondary) — to morning tea. Share the key issues in your schools. You may be surprised at the similarity. Then identify key issues in your neighbourhood, and consider how you might partner to address one of these issues.

You may like to invite local principals, business owners, community group leaders, civic representatives and others to a meeting, and to explore issues for the community, or for the enterprise, which might be addressed through partnership. Alternatively, you might hold a series of one-to-one or small group events to explore the same issues, looking for ways to partner together, or ways to connect one person with whom you speak with another. Being the linker of partners is an influential role.

5

Delegation, negotiation and collaboration

From delegation to negotiation

Where you stand depends on where you sit (Miles, 1978, p.399).

REFLECT

- In your school, how are responsibilities determined?
- Who makes the decisions?
- How do people feel about those decisions?

SHIFT THE FOCUS

Roles are often allocated based on expectation or delegation. Within one school, for example, the deputies may have been responsible for curriculum issues and for care and discipline in the past, and so it is expected that they will continue to fill these roles. In some schools, principals delegate those tasks that they dislike doing, and which they feel comfortable about letting go — which often means those which they feel are of lesser importance.

This is no longer an appropriate way of working. Executive staff are able to demonstrate a high level of knowledge, skill and experience. It is essential that the school makes effective use of these competencies. New positions should be created, and leaders given different emphases. There needs to be a shift away from expectation and delegation, to negotiation of roles to best develop leaders and meet the school's needs. Instead of the principal allocating tasks to deputies and others, the executive staff need to discuss what needs to be done and who is best equipped to do it.

Know how to negotiate

Negotiation is the key to building a successful leadership team. Existing leaders in the school need to discuss and negotiate responsibilities, according to skills, time, interest and appropriateness. For example, where the school has a staff member who has a strong curriculum background, perhaps as a writer or a consultant, it makes sense to create a curriculum leadership position to use their skills; a person with a passion for care of students could be given a caring focus; a leader with organisational and administrative skills could be given a role which uses these skills.

Some of those decisions may be built into the role description and appointment; some will be long-term, staying constant for a year or more; others may be renegotiated more often, because of changing needs and pressures. Executive staff need to meet regularly, discuss what things need to be done in the short and long term, and who has imminent commitments, then decide who will attend to what.

When these decisions are being made, problems commonly occur with the decision-making process. The principal may want to make the decision alone, or the other executive members may want the principal to make the decision alone. There may also be problems with the content of the decisions, if particular members of the team want to retain, or avoid, particular responsibilities.

Negotiated decisions are joint, consensus decisions, arrived at by discussion, not haggling or argument. Negotiation has failed unless all members of the team are confident that they have had the chance to contribute, that others have contributed honestly, and that all relevant views have been heard. Decisions should be agreed to by all members, and all members should ultimately be satisfied with the outcomes. Successful negotiation should ensure good relationships have been maintained throughout the process.

To negotiate successfully:
- Prepare. Know what you want from the negotiation, what you will and won't accept, and why. Think about what the others in the team will want, will accept and won't, and why. Consider what the school needs.
- Look for creative solutions. Avoid either-or and win-lose situations. Have other alternatives in mind, so that the discussion focuses on a range of options, rather than 'your' idea or 'mine'.
- Communicate effectively. Listen carefully to what is said or inferred. Use questions to clarify how others think and feel. Be assertive in expressing your opinions and feelings. Focus on issues not personalities

or positions. Avoid verbally attacking others, challenging their authority or position, or cornering them into taking a fixed stance.
- Reach agreement. As points are agreed to, state them clearly, confirm their acceptance, and document them.

This process does not deny the right of the principal to 'pull rank' in some contexts. There are some situations which the principal will decide need to be attended to by 'the Principal' (with a capital P). These situations may involve representing the school in certain forums, establishing particular partnerships, dealing with some difficult relationships, addressing the media, and so on. There are also some situations in which the school system or board expects the principal to represent the school. However, it is sometimes helpful to question these assumptions.

Emphasise purpose

Focus negotiations on achieving the school's goals, in an environment which all members of the school community find personally and professionally satisfying.

Consider which responsibilities need to be allocated to see that the goals and priorities are met, and which need to be the responsibility of the executive team. Discuss portfolios of responsibility, rather than tasks, so that tasks have a context and a purpose. If the distinction seems vague, test each responsibility by asking whether it leaves the responsible person with freedom to make their own decisions about how the responsibility may be exercised. Be clear about what is and is not a priority use of time and energy.

Match people with responsibilities

As the responsibilities are agreed upon, staff can be matched to each responsibility. Negotiate these on the basis of strengths and interests, along with time commitments. One of the key steps in this process is to identify and recognise the knowledge, skills and experience of the team members, their particular interests, and the areas in which they would like to grow or gain experience. Most people are reluctant to talk about their skills and achievements. If this proves so, you might exchange résumés, give each other a potted professional history, talk about the things you think you'll be remembered for by past students and colleagues, describe what you hope to be doing in your career seven years from now, or discuss your dreams for the school.

As you negotiate, be aware of areas of responsibility in which:

- traditional roles and stereotyping are strong. Consider whether these stereotypes need to be broken down. Be creative in negotiating responsibilities.
- all members of the team have an interest, or no member of the team has an interest. Provide a balanced role, which includes issues the staff member will relish, and those for which they have less enthusiasm but which are still important.
- members consider a particular responsibility theirs by right or appointment. Some matters may be clearly ascribed to the principal or the deputy (or other senior leaders) by system or board accountabilities, or by job advertisement and selection processes. However, most job descriptions define responsibility for oversight of certain functions, not for implementation of them. There is a difference between legal responsibility and functional responsibility.
- members are encouraged to take on unfamiliar responsibilities. It cannot be assumed that people will always want to be challenged. Some will prefer to retain familiar roles. Negotiate for such staff new roles which have inherent appeal for them; can be viewed as a 'next step' from their past role; are supported by training; enable them to achieve some personal goals; or relate to issues they are studying. This represents an opportunity for emergent leadership to thrive as well as initial leadership experience that may lead to a formal middle leader role down the track (more about these later). These individuals should be supported by colleagues with relevant experience.

Define the meaning of responsibility

There are several common misunderstandings that occur when people accept responsibility for an area of school activity, and these need to be negotiated to ensure leaders and other staff have a shared understanding.

Accountability

One common attitude about responsibility is seen when an individual thinks, 'I'm accountable. I should do it all myself.'

Responsibility should be negotiated for goals and outcomes, not work. It may require that we demonstrate that appropriate processes have been put in place, appropriate checks have been made or questions asked, and expected outcomes have been achieved. It requires that we can justify the outcomes in terms of goals, processes and resources.

If you are responsible for the school finances, for example, it is not necessary that you handle all the finances. Others may well determine and approve expenditure, maintain records, issue cheques, prepare statements and so on. Your responsibility is to ensure that the finances are used effectively to achieve the school's goals; to ensure that budgets are not overspent; and to ensure that the school's finances are handled responsibly and recorded in a way which is appropriate for audit.

This is not an unfamiliar concept. Principals are accountable for the school's most important activity: learning. Yet principals do not teach all students. They assign that responsibility to teachers. They demonstrate their accountability by ensuring that teachers are planning the learning in accordance with some acceptable objectives, are implementing appropriate and effective learning strategies, and are achieving acceptable outcomes.

Micromanagement

An extension of misconceptions about accountability can result in micromanagement, when a leader takes the view that, 'If I don't have time for that, I must ensure that others do it exactly as I would.' Or, in other words, 'You're responsible, but do it this way.'

For some school leaders, the most difficult aspect of working with others seems to be letting go. It's true for principals, for deputies, and even for teachers who have difficulty letting students go ahead and do a task their own way. Assigning someone a responsibility means letting that person do it. In negotiating the responsibility, define:

- the expected outcomes that must be achieved
- the non-negotiable parts of the process, including legal requirements or the principles that must be included in the process
- the budget or resources available
- who will be consulted in the process
- how the effectiveness will be measured.

As long as these things are in place, people should be encouraged to 'own' their responsibility; that is, to carry it out according to their own style and using their own strengths.

Abdication

At the other end of the spectrum from micromanagement is the misconception that assigning responsibility to a staff member means the leader never has to hear about it again. It's not appropriate for a leader to take the attitude that 'Because I've given you the responsibility, I don't want to know about it!'

Assigning responsibility to someone else does not mean yielding all involvement. For school leaders, it means continuing to monitor the progress of the person responsible, ensuring they are working towards appropriate goals, that appropriate processes are in place (not necessarily the processes you would use, but effective processes), that they are coping, that they have the resources and knowledge they need. It will also include coaching, guiding, advising as necessary, but without taking over the responsibility or dictating the process.

At the heart of this matter is the need for responsibilities to be shared in a way that ensures key responsibilities are allocated and carried out effectively, and that leaders within the school have responsibilities that are rewarding and challenging.

CASE STUDY: THREE TEAMS AT GREEN HILL PRIMARY SCHOOL

Green Hill Primary School is a large school in the urban-rural fringe of a large capital city. Their recent school review revealed several areas of concern that needed addressing. Some of these, such as numeracy in the early years, were carry-over issues from the last review that were being addressed by committees led by members of the executive. However, while the school has a very capable leadership team, a few of the new issues were outside the expertise of the executive team. Louise, the principal, saw these as opportunities to develop the leadership capabilities of teachers. Louise approached teachers whom she knew either had some expertise or a passion for the areas of concern. At a subsequent staff meeting, these key people were announced as team leaders and other staff encouraged to volunteer to create teams that would work through the issue over the coming year.

Literacy assessment group

Jean is an upper primary teacher who has had considerable experience in constructing tests for various aspects of literacy, including comprehension and spelling. While the school used national testing results, there was a recognised need for more regular tests and other assessment tasks for the purpose of tracking students, identifying emergent needs and organising needs based teaching. Under Jean's guidance, this team devised a series of cloze tests designed to identify levels of comprehension for each grade from Grades 1 to 5. Over time other members of the team began to share how they have learnt from Jean about assessments and how to construct fair tests. Jean is pleased with the speed with which the job of test construction was accomplished. Satisfied with the impact her work has had on the school, she is considering applying for formal promotion next year.

Social committee

The school review suggested that teacher morale was in decline. Barry knew this and had been an advocate for a return to the old days when staff used to get together on a Friday afternoon for a social gathering. Since that has stopped, Barry reasoned, staff morale has been dropping. Louise knows that other issues are also impacting on morale, such as increased administration workloads and more demanding and critical parents. However, Barry was chosen as the social committee leader because of his zest for the social and he eagerly accepted the mission: improve morale! Barry's team consisted of a mix of older and younger teachers. This group surveyed staff about preferred social events and chose to run a trivia night for staff, parents and friends. This was organised by two members of the team who describe themselves as 'trivia nuts'. While trivia nights aren't Barry's cup of tea, he was pleased with the turn out, and more events are in the pipeline. Louise has noticed cliques are starting to loosen, with some staff sitting with different colleagues, and the climate in the school seems to be shifting for the better.

Information and communications technology (ICT) team

ICT-assisted pedagogy has been lagging at Green Hill. Louise knew this before the review reported it. Adela, an assistant principal, would have been an adequate choice to lead changes development this area, but her list of duties is already overfull. Sue, one of the Year 3 teachers, was an enthusiastic user of ICT and even arranged a web page for the year group to publish work. She was an obvious choice and, after some hesitation because of self-confidence, agreed to lead a team whose aim it would be to professionally develop staff in the use of the internet as a research strategy. Before doing anything, Sue did some reading of recent journal articles about ICT in education and quickly realised the best was to get reticent teachers 'into' ICT was to invite rather than impose. So she began arranging times for an 'open classroom', when staff could visit her class and see her students using the internet for research. Louise supported this by arranging to look after those teachers' classes while they observed Sue at work. At first the take up was slow, with only three teachers coming to Sue's class in the first two weeks. But word got out and the following week was visited by six of her peers. Just the other day Louise was delighted to overhear students from Year 5 talk about how their teacher used the school set of laptops for the first time so that they could use the internet to help with short research topics on health. Sue has also been developing her committee so that colleagues can run their own open classes and also help with the professional development sessions that are planned for next term.

MAKE IT PERSONAL

The challenge for school leaders is to find ways to share responsibilities on the basis of skills and interests, rather than stereotypes, tradition or allocation by the principal.

Ask yourself, to what degree do I:
- know the skills and interests of other executive staff?
- know how to negotiate?
- actively negotiate roles with other executive staff?
- accept traditional or stereotypical roles?

FURTHER INVESTIGATION

Democratic leadership communication

Leadership staff in schools have a range of responsibilities. There are significant similarities and significant differences in how these responsibilities are distributed within schools. A discussion with colleagues or a survey of schools might provide interesting data. It would also be interesting to explore school leaders' level of satisfaction with their roles.

The notion of sharing responsibility for leadership appears several times within this book. Some researchers would argue that there is a difference between shared, democratic, participative, distributed, negotiated and collaborative leadership models (Goksoy, 2016; Harris, 2009; Youngs, 2017). Are the differences real or pedantic, and what are the implications for schools? Is a more detailed taxonomy appropriate to describe styles of shared leadership?

Democratic leadership communication refers to interactions in which leaders encourage input from staff or share decision making with staff. It is a manifestation of democratic leadership, but will also be associated with shared, distributed or collaborative forms of leadership too. Examples include interactions with staff that influence principal decisions, the work of teams and committees, and instances when leaders request staff input into policy or procedures (De Nobile, 2008; 2021a).

What are the likely effects of democratic leadership communication on the morale of staff, on student learning, on building leadership capability of aspiring or emergent leaders and on succession planning? How does democratic leadership communication relate to shared, collaborative or distributed leadership? Are there any potential downsides or things to be careful about regarding this type of communication?

Beyond negotiation to collaboration

It is well to remember that the entire universe, with one trifling exception, is composed of others (Holmes, 1927).

REFLECT

- Do staff members in this school collaborate? What does that mean? How is it evident?
- When did you last collaborate meaningfully with a colleague, and what were the outcomes?
- Is collaboration in your school seen as an imposition or an exciting opportunity?

SHIFT THE FOCUS

The authority of school executive staff has changed. All those with a stake in the school — staff, parents, students and the wider community — demand the right to a say in what takes place.

Rather than a threat to executive staff, this change provides exciting opportunities. Effective leadership involves others, because it enables and challenges others to share in defining and implementing a vision for the school. Those who 'own' the vision will support it.

Sharing of ideas develops commitment to the goals of the school and improved quality of ideas and decisions. All staff members have knowledge, skills and perceptions which can benefit the school. Most individuals know very little about most things, but a great deal about a few things. They share their knowledge, and allow others to contribute their knowledge, so that together the group knows, or knows how to find out, all it needs to know. Collaboration enhances the professional growth of teachers, by challenging them to reflect on their practices and experiment with new ways of thinking and acting.

There is a limit to what executive staff can achieve alone. Effective leaders are concerned to see that things happen, but they are less concerned about who does what. They have no compulsion to do everything themselves.

While delegation eases the workload of the leader, negotiation enables people to determine roles according to strengths. However, distributing or sharing of responsibilities involves the entire staff in leadership, according to need and opportunity. This makes the leadership of the school a collaborative process.

Distributed leadership

Distributed leadership is the distribution of leadership responsibility and opportunity throughout the school. While the principal may still be seen as the apex of power within the school, especially in terms of executive and legal responsibilities, other staff members share some responsibility for leading and managing the school. These include people in formal positions such as deputy principals and coordinators, and also staff in non-promotional positions, who may be described as teacher–leaders, organisers, committee heads or mentors or the like.

Key aspects of distributed leadership include the movement away from a top-down hierarchical approach to more democratic, participative interactions; interdependency between multiple people carrying out leadership tasks; and leadership practice that is shaped by leader qualities, interaction with followers and the situation in which they are working. Harris (2009) summarises the characteristics of distributed leadership as:

- broad-based involvement in leadership practice where there are multiple formal and informal sources of leadership
- emphasis on expertise rather than role, meaning that those with the expertise lead, and that this may vary according to school needs
- deep trust and reciprocal support among staff members
- power sharing (to varying degrees).

Harris also points out that the way in which leadership may be distributed can vary widely from school to school, with models including:

- division of labour, when a number of teachers accept responsibilities
- co-performance, when two or more leaders perform a role collaboratively
- parallel performance, when two leaders carry out the same role separately
- shared performance, when a group of teachers assume joint responsibility
- mutual responsibility, when all participants in a school or a particular context assert influence as and when appropriate.

Distributed leadership can develop organically over time, such as when two colleagues work closely together until their combined work impacts on the running of the school. This kind of development has been termed 'spontaneous alignment' and distribution of leadership by default. It can also come about for strategic purposes, such as when committees are required to review aspects of school curriculum or culture and executive members and other staff work with the principal. Development of distributed leadership in this form is termed 'planful development' or distribution of leadership by design (Harris, 2009; Spillane, 2006).

However, the concept of *mutual responsibility* is potentially the most powerful form of distributed leadership. It suggests that a leader is a person who leads when a leader is needed. Leadership is not just for those already in formal positions of leadership, nor does it require official sanction or appointment, but is the exercise of leadership initiative in response to a need. The need may be for role modelling, mentoring, encouragement, implementation, ideas creation, organisation, influence, challenging the status quo or the dominant thinking, and more.

The distinction is the recognition that leading and managing schools involves many people and that the practice of leading and managing is more important than the nature of the roles and responsibilities involved (Harris, 2009; Spillane & Diamond, 2007). Elsewhere in this book it is suggested that schools are communities rather than organisations. In some communities, such as virtual communities, there is little, if any, mention of leadership. That does not mean that no leadership is exercised, but rather that the leadership exercised is not consistent with a hierarchical power structure. Therefore, in thinking of schools as communities, it may be more appropriate to think of leadership as a sense of common endeavour by all, supported by specific leadership actions by particular people when necessary. Sharma (2010) explains:

> This ... is all about creating an environment and culture where *everyone* needs to show leadership. Everyone needs to drive innovation. Everyone needs to inspire their teammates. Everyone needs to embrace change. Everyone needs to take responsibility for results. Everyone needs to be positive. Everyone needs to be devoted to expressing their absolute best. And once they do, the organisation not only will adapt beautifully to the changing conditions, it will actually lead within its field (p.16).

Collaborative leadership

However, distributed leadership is not always collaborative; they are distinct ideas (Spillane & Diamond, 2007). There is even an inherent problem in distributing leadership throughout the school, if staff are seeking to influence others towards competing ends. Some may be working against the school's goals, either intentionally, or unwittingly through a misunderstanding of an issue or a lack of awareness of the consequences of their actions. However, even if staff members have an understanding of and commitment to the school's goals, potentially there is the possibility of confusion, with various staff members seeking to enlist colleagues to their particular emphasis or strategies.

Without wanting to argue the nuances of the various definitions, to us collaborative leadership implies the combination of thought and effort rather than parallel effort. How can distributed or shared leadership be collaborative?

Collaborate purposefully

Collaboration involves working purposefully together. It is sometimes used synonymously with 'sharing' and 'cooperating'. However:

- Sharing is allowing others to see or use what we have. In schools, it is the exchange of ideas, opinions, plans and resources. However, sharing involves no obligation on the listener to respond in any meaningful way.
- Cooperating is acting in a way which supports what others are doing. In schools, it is ensuring that our ideas, opinions, plans and use of resources do not compete with or frustrate those of our colleagues. However, cooperation often implies the expectation that others will endorse and enable our ideas.
- Collaborating is working together in purposeful ways. In schools, it is generating ideas, opinions, plans and resources jointly with others. Collaboration is not simply a communication process, but a creative process. Collaboration generates new ideas, not previously expressed by any of the individual participants, or the development and enhancement of ideas in ways not envisaged by the creator of the idea.

In the context of leadership, collaboration involves generating priorities and strategies together, and implementing them in consistent, coordinated and non-competing ways. The need for such leadership is real. Have you ever felt caught between contradictory priorities promoted by various committed and enthusiastic leaders within a school? Although staff may be travelling in a similar direction, their efforts are hindered when there is competition for their time or energies or for various school resources.

When people work collaboratively, each is aware of the plans others are putting in place; each is aware of what the others are doing, and why, and is monitoring how they are progressing; each shares the vision, principles, goals and priorities. This is clearly akin to the notion of partnering, discussed in an earlier chapter.

In a school, each staff member has something to offer their colleagues: experiences, strategies, knowledge, creative ideas, classroom management procedures. Teachers ought to collaborate creatively, to find better ways of working, better ways to help students learn, better ways to conceptualise and implement curriculum and teaching strategies. People can be creative in isolation. However, creativity is typically enhanced when people collaborate to share ideas, challenge ideas and build on ideas; and the implementation of new ideas is more effective when several are going through the process together.

Collaboration in this context is a process in which individuals contribute effectively to the work of a group by building shared understandings and resolving differences by negotiation (Scoular et al, 2020). It facilitates for professional growth, as teachers observe one another, listen to one another, try new approaches together and evaluate these together (Admiraal et al, 2021).

However, given the findings of researchers in school leadership and change (Fullan, 2013; Hargreaves & Shirley, 2009; Harris, 2014; Sahlberg, 2018; Sharratt, 2019) some cautions are worth considering:

- Collaboration is not simply doing things together or being together. Storytelling, help and assistance, and sharing are relatively weak forms of collegiality; but 'joint work' (team teaching, planning, observation, action research, sustained peer coaching, mentoring, and so on) is the strongest form of collaboration.
- 'Contrived collegiality' forces people together in ways which simply have the appearance of collaboration. Tokenistic collaboration, which is neither genuine nor desired, damages long-term collaboration.
- Collaboration is not 'group speak', in which individual ideas are quashed. To the contrary, collaboration involves encouraging teachers to express their individual ideas, and using the power of collaboration to develop both the ideas and the collaborators. We should encourage individuality, the individual expression of ideas, individual style of processing and individual ways of teaching; but discourage individualism, the desire to do everything alone, by oneself and for oneself, and to reject other perspectives.
- Collaboration does not mean that there is no division of labour. Collaborative frameworks and directions do not dictate group action on every task. It is pointless to collaborate on every task. Some things are done more efficiently and more effectively alone. Choosing when to

collaborate is as important as knowing why to collaborate and exploring how to collaborate.

Collaborate widely

The value of our collaboration depends not only on how we collaborate, but with whom. We tend to choose to collaborate with people with whom we feel comfortable — those who share our ideas and perspectives. There is significant value in collaborating with people who bring a different perspective and will challenge our thinking. This is especially so if we are seeking to create new ideas, wanting to genuinely critique our own practice, or wanting to ensure we have thoroughly considered a range of issues.

That means looking beyond the immediate group. Bring other staff into the leadership discussion from time to time and invite their perspectives. Structure discussions among staff so that the groups vary from time to time; for example, mix people across teaching levels, subjects, years of experience, or height!

Real collaboration among people who do not usually work together will only occur if two factors are present.

The first is *a willingness to collaborate*. Ensure staff are aware of what you are trying to achieve. Encourage them to give it a go. Then highlight the positive outcomes. You might even reward those who do it well, even if the reward is simply a movie ticket or other fun gift. If you persist, the idea of collaborating across divides will become part of the culture as people see value in the process.

The second necessary factor is *skills to collaborate*. It is unreasonable to assume that putting people together and telling them to collaborate will enable them to do so effectively. It may be necessary for staff to participate in a series of workshops on topics such as strategies for generating ideas, for analysis ideas, for making decisions, along with negotiation skills and conflict resolution skills.

It may also be useful to help teachers to understand personality and processing styles. People differ in the ways they process information, attend to tasks and make decisions. There are several tests which categorise these differences (e.g., Buckingham & Clifton, 2020; DISC Profile, 2023; Majors, 2012). The principle behind these is that people operate differently, and that by knowing our own preferred ways of processing information and acting, and being aware of others' preferred ways, there is an increased ability to use the strengths of the group members, rather than complaining that others in the group 'don't get it'!

While most of us understand this intellectually, it does not mean we accept this in others in the heat of debate. For example, knowing that a group member is a conceptual, 'big picture' thinker who enjoys exploring possibilities, may not of itself prevent frustration in meetings for the micro-thinker, who wants to fill in the detail, and the 'action man', who wants to get on and make things happen. Understanding and managing our feelings about people who operate differently from us, and finding ways to capitalise on differences, rather than be frustrated by them, requires mature relational skills. It may be necessary for a facilitator (probably from outside the school) to help staff to learn these skills.

Enable other voices to speak and to be heard

Collaboration involves more than one person. The potential quality of collaboration depends on the people available to collaborate. That is not a comment on the quality of the collaborators, so much as the number of people willing to collaborate and the quality of their interactions.

The challenge for school leaders is to find ways to encourage colleagues to contribute, to hear them, to engage them in the dialogue, and to draw deep and responsive contributions from people. The power of collaboration is that it has the potential to enhance the thinking of each participant. It is why we speak of the synergy of collaboration. The dialogue is not simply a sharing of what each contributor already knows, but the creation of new thinking.

To ensure quality contributions and interactions:

- Create a climate of trust, so that staff are comfortable to express not just what they confidently know, but also what they tentatively think.
- Facilitate the process, by including someone who is able to ensure all voices are heard, draw out people's ideas, challenge thinking in ways that encourage contributors to develop their own and others' ideas.
- Encourage progress, by affirming creative and collaborative thought and action.
- Provide time, so that these things can take place.
- Provide essential information. This requires transparent leadership. This is not about a lack of confidentiality. It's about not being secretive about knowledge and information. People cannot make responsible decisions about finance, for example, if they don't understand the budget: what's coming in, what's going out, where it's coming from, where it's going to. There will be a lack of trust if they think there is a secret agenda.

Engage non-principal leadership

Throughout this chapter we have referred to the work of others who may enact leadership roles as a result of delegation, negotiation or collaboration. Some researchers identify three levels of leadership in schools, which are described below.

Senior-level leadership

The senior-level leaders are the top echelon of leadership in a school. They include the principal, deputy principals, directors and others with significant whole school responsibilities (Cliffe et al, 2018; Cranston & Ehrich, 2009). Their duties and responsibilities reach across the school, often including active involvement in staff recruitment and performance management. Importantly, they are usually able to step into the principal role at any moment, and this is often made clear to them during the processes that prepare them for their position. Senior-level leaders may have some classroom teaching duties, but most of their time is devoted to matters of leadership.

While senior leaders may have been under-utilised in the past (Cranston et al, 2004), the research evidence is clear that they have become increasingly active in supporting principals to improve teaching and learning, as well as other aspects of school operations (Abrahamsen & Aas, 2023; Leaf & Odhiambo, 2017). Senior leaders can be particularly well-placed to collaborate with middle-level leaders and other staff to improve leadership capacity and teaching practices. They, in turn, distribute leadership to middle-level leaders so that initiatives are better implemented throughout the whole school.

Examples of senior-level leadership include:

- deputy principal leading a committee that will redraft the whole school behaviour support policy
- curriculum director who is facilitating professional development in problem based learning across the school, and
- assistant principal in a primary school reviewing NAPLAN results in preparation for a school review of curriculum.

Middle-level leadership

Middle-level leaders operate at a level below senior leadership. Their work is often overseen by senior-level leaders. In addition to their normal duties (such as classroom teaching), middle-level leaders have responsibility for a significant aspect of the running of the school. These responsibilities may vary from leading a subject area (such as a head of learning area), looking after a cohort (such as heads of years and stage coordinators), or another aspect of school organization (such as ICT or inclusion) (De Nobile, 2018; Grootenboer, 2018; Lipscombe, Tindall-Ford & Lamanna, 2023). They are generally not responsible for the hiring of new staff, although they might coordinate casual/relief/supply staff (De Nobile, 2021b).

In secondary schools, middle-level leaders will very likely be restricted to a subject area, cohort or other responsibility unlikely to affect all staff schoolwide. For example, the head of science in a school will not have responsibilities beyond that learning area. However, in primary schools, middle-level leader responsibilities may well be across the school. For example, a curriculum leader may have responsibility for leading the implementation of a science syllabus in all classes. Recent research makes clear that the major role of middle-level leaders is to influence teaching and learning, by leading instructional practices and developing the capabilities of colleague teachers (Gurr, 2015; Highfield & Rubie-Davies, 2022; Tang, Bryant & Walker, 2022; Wattam, 2021).

Examples of middle-level leadership include:

- subject heads organising the teaching scope and sequence for the coming year
- year advisor liaising with other teachers while investigating a student experiencing behaviour problems
- primary coordinators organising the timetable and activities for the annual school open day.

First-level leadership

The first-level leaders are perhaps the least recognised in leadership theory and literature, but there are many people who operate at this level. First-level leaders are those teachers (and other staff) who engage in leadership activities, but with a smaller span of responsibility and influence than middle-level leaders (De Nobile, 2023a). Their equivalent in other occupations would be front-line managers and junior leaders.

There are several ways in which first-level leadership may happen. Emergent leaders, those who are having an influence on other teachers for the first time, may enact it by mentoring peers or supporting colleagues to implement new pedagogical tools. We sometimes see early career teachers engaging in the latter with more experienced teachers because of their recent learning at university. First-level leaders might also be holders of formal positions who assist middle leaders with their responsibilities.

These individuals are often given job titles that are not officially gazetted in enterprise agreements or awards as they are filling in workload 'gaps' that other leaders cannot attend to (De Nobile, 2023b).

Examples of first-level leadership include:

- assistant heads of learning areas who look after the inventory of teaching resources
- deputy heads of house who support a specific cohort of students
- senior teachers and highly accomplished teachers who coach other staff.

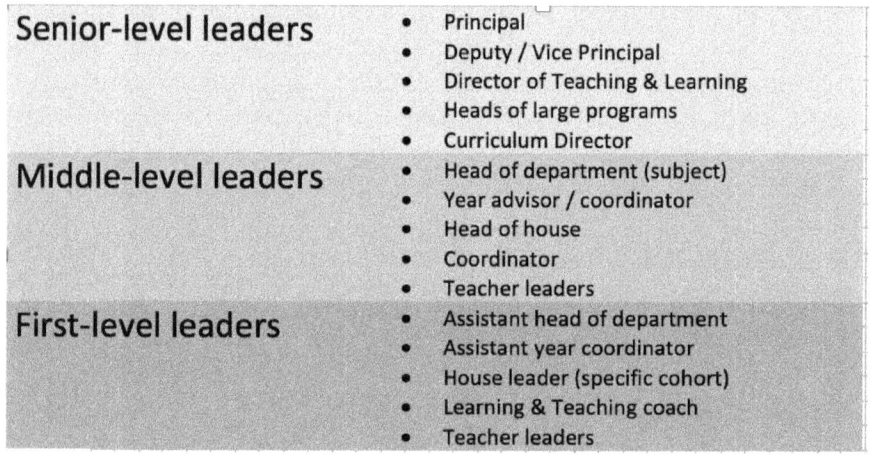

Fig. 5-1. Levels of leadership in schools
Adapted from De Nobile, 2023b, p.6

Fig. 5-1 illustrates the three levels of leadership described in this book. It is not really meant to make schools look hierarchical, though to some degree they are, especially large secondary schools and K-12 colleges. The point of the diagram is to illustrate how the three levels of leadership may manifest as formal positions. You will notice 'teacher leaders' listed twice. This is to acknowledge how this concept is applied in educational literature at the present time.

It should also be acknowledged that there are many staff who accept minor (first-level) leadership roles which are not acknowledged in any formal way by the system or even the school. That is, they typically attract no financial reward or time allocation, and are not acknowledged in the hierarchy of promotional positions, although the experience may be used to develop leadership skills and insights, and to enhance a resumé. These roles usually provide leadership to activities or programs which are outside the priorities of the leadership group. So in addition to enhancing the experience of staff, these roles enrich the curriculum or the life of the school community.

Reculture the school

Real change in schools, change which affects the teaching and learning, must come from teachers collaborating effectively to question the school's structures, processes and outcomes; create and explore possible alternatives; and support one another through the emotional, relational and practical difficulties which result. In some schools, this involves *reculturing*, described by Hargreaves & Fullan (1998) as 'changing the norms, values, incentives, skills and relationships in an organisation to support (and prod) people to work differently together. The goal is to create more collaborative work cultures' (p.118).

Senior and middle level leaders are particularly well placed to develop collaborative cultures. Deal & Peterson (2016) described a school where culture change was initiated first by bringing the school community face to face with negative aspects of school communication, followed by collaborative vision setting among staff. In a similar way, middle and senior leaders may be deployed to model collaborative practices as well as spearhead collaborative curriculum and policy development. It is easier for these people due to their closer relationships with teachers compared to principals.

CASE STUDY: NEW PRINCIPAL AT STENMOUNT HIGH

> Things have certainly changed since Roslyn took over as principal at Stenmount Secondary School this year. The previous principal, Michelle, was far more consultative and inclusive in her approach to running the school. The school leadership team and other staff members were usually asked for input on most decisions and the opinions of individuals, however different, were always respected. People generally trusted the principal and her leadership team because they were open, approachable and respectful. In the eight months since Roslyn took over consultative committees have been discontinued and staff meetings, rather than avenues for discussion about issues, have become briefing sessions where members of the leadership team inform us about things that are happening and decisions that have been made. Twice already, Roslyn has made it clear that certain opinions were not welcome by being openly critical. On top of this, the staff has been informed that from next year they will be undergoing performance reviews which will involve the principal

observing lessons. The process and the indicators have been distributed, which staff appreciate, but no-one has had any say in their development, other than the leadership team, and there is some confusion about what some terms and phrases mean, and concern about how the 'reports' will be used.

Morale at the school has plummeted to an all-time low. People are complaining that they feel disempowered, less 'in control' of their work, and trust in the leadership team is fast evaporating. Some teachers feel stressed and anxious while others report that they have lost their 'drive' for work. The number of staff taking sick days had increased slightly. A couple of staff members have openly announced intentions to look for jobs in other schools.

Something needs to change. After a discussion with her professional mentor, Roslyn realises that a new approach is needed. She calls her senior staff together. In a disarmingly honest presentation, she talks about the leaders with whom she has worked and on whom she has modelled herself, and she speaks of her own personality and preferred ways of responding. She then explains that it is clear that this staff is used to operating differently, and admits that her style has created disharmony and tension. Then, acknowledging that this is a difficult process for her, she invites her colleagues to talk about their understandings of leadership, and how they would like to see leadership enacted in the school. It takes a few minutes as people process her speech and the context, but gradually the conversation begins.

MAKE IT PERSONAL

The challenge for school leaders is to find ways to tap into the synergy of collaboration as a tool for enhancing the quality of education and life in the school.

Ask yourself:
- To what degree do staff in this school collaborate? Are they truly collaborating, or just sharing or cooperating?
- What collaborative ideas or actions have emerged from groups of teachers?
- To what degree are my actions or other factors impeding effective collaboration within the school?

FURTHER INVESTIGATION

Directive leadership communication

There are times when a leader needs to make 'executive decisions': When an issue is sensitive, when an urgent decision is needed, when the decision has few ramifications, when the principal needs to declare what is acceptable and what is not, when clear policy or procedures determine the response, and so on. There are also many situations when staff members want a clear and prompt decision from a leader. Directive leadership refers to leader behaviour that aims to direct, control or persuade staff members to comply with expectations. It is part of a principal's job.

In classic studies of how primary and secondary school principals interact with colleagues by Bredeson (1987), Collard (1990) and Arlestig (2007), principals were frequently reported to engage in directing staff members concerning policies, regulations and tasks. Eden (2001) described how principals engage in directive leadership, through actions such as stipulating policy directions at staff meetings, monitoring teacher lessons with personal inspections, reminding teachers about expectations regarding professional behaviour and reprimanding staff members who did not comply with school regulations on professional dress.

From his nation-wide study of Australian primary and secondary schools De Nobile (2015) identified five types of directive leadership communication. These included 'Guidance' interactions in which principals offered suggestions or advice; 'Collaboration' interactions in which the principal worked with staff to address issues; 'Delegation' interactions in which they guided staff through senior or middle leaders; 'Indirect' interactions in which they influenced staff by their example; and 'Command/control' interactions in which forceful and overt demands were used.

While directive leadership communication is beneficial because staff members have the information and advice to get things done, too much can be harmful. Excessive use of the 'Command/control' interactions, in particular, can be damaging to morale as people start to feel micromanaged and pushed around and feel they have less autonomy (De Nobile, 2021a).

You might explore how balanced the communication is between leadership and staff in your school. Do the interactions suggest a leaning towards directive leadership or a more democratic type of leadership? Or is the balance 'just right'? Why do you feel this?

6

THE CLASSROOM, THE SCHOOL AND THE WORLD

From the classroom to the school

The 'cathedral builders' amongst us don't talk about how little time we have to lay bricks and make walls. We know we're building a cathedral (Sackson, 2011).

REFLECT

- Do you think of yourself as a teacher or a school leader?
- Do you resent the time you spend teaching, because it takes you away from leadership responsibilities; do you resent the time you spend in leadership, because it interrupts your teaching?
- Are there particular times when you think of yourself as a teacher or as a leader?

SHIFT THE FOCUS

The school of the past was like a group of hotel guests, who simply happened to be on the same site at the same time. The principal was the 'head teacher', identified by their superior teaching skills or greater experience. But now the school needs to be a cohesive, coherent organisation, planning and acting collaboratively to achieve agreed goals.

Many school leaders have classroom teaching responsibilities as well as school leadership responsibilities. Some have ambivalent feelings about this. They bemoan their lack of opportunities to take on whole-school responsibilities, but complain that their administrative role takes them away from teaching. These dual responsibilities present particular role problems for leaders who see themselves simply as teachers who have some added responsibilities.

School executive teams need to change that orientation, and to be seen, not as teachers with leadership responsibilities, but as school leaders who also teach a bit. This means shifting focus from the classroom to the school; planning and acting not from the narrow perspective of your own class, but that of the whole school; making decisions, establishing priorities and allocating resources from a whole-school perspective.

Manage dual roles

School leaders must have a whole-school orientation in their thinking. Concepts of culture, educational philosophy and platform, school development, accountability, participative decision-making, community involvement in schooling, public relations and performance management need to be part of their thinking. They need vision, courage, self-confidence, persistence, political astuteness, willingness to take risks, confidence in autonomy, and the skills to empower others, analyse, monitor, build culture, motivate, and communicate to all members of the school community.

There is no doubt that leadership roles in schools have become more demanding. Deputy principals, for example, are involved in almost all of the principal's responsibilities: staff selection, staff performance reviews, curriculum innovation, professional learning of colleagues, dealing with parent, student and staff issues, conducting information and education sessions for parents, visioning and strategic planning, and so on, and carrying full responsibility for some of these. Teaching, too, is increasingly demanding, with external accountabilities and greater parent and community scrutiny adding to a teacher's load.

Many school leaders with teaching responsibilities experience the frustration of feeling that they're performing neither role well. In the classroom their teaching is interrupted by school matters and their mind distracted by school concerns. When they're attending to school matters, they are distracted by concerns about the classroom. Successful leaders use strategies to cope with these situations.

Plan roles carefully

Some teaching responsibilities are less demanding than others. A teacher with prime responsibility for a group of students has a lot to think about: their progress, the class conflicts, class structures and organisation that might work better, interactions between students, parent interviews and reporting procedures, and other individual and group problems. A more manageable teaching role is one which avoids prime responsibility for a particular class. However, a teacher in a 'support' role needs to be dependable, irrespective of other demands on their time. Whatever teaching commitment you negotiate, fulfil it reliably and effectively.

Similarly, leadership responsibilities need to be appropriate. Deputy or assistant principals with teaching responsibilities, for example, often have responsibility for student discipline–but this may be an inappropriate choice of role for someone with teaching commitments, because either their classroom teaching will be interrupted when they are called on to handle disruptive incidents, which is unfair on the students they are teaching, or they will delay dealing with the disruptive incidents until they are free from classes, which is poor discipline practice.

Executive staff with teaching commitments need to have responsibilities which are shared with others or can be carried out at times convenient to them, such as professional development planning, teacher mentoring or curriculum management.

Focus on one role at a time

Make it clear to everyone — including system or board executives — that when you are in the classroom, the students deserve your best and have prior claim upon your time. Make it clear to your colleagues that, while teaching, you are not to be interrupted except for a major crisis. Train staff, parents and students to deal through clerical staff or others when you are in the classroom. Similarly, keep classroom issues to classroom time.

Although this is a little simplistic — life isn't always as neat as this — it is essential to give your best attention to whatever you are doing at any moment. This includes never interrupting a face-to-face conversation with someone simply because the telephone rings; it is disrespectful to interrupt a conversation for a phone call of unknown importance.

Organise time

Ensure that you manage time well. Keep a time log for a week or two and look at how you have spent time. Complete things. Focus on achieving things. Do less better. In addition:
- Plan the timetable so that you have some time every day to attend to management issues. If there is some particular time of the day when these seem to be most demanding, make that your administration time.
- Display your teaching timetable in a prominent place, so that everyone knows when you are available.

- Do only what is worth doing. With a focus on outcomes, be ruthless in discarding tasks that are not productive.
- Say no. Be willing to say, 'This is not a high priority for my school, and therefore for me, so I don't have time for it.'

Let go

Avoid trying to do everything yourself. Trust others with responsibilities. Do only those things that you alone can do:

- Allow clerical staff to open your correspondence.
- Give your clerical staff real responsibility. Teach them how to prepare certain types of letters for you.
- Let clerical staff have your diary. Let them make appointments for you, and to book return phone calls for the time when you're available.
- Trust others. Be prepared to let other staff do things without your constant presence or interference. Provide feedback when it's done, so that staff learn.
- Share the problem of keeping up to date. There is a vast amount of material you need to keep in touch with. Allocate colleagues to be responsible for reading certain categories of correspondence, such as teaching materials, camps, curriculum innovations, excursions and cultural events. Encourage them to display or circulate materials of general interest, and to bring to your attention items that may be significant for your school.

Spend your administration time on tasks that have large potential payoffs, such as: coaching staff to handle discipline problems; training colleagues to handle various responsibilities; talking with parents who are looking for ways to assist in the school; and liaising with the community.

Draw the school community together

Encourage all members of the school community to feel a part of the school, working together for students. Focus their attention on the whole school and not just their classroom or child.

Help people to understand the school culture, which is defined through the school's defined purpose, values and beliefs. Consider questions such as: What is unique about us? Why do we do things the way we do? What is my specific, even unique, contribution? How do I fit into the larger picture of the school, and how does the school fit in the community and the world?

Articulate and model the culture to every audience at every opportunity.

Build a stronger understanding of the school's culture:

- Seek staff opinion. Involve staff in exploring problems and recommending solutions. Ensure that support staff such as cleaners, gardeners, clerical staff, aides and technicians are acknowledged as colleagues by yourself, teachers, parents — and themselves — and that they see their role as contributing to student learning and wellbeing. Share decision-making where possible, so that staff members see themselves as important and as owners of the decisions.
- Ensure that parents are accepted as part of the school community, with a legitimate influence, interest and involvement in what happens in the school. Vigorously counter the stereotype of interaction between the school and parents is as a confrontationist 'them and us' relationship.
- Ensure that students are accepted as an active part of the school community. Schooling is not what is 'done to' students. It is the process by which they interact with people and curriculum to achieve certain outcomes. There are positive effects on learning outcomes when students are involved in the school community in other ways than simply as learners.

CASE STUDY: THE TEACHING–LEADERSHIP BALANCE

Teresa has been the Year 8 coordinator at an independent community school for the last three years. Her teaching responsibilities include mathematics classes for Years 8, 9 and 10 and one technology class in Year 8. While her teaching workload has been consistent over the three years, she has found her year-level coordinator role is demanding more and more of her time. Her dilemma is that she would like to spend more time developing better lessons and resources for her classes, but the coordination load takes up all the time she would have for this. She is required to demonstrate leadership in her area, but feels she is losing her edge to what she calls 'administrivia'. Her year-level coordinator role typically involves:

- responsibility for the academic progress of each student in Year 8
- responsibility for managing challenging behaviour issues in all Year 8 students
- liaison between teachers and the learning support team to assist students who are experiencing difficulties
- working with the other coordinators to develop class timetables and exam timetables

- writing comments on student reports each semester
- dealing with parent inquiries
- chairing the academic prize committee, which determines annual prize winners
- preparing and chairing meetings of Year 8 teachers
- organising Year 8 camps and social events.

While she could get some help with some of these responsibilities, it would not free up much extra time. At the moment she feels spread too thin and, on top of that, does not feel she is doing her best job as a teacher.

Teresa knows there might be people willing to take on some extra responsibilities. She knows Antonette, one of her colleagues in mathematics, is looking to get promoted in a year or two, and would surely accept any opportunity to demonstrate her abilities, but is not sure how to go about pursuing that. Teresa asks her principal for a meeting to discuss the situation.

Teresa and the principal approach Antonette, who agrees enthusiastically to take on responsibility for the prize committee, camps and social events. At the following staff meeting, the principal announces the new arrangement.

The principal also initiates a new school-wide timetabling committee, and asks for volunteers from each year level to become members. This committee will take on the class and exam timetabling duties once ascribed to year coordinators in that area.

Teresa effectively communicated her workload issues to the principal and the principal took a school-wide view of leadership by inviting other staff members to take on responsibilities. This has allowed Teresa to better balance her Year Coordinator and teaching responsibilities, and she can continue to teach effectively.

MAKE IT PERSONAL

The challenge for school leaders is to see the school not as a cluster of individual classrooms, but as an integrated and cohesive organisation.

Ask yourself, to what degree do I:
- recognise and understand whole-school issues?
- bring the whole-school perspective to parochial discussions and decision- making?
- cope with the dual roles of school leadership and student teaching?

FURTHER INVESTIGATION

A whole-school perspective

The influential International Successful School Leadership Project (ISSLP) (Drysdale & Gurr, 2011; Gurr, 2015), and other studies in Australia and New Zealand, have defined a set of key variables that contribute to whole-school transformation, including, vision, distributed leadership, quality teaching practice, professional learning, and good use of data (Boyd, 2012; Gurr & Drysdale, 2020; Hogan, Carr & Down, 2020). These reports build upon earlier research by the Organisation for Economic Cooperation and Development (Pont et al, 2008), which found that the policies in many OECD countries focused on defining leadership responsibilities, distributing school leadership, developing the knowledge and skills of leaders, and making school leadership a more attractive profession (e.g., Day & Gurr, 2014).

Discuss with leadership colleagues in your school the degree to which a whole school perspective is evident, and the distribution of leadership within the school.

Beyond the school to the world

It is critical for school leaders to understand the context within which schools function. While the context is not something that can be changed, it does provide the drivers for change that need to be understood and used in creating the schools of the future (Caldwell & Loader, 2011, p.5).

REFLECT

- In what ways have big-picture issues at the local, state, national or international level had trickle-down effects on your school?
- What international educational trends are likely to impact on educational policy in Australia?
- Do staff in your school have an awareness of the big picture issues?
- Do you and your colleagues have a conceptualisation of the school of the future? What does it look like?

SHIFT THE FOCUS

It is easy for teachers, and even school leaders, to become micro-focused. In the previous section we explored the importance of understanding educational issues beyond the walls of the classroom.

However, while essential, a school-wide perspective is no longer sufficient. Increasingly, educators need to see their work in a global context. Leaders cannot act in a vacuum, but need to be aware of the educational, political and economic factors at local, state, national and international levels that have influence on schools.

It is not just present influences that impact upon schools. Conceptualisations of the future are influencing thinking about schools in the future, and the future will not wait. It is impatient to be heard and its voice is echoing down our school corridors now.

The big picture

What happens in the classroom and school matters. However, increasingly, what happens in your classrooms and school is influenced — even dictated — by what happens far beyond your school.

There are many examples:

- The global financial crisis of 2007–2008 had its source in the financial decisions of lending institutions in various parts of the world. Though now in the rear view mirror of history, its ripples have had impacts on individuals, businesses and governments throughout the world (Aparicio et al, 2019).
- The COVID-19 pandemic greatly disrupted all aspects of life on the planet, especially during the years 2020–2022, Not only were there business and economic repercussions, but the very nature of schooling had to change overnight and the effects continue to be felt (Ryan et al, 2023).
- From 2008 Australia adopted an approach to national testing and the publication of data about schools which was modelled on similar systems from other countries (Hargreaves & Shirley, 2009). Interestingly, Australia adopted (and still implements at the time of writing) ideas which were roundly criticised in the countries from which they were adapted (Hardy, 2021; Lingard et al, 2016; Long, 2023; Rimfeld et al, 2019; Sahlberg, 2018; Taylor, 2019).
- The development of information and communications technology (ICT) in other parts of the world, including the creation of internet social networking sites, and, more recently, AI based applications, has had a significant impact on the resourcing of schools with ICT facilities, and the implementation of policies and procedures relating to the use of ICT for learning and management, as well as for inappropriate purposes such as bullying and cheating (Karan & Angadi, 2024).

It is easy to feel that the difficulties and frustrations we face are unique to our school, our district or our sector. It is easy to assume that what happens on the other side of the world need not affect us. It is easy to assume that the current government (whichever it might be at the time) is to blame. The reality is different. Governments are influenced by global circumstances, and the solutions they implement are influenced by ideas generated in other parts of the world. Those same governments are responsible to ensure that education systems continually respond to changing circumstances throughout the world; meet the expectations of the community; achieve appropriate outcomes for students; and do all this in a context of rapidly changing circumstances, expectations and anticipated outcomes necessary to prepare the young for an uncertain future.

It is important for leaders to understand the 'big picture'. This includes the following strategies.

Recognise the influences

It used to be common to hear school principals say, 'I've seen all this before. Keep your head down, and it will blow over.' (Perhaps it's still common!) There are certainly changes which come and go in a way which appears cyclic. However, it is more correct to see it as helical, with some issues being revisited, but from a different perspective, or with different understandings.

Education is a core value or expectation of our society, so there are many influences which impinge on schools:

- Some are political. Watch for trends in messages in political rhetoric, expressed by a variety of politicians from both sides of the parliament. One such message in recent years has been accountability — the idea that schools cost governments a great deal of money, but no-one is quite sure about what they are getting for their money. Each country, each government, each political party, is addressing the issue in its own way, but they *are* addressing it, and it *is* having an impact on your school.
- Some are economic. Whether the economy is in boom times or crisis, there is consistent touting of the need for a better-educated workforce. This may be expressed in a variety of ways, which include a more relevant curriculum, more vocational experience and course options for school students, improved standards (which usually means more standardised testing), and the promotion of the languages of neighbouring countries, such as an increase in the teaching of Asian languages in Australian schools.
- Some are social. As our society has changed, for example, there has been a growing perception by many that we are becoming more violent, that values are not being taught to our youth, that breakdown of families and other factors are resulting in youth without clear moral codes to guide their behaviour. As a result, for some years there have been trends in Australia towards increased enrolments in private schools, where, many consider, students will be taught values; to the publication, by state and national governments, of statements of values to be taught; and to the requirement for schools to teach a prescribed course in Australian history to all students.
- Some are research-driven. For example, research into the way the brain processes information, and the need for learning to integrate information in problem-solving contexts rather than to focus on isolated pieces of information, has influenced the nature of curricula, and the application of teaching and learning strategies which increasingly emphasise understandings and problem-solving.

- Some are technological. One obvious influence is the impact of information and communication technology on access to knowledge, allowing for instant access to knowledge and opinions, and creating new ways for learners to connect and collaborate.

In 1999, Australia's education ministers agreed to *The Adelaide Declaration on National Goals for Schooling in the Twenty-First Century*. This was a refinement of the earlier *Hobart Declaration* from 1989 (MCEETYA, 1999). The three overarching goals were that:

- Schooling should develop fully the talents and capacities of all students.
- Students should achieve high standards in an expanded range of core curriculum areas.
- Schooling should be socially just and contribute to social justice in a wider sense.

Principals Australia (APAPDC, 2003) identified a number of major issues, priorities and challenges which they saw as emerging from the Adelaide Declaration. These were:

- reconciliation between Indigenous and non-Indigenous Australians
- equity for Indigenous students
- accountability
- quality teaching
- innovation, the knowledge society and information and communication technologies
- teacher demographics and current/impending shortages
- middle schooling
- international comparisons
- literacy and numeracy
- civics and citizenship education
- pathways and vocational education
- articulating and assessing professional standards.

Two decades later, it is interesting to consider how accurate the writers were. Some of these issues continue to impact schools. Equally importantly, it is interesting to consider which emergent issues which were not part of that list, and what has precipitated them.

The 2008 *Melbourne Declaration on Educational Goals for Young Australians* (MCEETYA, 2008) further refined the Adelaide goals to just two, and added further meaning to them by way of deeper explanations of what each goal entails and how it can be achieved. The goals are:

- Australian schooling promotes equity and excellence

- All young Australians become successful learners, confident and creative individuals, and active and informed citizens.

Subsequently, Caldwell & Loader (2010) described the following four forces for change which are so strong they can be described as 'revolutions':

- knowledge revolution, including issues of new knowledge, access to knowledge, shape of knowledge (new disciplines and interconnected knowledge), lifelong knowledge and priorities in knowledge
- economic revolution, including the interdependence of national economies and uncertain economic futures
- social revolution, including changes to authority structures, the expectation of immediate gratification, the influence of technology, extended adolescence and changes in family and community life
- technology revolution, including changes to the ownership of knowledge, access to knowledge, the management of knowledge, how people communicate and interact, and changes to the way people learn.

The most recent national statement is the *Alice Springs (Mparntwe) Education Declaration* (Education Council, 2019). This document, again signed by all state and national ministers of education echoed the Melbourne goals word for word, but expanded a little on explanation for each aspect of each goal, particularly those relating to the second.

The impact of these changes is being felt in such areas as school curricula, building design, educational facilities, pedagogy, curriculum design and publication, and relationships within and beyond the school. (Some of these changes are addressed in this book.) Even educational writers, with a commitment to schools and a heart for teachers, are recommending changes to schools in response to the impact of these influences. Degenhardt & Duignan (2010) expressed it this way:

> We believe that schools need to change radically if they are to meet the needs of young people in the 21st century. The external context within which schools operate has changed and continues to change at ever-increasing speeds. The internal context of schools has also changed considerably since the 19th century, when modern-day schools were first established. Yet it can be argued that the prevailing model of schooling is still that of the 19th century. We agree with the OECD assertion that nothing short of reinvention will deliver the type of schooling required for the knowledge society and for young people of the new millennium.

Watch for the next 'big thing'

How do we recognise influences in our society which are likely to impinge on our work as educators? How can we see the arrows pointing to the 'next big thing'?

More than thirty years ago, Guthrie & Koppich (1993) offered some useful guidelines that still apply today. They argue that:

- Education reform is a delayed political response to social disequilibrium.
- It is likely to be a response to a problem recognised by politicians.
- Education is seen as a solution to the problem.
- The reform will have been proposed earlier, but not successfully taken up.
- Its implementation coincides with a significant political shift.
- Reform occurs during periods of when values are confused or unstable.
- Reform depends on a policy entrepreneur or champion (p.26).

Therefore, the questions to ask are these:

- What are the areas of social disequilibrium being highlighted by politicians? For example, unemployment, youth crime and disorientation.
- How could education be a solution to the problem? For example, a vocational training emphasis in schools or a renewed emphasis on teaching of values and religious education.
- What reforms have been proposed earlier, but not well implemented, which could be re-applied to the problem?
- Is there a significant shift in political ideology, decision-making powers, regulatory mandates or prohibitions, or the distribution of resources? For example, a change of government, a change of leadership or power groups within government, significant funding initiatives in a particular field, new laws or regulations.
- Is there a values disequilibrium? For example, a division within the community about the success of schools in preparing young people for employment.
- Is there a policy champion, such as a new government minister or a community leader being outspoken on this issue?

Of course, this process is not an exact science. Some issues will disappear because of economic or political changes, or the arrival of a newer social imperative, or the discredit of a particularly influential person or the rise of another. We cannot predict disruptive influences, factors which disrupt the deep-seated ways in which the world functions, such as the recent pandemic, international conflict, and unexpected technological innovations. And we cannot fully predict what changes the future will bring to education, nor can we predict how insistent those changes will be. However, as educational leaders we can move from a defensive stance, from which we complain of persecution, to a proactive stance, from which we seek to be informed about the current and impending changes.

Broaden your outlook

It's a human characteristic that we like to spend time with familiar people, people we are comfortable with. We also like to spend time with familiar ideas. Conversations with friends often cover the same topics. The challenge for leaders is to broaden their outlook. How do you do that?

At conferences, sit with someone you've never met. Join a group of strangers at lunch. Introduce yourself and listen to the things they are talking about. Go beyond names and locations. Ask, Why did you come to the conference? What are the messages that are challenging you? What are the issues you're dealing with at work? What keeps you awake at night? What have you celebrated recently? By all means, 'keep it light', but find ways to explore the issues others are dealing with and how they are thinking about them.

Join professional associations which attract people from a range of education sectors, and even people from outside education. When you meet, listen to different perspectives. Read journal articles on topics you are unfamiliar with.

Find a mentor or professional supervisor who thinks differently from you, and may not even be in education. If, when you meet with them, you both find yourselves nodding and agreeing with one another, find another mentor, someone who will challenge you with unfamiliar ideas and unfamiliar ways of viewing issues.

Appoint staff who will challenge your thinking and that of others — not those who cannot fit the school culture, but those who are not afraid to offer a different perspective, and alternative solutions to problems. If the people on your leadership team are always agreeing with you, then broaden the team or change the culture of the group. (You can't always be right!) If it is not possible to add to or change the group, then invite into your leadership team meetings a couple of divergent thinkers, with the explicit role of challenging the thinking of the group and questioning decisions.

In summary, get out of your bubble of like thinkers, and broaden your outlook.

Adapt or amend

By identifying the essence of the influence, school leaders can explore ways to address the issue, rather than to simply respond to the solutions proffered by others.

Whereas past generations of school leaders waited for system leaders or other authoritative sources to provide the answers, Caldwell & Loader (2010) suggested that,

> The way forward is not linear; the answers to the questions that challenge schools will not be simple. School leaders cannot rely on others to do the work and most importantly the answers will not be delivered to school leaders from on high, engraved as it were on stone tablets to stand forever into the future (p.6).

It appears, from a schools perspective, that governments have a poor record of seeking solutions to educational problems from educators. With each new expectation from government comes a directive on how this will be implemented by schools. The solutions often appear to have been designed by people with no understanding of schools. Perhaps educators are to blame. Perhaps we spend too much time trying to oppose the impositions on schools, rather than acknowledging the oncoming tsunami and offering our own suggestions for surviving it.

If we understand the essence of a new influence, we may have the opportunity to adapt our practices to accommodate the issue, before being told how to do so. We may also be able to reshape or mould the influence itself, by implementing educational solutions which may be accepted as an adequate response to the issue (Ridden, 2011, p.24–26).

Influence the debate

We might even be able to influence the debate itself. In the past, educational leaders have often left it to academics to argue the issues on behalf of schools. Increasingly, peak educational bodies, such as principals' associations and educational associations, are actively participating in the discussion. What's more, their voices are being heard, and in some cases, their opinions sought. School leaders ought also to participate. We can do this at a macro level by providing submissions to enquiries, by writing or speaking to policymakers and politicians, and by writing to newspapers. At a micro level, we can speak or write to parents, ensure that staff are informed, and encourage staff participation in discussing the issues.

Whatever the approach, some key principles apply:

- Focus on the essence of the issue, as understood by most, rather than being distracted by an isolated (and sometimes unreasonable) suggestion for implementation offered by one politician.
- Be articulate. Understand the issue, and be able to write or speak about it, as best you understand it, for a range of audiences, including colleagues, parents, local community members and students.
- Invite input from others, within or outside the school, who might understand or explain the issue better than you.
- Be seen to be actively exploring the implications of the issue, not simply promoting your own political view, or being negative or defensive for the sake of it.
- Focus on student learning and welfare. Be seen to be concerned, not simply because the change may inconvenience teachers, or impede your career, but because it has the potential to impact on students.

Be future focused

There is also a need for the school to be future focused, to have in place processes which allow the school to understand the forces at work on the school, identify the likely impact on the school's future, explore these and respond. The strategies involved are related to several of the concepts explored in this book concerning the ways in which the school is led, people relate and issues are explored.

However, Caldwell & Loader (2010) provided interesting insights into this issue. They reported that a school with a future focus has a clearly defined set of values and beliefs about learning, which link the past, present and future; incubates innovation; gathers intelligence about the future and acts on this information; and has structured review processes. They go on to explore a range of strategies, and then to highlight three themes: responsiveness, autonomy and partnering, arguing that 'It's time for schools to "take charge" if they are to proceed with confidence in creating their futures' (p.125).

Hargreaves & Shirley (2009) identified three ways that education has been shaped in the past, and suggested a fourth way that we might take in creating the future. As they describe it:

- The first way to implement change involves state support and professional freedom and innovation, but results in inconsistency between schools.
- The second way to implement change is through market competition and educational standardisation in which professional autonomy is lost.

- The third way tries to navigate between and beyond the market and the state and balance professional autonomy with accountability.
- The fourth way seeks change through democracy and professionalism. It places trust and confidence in the expertise of highly trained professionals, a fundamental shift in educators' professionalism that offer schools greater autonomy and introduces more openness to and engagement with parents and communities.

Their 'fourth way' similarly identifies a future in which schools act with confident autonomy, using their professional knowledge, insights and opportunities in partnership with others.

CASE STUDY: THE CHILDREN'S CONFERENCE

For some years now one of the local universities has hosted and sponsored an international children's conference. The conference is organised by an internationally renowned professor and his team. At this conference students from local schools are able to have real time discussions with their peers in Kenya and the United States about technology, health and environmental issues that affect them. Many issues were discussed and possible solutions arrived at together and draft resolutions produced for publication on a dedicated website that all could share. This was all done through video cameras and the internet. Several of the teachers who observed the conference were amazed at how much work could be done between people who were not physically in the same room but connected by interactive technology.

Bruno, one of the local principals, was there to observe all this. For him the experience was paradigm shifting. He quickly came to the realisation that the business of education is no longer something that only happens in a local context. Technology can bring down barriers of distance and politics. There is a wider world out there that students can interact with when producing their work and sharing their work. Indeed, the possibilities for interaction between people for a common good seem limitless. Bruno left the conference with a question he still hasn't answered yet: How can I take advantage of these possibilities in order to provide my students with a truly world-class education and take my staff along with me?

A few things have happened in the year since then:
- Bruno invited other staff and students to come to the next conference the following year.
- A committee has been looking at ways in which the curriculum can incorporate interaction with other students, organisations and even

celebrities using technology. Students are already able to combine video, photos and other images to produce works for assessment that are interesting, interactive and allow for critical peer review, using social networking software.
- The values education curriculum, already implemented in the school since 2006, is being redesigned to incorporate intercultural understandings of values. To this end a series of link-ups using Skype software are being organised with a Malaysian school so students can exchange ideas about their values and lifestyles, which feeds nicely into the personal development and health curriculum.

For the next school review, Graham has set 're-imagine the school ethos' as one of the major priorities to work on. He envisages a school commitment towards global citizenship and cooperation which is not only aligned to national schooling priorities, but will help educate the wider school community about tolerance, understanding and cooperation.

MAKE IT PERSONAL

The challenge for school leaders is to be aware of issues globally and nationally, while working with students who are here, but whose minds and futures are somewhere out there.

Ask yourself, to what degree do I:
- understand the socio-political influences on the school?
- help colleagues to understand influences on the school, and encourage debate about them?
- create an environment in which staff can respond creatively and confidently to the current and future influences and opportunities?

FURTHER INVESTIGATION

Teacher activism

Influences from outside the school, and even the nation, will have more and more impact on schools. Pressure from the community and governments for schools to provide the solutions to various real or perceived social problems will be intense. How can school leaders walk through these issues with a level head and, importantly, still have a balanced perspective on the real educational priorities?

Sachs (2003) advocated teacher professional activism as one way of dealing with this dilemma. The teacher activist is someone who collaborates with key people to improve trust in the profession and establish the key issues that need to be addressed in education. It is not about protests and marches as the term might suggest; rather, it is about interacting with colleagues and the wider community in order to establish an agenda based on what is right and good for the profession and, ultimately, for students that can potentially influence those external forces.

The future

Hargreaves & Shirley (2009) and Fullan (2013) have written about possible futures for education, and Caldwell (2023) provides a succinct list of likely influences, but a search of the internet or library will identify many more writings about the future, and the key influences which will determine decisions by governments and other authorities. It is interesting to note:

- the source of the information, such as the country or geographical location, and the political or social group articulating the influences
- the common threads between lists from different sources
- the implications of the influences for your school.

7

Dependency, empowerment and succession

From dependency to empowerment

You can't tell how deep a puddle is until you step into it (Shaw, 1978, p.49).

REFLECT

- Where does your role fit in the scheme of things in the school? What are the special, if not unique, opportunities you have?
- If you had the freedom to write your own job description, what would it say?
- If present reality doesn't match your ideal role, who or what is inhibiting it?

SHIFT THE FOCUS

Schools in general, and leaders in particular, have been trained over many years to depend on central authorities for decisions and resources. Historically, leaders in government schools and other systemic schools have looked to the system leaders for answers not defined in the volumes of policies, procedures and regulations; for resources, and decisions about how they'll be used; for allocation of staff and resolution of staffing issues; and so on. Dependency continues through the school. Deputies do tasks that principals decide for them; teachers plan, teach, use resources, evaluate and report in the way the executive staff decide and instruct; difficulties with students and parents are referred to executive staff for resolution. An outcome of dependency is to blame others for the cause of problems and for inadequate resolution of them.

Fullan (1997) argued that the pressure for dependency comes from below, through teacher expectations, and from above, through central office directives, and through the constant bombardment of new tasks and continual interruptions. 'Overload fosters dependency,' he said. 'Principals are either overloaded with what they are doing, or overloaded with all the things they think they should be doing.' But the key to the issue is that 'Dependency ... may also be internalised or too easily tolerated by principals themselves' (p. xi).

Schools must break free from dependency, and become proactive in seeking to change things that frustrate them; to focus instead on a forward-thinking, goal-oriented approach to solving the problems they face. Schools need to accept the opportunities that are before them, to accept that change is dependent on themselves and not others, and to act without fear. When you are prepared to take risks, to justify your action and be accountable for it, you are in control of your professional life.

Make things happen for your school

Imposing conditions, wishing, waiting and hoping are all ways of avoiding action. But change will continue, and you'll be caught constantly reacting and catching up. The alternative is to make things happen. Schools and education systems are ripe for leaders who are prepared to use initiative and to take control of their schools and their own professional destinies.

Being prepared to make things happen involves taking risks. In large organisations, if you ask enough people, someone will say no! Those leaders who manage to push the barriers work on the assumption that if you don't ask, no-one can say no. Ensure that your risk-taking referred to here is strategic: not irresponsibility, blatant rule-breaking nor contempt.

Act within the parameters set by regulatory authorities

The school and central authority are interdependent, each relying on the other to play an essential part in the process. The most powerful people in the education system are teachers, with direct access to students; the least powerful are those in the central authority or governments, furthest away from direct access to students and teachers.

Be clear about what you are trying to achieve

Change for change's sake is unlikely to lead to benefits for schools or for leaders of them. The focus for change must be the achievement of appropriate goals, and, specifically, goals that benefit students. In that sense, your action is intelligent, knowledgeable, professional action, taken because of a belief that students will benefit.

Be innovative and creative in considering actions and seeking solutions

Innovative risk-taking actions usually result from clever thinking about a problem or a perception that something is not happening as well as it might. Involve others in helping to generate a range of options: sound and harebrained, traditional and radical, detailed and sketchy. Explore all the possibilities you can find, before deciding on a particular course of action.

Be prepared to involve others and to listen to their opinions. In particular, involve in the discussion those people who will implement the idea and those who will be most affected by it. Listen to their views initially, and as the action is implemented.

Be aware of the possible consequences of the action

In addition to the anticipated or desired outcomes, an action will almost certainly have other consequences for students, staff, parents, yourself and others. Think these through. No matter how cautious you are, unanticipated consequences may still occur, but you can reduce the impact of these by carefully considering possible consequences beforehand, and considering how you will retrieve the situation if things go awry.

Be convinced that the potential advantages of the action outweigh the potential risks. The two sides of the ledger can now be evaluated rationally. How likely is this action to succeed and what are its potential advantages? By contrast, what are the potential risks, how disastrous will their effects be, and what is their likelihood of occurring? Is the risk worth it for the outcomes?

Expect results and watch for them. Be clear about what you are hoping to see. Define and watch for indicators that will show whether the action is having the desired effects. However, be honest and objective. Be willing to admit when actions don't have the effects desired. If this occurs, intervene to provide additional resources and guidance, to revise the intentions, or to discard the idea altogether.

Be willing to learn

If an innovation does not succeed as expected, try to identify the reasons. It's very easy, when innovations don't work, to simply dismiss the reasons as beyond your control; to say, for example, 'It will never work until we are given more money' or 'People here didn't want it to work.' Would more money really have made the difference? How much more and for what purpose? Did you underestimate the changes in people's attitude, knowledge or skills needed to make the idea work? Did you fail to support people through the change, to communicate effectively, to provide opportunity for involvement in the initial decision or the change process, or to provide feedback mechanisms?

Don't allow a lack of success in one action to destroy your willingness to keep searching for excellence. Learn, and move on.

Be accountable

Be accountable for the actions you take, whether or not they are taken with the knowledge and endorsement of the central authorities. Being accountable means being able to justify that the process has been sound: that the purposes were clear and appropriate, the action carefully selected and considered, and the effects monitored, evaluated and used as a basis for further decision-making.

Make things happen for yourself

What prevents you taking control of your own professional life? Perhaps it is your expectations of yourself: your self-esteem, knowledge and skills, or understanding of your leadership role. Perhaps it is others' expectations of you: their perception of your capabilities, motives or your role. Perhaps it is your perception of what others expect of you.

You can change these expectations by actions such as these:

- Recognise your skills. Make a list of your past achievements in your work and beyond it. Identify anything that made you feel satisfied at the time. Identify the skills you used to achieve those things.
- Enhance your skills. List tasks you've found difficult or intimidating lately. Decide whether the reasons were due to the unfamiliarity of the task, the intimidation of others' expectations, or a lack of knowledge or skill. Identify from this list knowledge or skills you need to enhance. Look for professional learning opportunities to achieve this.

- Question your own perception of your role. Hold a dialogue with a colleague to question what you do and why.
- Be creative in finding new things to do and new ways to do them.
- Attempt something new in your job every week.
- Take hold of opportunities to do new things. Offer to take on new responsibilities. Have a go at things you're uncertain of.
- Demonstrate your skills and successes. Do some things you know you can do well and let others see you. In some way that fits your personality, let others know of your successes.
- Learn to negotiate effectively. Then use those skills to negotiate a new role for yourself.
- partner with others. Find a partner whose skills differ from yours, who will see things differently from you, who will challenge your thinking wisely, and who will motivate you when you need it.

Provide the context for others to be empowered

When people feel empowered, they feel they have some control over their work, with the 'power' to innovate and explore, to think differently about their work, to make decisions which enhance the success of the organisation. Consequences include increased initiative, creativity and commitment, and a strong sense of worth. There are also benefits for leaders:

- Leaders are able to focus on what no-one else can do, and on monitoring, supporting and networking.
- Available skills are better identified, used and enhanced, the pool of knowledge and experience is increased, and individuals become more flexible and adaptable.
- Inefficient, tedious, frustrating work practices are likely to be eliminated.
- Because self-esteem, confidence and peer credibility are enhanced, collaboration is improved.
- Trust in staff is demonstrated, and their worth recognised. Commitment to the organisation is developed.

How is an 'empowering workplace' achieved? It requires more than a call to, 'Roll up your sleeves and get in there — and may the force be with you!' In practice, you can empower no-one. Empowerment comes from within, and leaders must provide the environment, opportunities and encouragement for people to assume the power which is available to them.

Changing people's perceptions from one of dependency to empowerment takes time, and conscious strategies such as these:

- Give meaningful power. Do not give a responsibility to a colleague, then continue to direct them. Monitor and coach, but do not give pseudo-responsibility. Let go. Let others have the power to make meaningful decisions about how things will be done, and how resources will be allocated.
- Enable staff to examine and restructure their own roles and learning environments. Avoid simply delegating responsibility for things you don't like doing anyway and don't consider particularly critical.
- Warn of bear pits. Don't encourage staff to take control of a critical aspect of their work that you know that a superordinate has set views about; or in which you won't support them; or where you know there is such strong parent feeling that the teacher can't win.
- Negotiate the parameters. Make sure that staff members know the non-negotiable expectations.
- Explain the costs. Staff need to be willing to devote time and energy; listen to others; share ideas; collaborate; accept responsibility for ensuring high standards; be accountable for their decisions and actions.
- Demonstrate trust. Make it clear, not only in your words, but also in your actions, that you trust staff to act in the best interests of their students and the school.
- Encourage initiative. Help staff to identify new approaches. Accept the validity of risk, of trying something for which there are no guarantees of success.
- Allow error. Error is a fundamental learning tool, for students and adults. Use errors to learn about processes, strategies and people. Avoid seeing error as the end of a project. Rather look at it as the launching pad for a potential breakthrough.
- Provide training. Identify skills or knowledge staff members need to move forward successfully. Encourage them to analyse their own needs. Find ways to provide the necessary training.
- Provide resources. Use resources to encourage and foster teachers who are prepared to be proactive in improving student outcomes. The key resource is time.
- Provide support and feedback. Monitor progress in a non-imposing way. Commend achievements. Report successes to the school community. Talk through problems with teachers. Provide constructive feedback on actions. Coach where appropriate, or match teachers with a colleague for coaching.

Let those who achieve enjoy the reward. When others complete a task or project so effectively that people praise it, let those responsible claim the credit and enjoy the praise

CASE STUDY: THE LEADERSHIP COMPROMISE

Linda was appointed deputy principal at Mornang Road Secondary College eight months ago. While the first few weeks were good, Linda steadily came to feel disempowered, negative, dissatisfied and stressed.

Linda felt that Kate, her principal, didn't trust her. For instance, when Linda had finished checking the early years teachers' mid-year reports, Kate requested to see those reports with Linda's feedback to the teachers. In another case, Kate asked the teachers about Linda's supervision of their teaching and in particular how she conducted area meetings. Often, after Linda had telephone conversations with parents or educational suppliers, Kate asked Linda to justify the calls. Kate often corrected Linda or clarified her meaning at staff meetings, interrupting her while she was addressing staff or reprimanding her if a staff member had a complaint about her, which some felt they could do for things as trivial as non-preferred times on the yard supervision roster. Linda had not experienced this kind of interference when she was the deputy principal at her last school.

By September Linda was fed up and asked for a meeting with Kate. Before the meeting she wrote down her concerns and listed the things she wanted to discuss in order. At the meeting Kate was taken aback, but composed herself and explained that her questioning of staff was how she showed interest in her staff as a 'hands-on' leader. Kate explained her corrections of Linda, and others, as simply the way she operated to avoid misinformation. Kate also said, though, that the other staff members' complaints over issues such as the roster were evidence that Linda was not a strong leader. At the conclusion of the meeting Kate advised Linda had best develop a 'thicker skin' as leadership is a 'tough game'.

Linda thought hard about what Kate had said. She realised that her leadership style was very different from Kate's, and that if she was going to find a way to work with Kate, she needed to better understand her own style and perception of her role.

First, she made a list of what she perceived to be her strengths, as well as those areas in which she was less confident. Next, she contacted a trusted colleague from her previous school and asked for a real, honest discussion of her leadership style. Through this process, Linda realised that her style relied on communication with her colleagues, but that because she had lost confidence and closed herself off, she was functioning less effectively as a leader in her new school. She also realised that, in a way,

Kate had been right: realistically, Linda didn't expect every staff member to agree with her every decision, and that complaints over matters such as rosters would not have bothered her in her old school, when she had felt more confident in her actions.

Linda had two options: she could blame Kate for her loss of confidence and resign; or she could empower herself, reconnect with her colleagues and reassert her leadership.

Linda made a list of the issues other staff had complained about, and approached the relevant staff to discuss their concerns. She found that some of the concerns were valid, and made plans to address these. Others concerns, she saw, were unreasonable, and she explained frankly and firmly to these staff members why changes would not be made. Linda found that there were a few staff members who did not agree with her decisions, but they seemed to respect her for explaining them. She also discovered several colleagues who had similar ideas about leadership, and with whom she felt she could work collaboratively in the future.

Linda also took into account Kate's approach to communication and avoiding misinformation. Linda made a habit of reporting in regularly to Kate about her day-to-day decisions and actions. Although it went against Linda's leadership style, she understood that compromise was necessary. This seemed to make Kate feel more secure and resulted in a more trusting working relationship between Linda and Kate.

MAKE IT PERSONAL

The challenge for school executive staff is to empower themselves and others to be proactive and entrepreneurial in making their own work meaningful and rewarding, and in achieving the school's goals.

Ask yourself, to what degree do I:
- encourage and motivate staff to use initiative and take risks in order to achieve their goals?
- encourage and support others to push the limits?
- make things happen?
- let go of control and let others take responsibility?

FURTHER INVESTIGATION

Dependency

There are a number of sources of policies and procedures for schools. Some government systems may have a regulatory framework online. Smaller systems or individual schools may have hard copies of regulations, policies and procedures. Examine these to identify the style in which they are written (are the parameters narrow or broad, for example?) and the content of them. Consider how much is essential for safe and legal operation of schools, and how much is promoting dependency.

Improving your own skills in business and management may give you an advantage when deciding when and how to make decisions for your school rather than referring to centralised bureaucracy. Smith & Riley (2010) suggest some strategies.

Fullan (1997) wrote about the impact of school systems in creating dependent principals. He cites Louis who, in discussing school district relationships with principals, argues for tight 'coupling' but non-regulatory bureaucracy. Louis explains that, 'By coupling I mean a relationship which has some shared goals and objectives, reasonably clear and frequent communication, and mutual coordination and influence. By bureaucracy I mean control through rules and regulations.' Fullan said in summary: 'It is imperative, then, that superintendents understand that closeness does not mean control, and that autonomy does not mean neglect' (p.43). It is generally assumed that change in the relationship between system leaders and principals has paralleled the change in the relationship between principals and teachers, but it may be helpful to explore whether this is so in your context. The question can be extended to whatever authorities your school answers to.

Beyond empowerment to succession

You can't hold a man down without staying down with him (Washington, 1990, p.803).

REFLECT

- If you were to leave your role — due to sickness, death, retirement or a new job — who of your colleagues would be able to step into the role? Is there at least one credible candidate for the position when it is advertised?
- If you leave suddenly, will the school suffer through a lack of appropriate leadership or a lack of knowledge?
- How do these questions apply to other leadership positions within your school?

SHIFT THE FOCUS

A natural consequence of empowerment is that people not only take control of their current role, but seek to move to new roles, where they can be even more effective. This is succession, the notion that people are willing, competent and prepared to assume the next level of leadership in the school.

We must involve colleagues in leadership, to encourage them into leadership roles, to honour their leadership gifts and grow their leadership insights. We must see leadership not as a possession, but as an opportunity and a trust, which we share, grow and then hand on to others.

Succession

Some school leaders have made their roles seem unattainable except to the most skilled and experienced. Some have been possessive about their power, handing out leadership titbits to those who are honoured to be allowed to participate. Others have made their roles appear stressful and complex, roles which no-one in their right mind would ever choose. Even the notion of empowerment has been seen by some as benevolence, or as enlisting others to do the leader's work for them. As a consequence, school leadership is seen by many as inaccessible or unattractive.

Leaders who commit to succession have a different mindset. They are passionate about helping leaders to develop, about ensuring that they are responsible for the growth of those who are accountable to them (Goldsmith, 2009). The measure of our commitment to succession is the presence of a pool of aspirants willing and able to fill any leadership position which becomes vacant, in our school or in others. It is rewarding for a leader to see colleagues assuming a leadership role which is valuable to the school and fulfilling to the individual. While we cannot ensure our colleagues do this, we can provide the environment and opportunities for them to do so. Their readiness includes being:

- willing to accept, and even seek, leadership opportunities
- aware of the nature and expectations of leadership, and emotionally and mentally prepared and capable
- experienced in many aspects of the role, and appropriately knowledgeable and skilled.

Being willing

The ability to assume leadership positions is insufficient without a willingness to do so. The willingness is influenced by the images of leadership conveyed by leaders — consciously or unconsciously. Put simply, the behaviour and attitudes of leaders have a significant impact on the leadership aspirations of others. When principals and other school leaders consistently display signs of stress and job dissatisfaction, this discourages others who might aspire to such positions.

Bywaters et al (2007) suggest numerous actions which may encourage leadership aspirations, including communicating the positive aspects of the role, providing leadership experiences, supporting the leadership of others, and coaching people in leadership roles.

Being capable

Willingness is not enough without capability. Leadership capability is more than competence. Whereas competence is about performing adequately with current responsibilities, capability reflects the ability to lead in any circumstances or situation. Capability is an all-round quality, an integration of knowledge, skills, personal qualities and understanding used appropriately and effectively: not just in familiar and highly focused specialist contexts but in response to new, changing and unfamiliar circumstances (ACEL, 2023).

Defining the essential qualities of capable school leadership is a field of study of its own. Leaders are called upon to do so many things that defining a skill set for them is contentious. This is especially so in schools, where principals do not usually have the support of other leaders skilled in finance, human resources, facilities management or the like, let alone access to experts in counselling, assessment, strategic planning or change management.

Yet the problem may not be as difficult as we may make it out to be. School leaders often impose on themselves limitations in their thinking and expectations in the role that leaders in other fields would not. Breakspear et al (2009) highlighted this issue, when writing of the challenges in attracting and retaining highly skilled young teachers. They argue that:

> For too long, educators have operated with the problematic mindset of 'terminal uniqueness': that somehow education is 'different' from the private sector in having to respond to changing labour market conditions and staff expectations. They also dismiss the notion that schools can learn from industry responses to these challenges (p.11–12).

Some time ago, Principals Australia created a course which was premised on five propositions that describe the nature, scope and work of school leadership (Bywaters, et al, 2007). The inherent elegance of these five propositions is that they focus on leadership thinking first, and leadership action as consequence. Where school leaders come adrift is when they focus on actions, a large percentage of which are reactive, and then try to justify to themselves where these fit in their own perception of the role.

Put simply, leaders are as leaders think. Leadership is an intellectual activity. Leaders are constantly thinking about their organisation — its purposes, its achievements, its people, its structures and its resources. They are constantly evaluating the organisation and the integration or synergy of the policies, plans, programs, procedures and practices, and intervening to redirect or refocus these.

Those people in schools who are not in formal leadership positions but are future leaders should be identified not by their teaching ability nor their administrative efficiency, but by their thinking. They think school, not just classroom; they think general policies, not just idiosyncratic procedures; they think culture, not just isolated incidents; they think growth, not just industrial peace; they think influence, not just personal venting; they think us, not just me; they recognise past and think future, not just present.

Ability to lead, then, is not just about specific skills of organisation, time management, public speaking and report writing. Clearly, if a leader lacks key skills, this will impair their effectiveness and the respect they receive from others; therefore, they matter. However, particular skills can be learnt, and, in larger schools, partnerships with others can provide the requisite skills within the school. However, a leader cannot operate without a leadership mindset.

The Australian Council for Educational Leaders' Capability Framework (ACEL, 2023) is designed to provide pathways for the development of particular skills and insights into leadership. Eleven leadership capabilities have been identified from a synthesis of many leadership programs from around the world, and are grouped under three categories relating to the leadership of self, of others and of the school.

In 2011, an alternative framework was created by the Australian Institute for Teaching and School Leadership (AITSL, 2014). The Standard for Principals aims to provide a framework for professional learning, to guide self-reflection, self-improvement and development, and the management of self and others. The Standard is based on three leadership requirements: vision and values; knowledge and understanding; personal qualities and social and interpersonal skills. These requirements are enacted through the following five key professional practices:

- leading teaching and learning
- developing self and others
- leading improvement, innovation and change
- leading the management of the school
- engaging and working with the community.

Being experienced

Leadership experience can be claimed or awarded. Those who aspire to leadership are often identified by their willingness to assume leadership in particular context. They reflect the notions that:

- Leaders are often leaders long before they become leaders!
- Leaders are people who lead when a leader is needed.

Such people volunteer to lead or participate in ad hoc groups formed to organise an event, review a program, generate ideas for a particular purpose or oversee the implementation of an innovation. They may approach the principal or other leader and offer to take on a particular challenge which they see as benefiting the school, such as a project on cyberbullying, a thinking skills program or an idea for involving students in leadership. They don't always wait to be asked, but see needs and opportunities and seek to lead them.

These people do not necessarily do so to 'score points' with the school's leadership or their colleagues. More typically, their motive is passion: they see a need, it interests them and they want to see it addressed, so they are keen to play their part. Such actions exhibit leadership thinking. Whether they have the leadership skills of influencing others, dealing with obstacles and opposition, negotiating with others, communicating effectively, planning appropriately, and so on, will become evident in time.

Leadership experience can also be awarded. Opportunities arise in schools for temporary (relieving or acting) leadership positions. In some of these cases, the principal may have power to offer the role to someone. Sometimes we yield to politics rather than leadership development; for example, we offer the position to the person with the most experience, or who for some other reason assumes the role of heir apparent. However, it is often more valuable to provide leadership experience to someone who has shown their willingness and capability to lead, and for whom this would be an opportunity to provide experience at the next level.

Be courageous about dealing with the politics if leadership development is more important. It may be possible to get the 'heir apparent' to support another appointee, by explaining to them that you want to challenge and develop leadership in your chosen person, and would like them to act as mentor and sounding board. You might even make this a formal arrangement between the mentor and the appointed leader, with the clear message that success in the role will reflect well on both leader and mentor. Opportunities also arise for ad hoc leadership opportunities, with a clear purpose, and a defined timeline. These might be dealt with in the same way as above, used as an opportunity to provide experience and develop leadership in someone who would benefit from the opportunity.

Encouraging and developing aspiring leaders

Pritchard (2003) found that disincentives for the principalship, as described by principals and aspirants, differed between government, Catholic and independent schools. However, there were common threads. They included:

- the nature of the role of the principal, including the impact on family and personal life, accountability issues, people management issues, legal vulnerability, isolation, uncertainty of tenure (in independent schools), the pressure of expectations, workload stress, and keeping abreast of educational issues
- the selection and transfer process (in systemic schools)
- mentoring and preparation for the principalship
- financial rewards for the complexity of the role.

These disincentives impact on the strategies designed to recruit, develop and retain potential leaders, which are at the core of succession planning. While there are some responsibilities here for systems and governments, at the school level succession planning includes ensuring that people are not discouraged by the role modelling of leaders, nor the process of selection; that staff with the interest or the capability to lead are encouraged and developed by experiences, training, mentoring and coaching; and that those already in positions of leadership are encouraged to continue in school leadership roles.

There are leaders who like to think they are indispensable. If the organisation struggles if they are take leave, or if they move on, they see it as an affirmation of their exceptional leadership. This is conceit, not leadership. Effective leaders seek to develop the leadership of those around them, and to ensure that the organisation continues effectively beyond the departure of any leader.

CASE STUDY: THE COWBOY AND THE OTHER GUY

Alison has been a teacher at her current school for 10 years. She has worked with three principals, but regards the contrast between the first two as quite remarkable in terms of impact on the school.

Roger, who was principal for the first six years, was what Buchanan & Badham (2003) would call a 'cowboy'. He was charismatic, very persuasive, and tended to get excited about new ideas. He implemented several changes, including a chess competition, tournament of the minds and other co- curricular activities. After attending a professional learning experience, he instructed the junior classes to adopt a new spelling program, replacing the other program that had been in place for a long time. He also introduced a series of science textbooks for Years 7 to 10. He would consult with people before implementing, but the consultation was more a 'sell' to get staff to adopt the new idea than a real discussion about the pros and cons.

Stephen, the deputy principal from a neighbouring school, took over after Roger retired. By the end of Stephen's first year, many of Roger's initiatives had disappeared. The chess club disbanded, tournament of the minds took place for the last time and the spelling program followed suit. It wasn't that Stephen had abolished them — although he did question the rationale behind them, more out of curiosity about the history than any judgement on his part — it was just that without Roger there to champion them, the initiatives didn't have momentum of their own. By contrast, many of Stephen's initiatives remain. The sports competitions, school choir and primary years literacy program are still going strong two years after his departure.

Alison puts this impact down to Stephen's approach. While Roger tended to get initiatives through on the basis of his strong personality and great enthusiasm, Stephen initiated steering committees for the literacy program and sports competitions. He contributed ideas and indeed kicked the conversations off with his descriptions of his 'vision' of how things should be. However, he gave the committees the job of looking at possibilities, comparing alternatives and leading the staff decision-making processes. Sometimes the result was not exactly in keeping with Stephen's vision, but he was intuitive enough to realise that the other ideas would work too and did not try to change people's minds unless he saw some negative impacts ahead (about which he would become vocal). What's more, both of Stephen's deputies have now moved into principalships, and a teacher has moved into a position as deputy principal in another school.

Rafaella is the principal now. She recently commented to Alison about how committed staff members were to the sports competitions and especially the literacy program. When she asked Alison why she thought this was so, Alison began to tell her a story about 'the cowboy and the other guy …'

MAKE IT PERSONAL

The challenge for school leaders is to grow leaders — to mentor and encourage colleagues with the will or the capability to assume formal leadership roles, and to share the exhilaration of leadership.

Ask yourself, to what degree do I:
- know those staff who aspire to leadership?
- recognise those who have the capability, if not the awareness at this time, to grow into leadership?
- encourage and grow leaders?
- model leadership as a worthwhile and rewarding career pathway?

FURTHER INVESTIGATION

Succession planning

The transition from one leader to another in an organisation is best facilitated when there is a positive mindset from the outgoing person, and a 'pass the baton' mentality. This means helping things along by nurturing aspiring leaders and knowing that now is the time for someone else to do the job. (Goldsmith, 2009).

In the introduction to a report on research into succession planning, Ridden (2003b) stated that schools in Australia, and other countries, have often struggled to find qualified, prepared and interested applicants for leadership roles. He asserted: 'Now, more than ever, systems need to review and strengthen their succession planning to ensure that there is a pool of willing, competent and prepared aspirants for positions of leadership at every level of the school, especially the principal leadership' (p. v).

Useful writings on this topic from Australia include d'Arbon et al (2002), Duignan (2003) and Ritchie (2020); and from the United States, Delaware School Leadership Taskforce (2001). Is the availability of Principal aspirants still an issue? Does the availability of willing, competent and prepared aspirants continue to be a problem for schools?

Cieminski (2018) offers a number of recommendations for systems and schools, included shared leadership and leadership modelling.

What might be other practical solutions to the identified (and other) disincentives?

8

ROLES, RELATIONSHIPS AND COMMUNITY

From role to relationship

It's never been so important to be trustworthy. It's never been so important to be someone others respect. It's never been so important to keep the promises you make ... And it's never been so essential to be authentic (Sharma, 2010, p.75).

REFLECT

- How well do people know you? How well do you really know your colleagues and students, and your family?
- Are you authentic — the same person at work as you are at play?
- Are you true to your values?

SHIFT THE FOCUS

It is not so long since principals and teachers were expected to leave their personal issues and personal style at the school gate, and to perform their role in a prescribed way. Of course, that doesn't mean they did! Good teachers, effective leaders have always left their mark, not so much for what they do, but for who they are.

As a leader, there are times when we play a role, doing what is expected of the role, no matter how comfortable we are with it. But schools are communities; relationships matter. They are also places of learning, and watching others is a key way in which we learn.

In schools, it is important that we are authentic people, able to be true to ourselves and truly ourselves. As Sharma (2010) has commented, 'It's about feeling really safe within your own skin and learning to trust yourself so that you work under your values, express your original voice, and be the best you can be. It's about knowing who you are, and what you stand for, and then having the courage to be yourself — in every situation rather than when it's convenient. It's about being real, consistent, and congruent so who you are on the inside is reflected by the way you perform on the outside' (p.75).

There needs to be a shift away from a prescribed leadership style and towards leadership based on individual personalities and styles. Our students, colleagues and families deserve to know us and be known by us as authentic people, not just actors playing a role. Powerful learning and growth occur when we authentically engage with others.

Engage with others

Leadership is a relational activity. Leaders do not lead organisations; they lead people. We may refer to someone as leader of a school, but this sometimes represents their title or function, not their actions (Ehrich & English, 2024). It is important that we engage with others.

Good teachers engage with their students. They do not teach mathematics or English or science; they teach students. From the students' perspective, an old maxim says that students do not learn subjects; they learn teachers. Students learn best when they engage with the teacher, when they relate to the teacher, when the teacher is a person whom they respect, like, and are interested in.

Good leaders engage with their colleagues. They are interested in their colleagues' lives as well as their work: their families, interests, health and stresses. And they reciprocate by allowing their colleagues to know something of their lives. That does not mean that people need to know the intimate details of their colleagues' lives: too much information can make relationships awkward. Some people are so open about their issues and feelings that others find themselves taking on their burdens for them, which is inappropriate. Conversely, leaders need to be respectful of people's privacy, and their right to share limited information. Trust your instincts and strike a balance that feels comfortable for you and your colleagues.

Good leaders and teachers also engage with parents. Parents want a relationship with the people in the school they have to deal with. They want to know them and be known by them. They want a relationship of reciprocal trust. If things go awry for their child, they want to feel comfortable with the people they need to talk to, to communicate with them in a trusting and respectful relationship.

Sheahan (2007) wrote of the importance of 'buy-in', the desire for talented individuals to connect to the companies they work for, and the people they work with. He argues that two key things attract and retain top people: the work they do — whether they find the work interesting, whether the work challenges them and forces them to grow; and the relationships they build with people.

Relate authentically

Authentic relationships are genuine relationships. They are not staged or acted, but come from a confidence in being oneself and a genuine interest in others. They are not based on acting out a role expectation; rather, they allow people to be their authentic selves.

In schools, many of our communications are impersonal, focused on the content of the message and revealing little about the writer. There are certainly contexts in which this type of communication is entirely appropriate. However, when people relate authentically, their communication reveals the character and personality of the people involved, enhancing relationships and connecting people. Within a school community, this means that parents, staff and students are able and comfortable to converse as people, not simply as role players; conversations come from the heart, not just the head; communication is sometimes 'deep', rather than superficial. Blanchard & Shula (1995) offer this challenge, which is relevant to school leaders too:

> What would happen if you looked at your job as a manager, teacher or parent as an opportunity to share yourself? Usually we're so busy with our tasks, we forget that, above all else, what our people get from us is *us* — our values, our attitudes, our perceptions. In the long run, it's not our skills or our know-how or our long experience that makes the biggest impact — *we* are the main message! (p.59)

Some will ask: where is the line that defines the boundaries of a professional–personal relationship for a leader? A measure may be this: Sometimes, as a leader, I need to hold a disciplinary conversation with a colleague. If my relationship with them is so familiar that I cannot hold such a conversation with them credibly, in their eyes and in mine, then the relationship has 'crossed the line'. Relationships can be authentic, without being so flippant or intimate that they become inappropriate.

Relate ethically

Leadership is about influencing others. The effectiveness of our leadership is a measure of our impact on people. It is possible for leaders to influence others strongly, through coercive or manipulative strategies, but to do so for their own gain, or for the achievement of their own goals, without consideration for the consequences on those they influence.

History is replete with examples of people who attempt to lead by command and control. They also exist in our own communities. The question of whether it is ethical to force anyone to do anything against their will is not an easy one to answer and this is not a book about philosophy. However, looking after the interests (including the welfare) of people is an expectation of school leaders (AITSL, 2014; Fullan, 2019; Starratt, 2004). The concept of ethical leadership can help us to better understand this responsibility.

Ethical leadership

Ethical leadership has been the subject of increased focus in the literature in recent times. The reason for this might be a decline in positive regard for leaders in the community, some spurred by scandals and some, perhaps, due to low opinions about motives. There has certainly been more questioning and critique about the motives and competence of educational bodies in Australia over the last decade. Recent controversies in the media involving literacy testing and standards, one could argue, reflect a lack of trust in the judgement and competence of educational authorities and teachers.

The notion is related to the concept of moral leadership. Leadership is closely bound to ethics and morality because the actions of leaders impact on others, both within the organisation and the wider community (Sergiovanni, 1996; Berkovich & Eval, 2021). Because of this, the consideration of this impact is a value-based judgement, often in response to a moral dilemma. Morality may be defined as the way one behaves based on prevailing principles about right and wrong, while ethics is the understanding or critical analysis of morality. Beyond semantics, moral and ethical leadership are both concerned with values-based behaviour and its effects on people and organisations or communities (Banks et al, 2021).

Ethical leadership may be broadly defined as leadership behaviour which is grounded in clearly understood values and reflected in actions which seek good for others, rather than oneself. Ethical leaders develop and promote a vision for the school based on their own values and those of the school community. The leader's decision-making and action must be consistent with these espoused values (Ehrich et al, 2015; Starratt, 2004).

In practice, this may be characterised by:

- involvement of teachers, students and parents in review and consequent decision-making about the vision, mission and values of the school
- integrity between the leader's espoused values, their own actions, and the behaviours they do and do not accept from others
- reflection on and analysis of the community's values and comparison with one's own
- reflection on the school's existing norms and values and challenging others with the questions: Why do we do things this way? How else can we do it?
- a tendency to serve the needs of the staff and school rather than cater to the leader's own or vested interests, involving an element of self-sacrifice, and encouraging staff members to do the same in improving the school
- a clear sense of responsibility to achieve the best possible educational outcomes for students, and strategies to achieve this that do not impact negatively on students or staff
- openness of communication, including timely disclosure of information and genuine appeals for staff input extending to allowance for and acceptance of staff critique
- clear focus on justice when issues are being dealt with, including doing what is right even if this is not procedurally correct
- demonstrated respect for people and commitment to human dignity
- active involvement in the development and further education of staff members
- developing a high level of trust and positive regard between staff and leaders
- servant leadership.

In schools, leaders are often required to make decisions quickly and under pressure. In such situations there is a high risk of erroneous judgement. Decisions may be made which appear to solve the immediate problem, but are harmful to people in the longer term. Ethical leadership can minimise the chances of poor decision-making, by maintaining a focus on a set of values which help leaders to make the right choices for the school community.

Servant leadership

A concept related to ethical leadership is that of servant leadership. Introduced in academic literature by Greenleaf (1977), servant leadership is characterised by service to others. The primary goal of servant leadership is for those who are served to grow as people, become more knowledgeable, more autonomous and willing to become servants themselves. Servant leaders are more selfless than selfish and have followers whom they have helped develop professionally. They make the people they work with better than they otherwise would have been, through care, support and an ability to know what their needs are and help meet them. Servant leaders use power in the spirit of assistance and compassion rather than political gain or advantage (Neuschel, 2005).

As a result of selflessness, servant leaders tend to share things that others might keep for their own gain, such as hints and tips about how to do things better, rare information, credit for achievements, and power. Servant leaders 'look after' the school as well as lead it. In the context of schools, servant leadership may be typified by any of the following:

- placing the needs of staff members before self-interests, which includes sharing knowledge, skills and time in order to improve the capacity of staff
- providing all the resources, including staff development, to enable teachers to perform their work and meet new challenges
- actively listening to empathise with and better understand the needs and concerns of staff members, students and parents
- inspiring trust from staff and others by being trustworthy, honest and open
- being idealistic in the vision for a better school, but realistic in consideration of the capabilities of staff to help achieve the vision in exact terms
- giving people time and providing assistance when staff members, students or parents need help, thereby establishing that the leader is not 'above' others
- committing to people and building community
- doing what is accepted as morally 'right' and being an active role model for professionalism as well as humanity
- defending the rights of others.

Through the development, support and nurturing of staff members, servant leadership contributes to the improved performance of teachers, and, ultimately to better teaching and a more effective school; creates more leaders and assists with succession issues; helps people to feel empowered and more confident about their jobs; and impacts on staff morale and the school climate.

CASE STUDY: EMOTIONAL LEADERSHIP AT MOUNT JANE COLLEGE

> Vince is the principal at Mount Jane College. This is his third appointment as principal. One of the things he has learnt about leading schools is that it's a lot about dealing with emotions — his own and those of others. He confesses that he learned much of what he knows from his own mistakes. Vince strongly believes effective principals are those who 'look after' teachers and other staff and that emotions are an important part of this. He thinks that self-awareness and empathy are the two most important skills when dealing with staff.
>
> Vince had noticed, for example, that in difficult discussions, people responded to him even before he had a chance to speak. He was expressing to others emotion that he hadn't consciously recognised himself, through his defensive body language. He found that by learning to read his own emotions, to recognise when he was reacting emotionally, and to control his facial expressions or body movements, he was able to participate in discussions calmly and productively.
>
> Self-awareness led to empathy: Vince improved his ability to relate to others and understand how they felt, and to echo that feeling to show his understanding. He uses this skill often; today, for example, when a librarian came to see him with a concern about a history teacher making what the librarian saw as an unreasonable demand. Vince repeated the essence of the complaint back to her calmly, and added, 'I can see why that would upset you.' The librarian felt understood, and Vince was able to get her to agree to a mediation meeting with the history teacher to come to a compromise. Vince understands that emotional leadership in a school is time-consuming, but he makes it a priority over administration work, much of which his leadership team can handle, because he'd rather spend time helping staff members to get along and work for the common goal of the school than see conflicts and low morale.

MAKE IT PERSONAL

The challenge for leaders is to understand and act in accordance with their own morals, and to act authentically in every aspect of their lives.

Ask yourself:

- Would others say that I act ethically and morally? What evidence could they cite?

- How do I feel about the notion of leadership as service, and leaders as servants to others?
- When have I had a strong emotional reaction to something someone said to me? How did I manage that? Would I have done anything differently and what?

FURTHER INVESTIGATION

Supportive leadership communication

Well-developed knowledge and skills about relationship building are necessary for leaders seeking to develop cohesive school communities. A key factor in the development of positive, productive relationships is supportive communication. Supportive communication happens when leaders offer support to their staff, when staff support one another and when staff offer support to their leaders.

Upward supportive communication includes providing encouragement to persist with a project, checking in to say hello, asking about family issues and questioning stress-related behaviours (De Nobile, 2013). *Downward supportive communication* from leaders to staff has been shown to be vitally important to relationships as well as the morale of staff (De Nobile & McCormick, 2008). It includes providing affirmation or encouragement, offering constructive feedback and showing personal concern or care (De Nobile, 2021a). This type of interaction can be informed by a leader's emotional capabilities.

The concept of emotional intelligence has been around for some time, but has increased in popularity since Daniel Goleman's acclaimed work (Goleman, 1995). Emotional intelligence relates to an awareness of one's own emotions and ability to manage them, awareness of the emotions of others and ability to influence them, and using emotions productively.

You may find it helpful to explore concepts of emotional intelligence, and consider who among your colleagues uses emotional intelligence, how they do so, and how you could foster emotional intelligence in yourself and your staff.

Beyond relationship to community

We need to be regularly 'taking the pulse' of what is happening in our classes and schools. We also need to be communicating respectfully and openly with the various groups that make up our school community (Dinham, 2016, p.128).

REFLECT

- Do you feel a sense of belonging within your school?
- Do staff, students and parents feel they belong? How do you know?
- What in your school contributes to or inhibits people's sense of belonging?

SHIFT THE FOCUS

Relating matters. People want to feel that they connect. Some people may say that they don't care about their colleagues, that they just go to work to do their job, and that they don't need to talk to colleagues except as necessary to do their work. However, most people want to feel that they belong, that they share a common purpose in their work, and that they are part of a group.

This requires a shift in thinking. Rather than viewing the school as an organisation, defined by roles and accountabilities, it is more useful to see the school as a community, defined by relationships and responsibilities. Rather than seeing individual staff and students as people who attend the school, it is more helpful to see them as members of a community who belong within the school.

The school as a community

For several decades, a host of writers have defined the qualities of the successful organisation, applied these to schools, then lamented that contemporary organisational theories of management, efficiency, accountability and change have failed to transform the basic nature of schools or education. Perhaps the reason is that schools are less like organisations and more like communities. This echoes a view expressed by Wise (1977) several decades ago:

> Educational policies fail because they are premised on the idea that the school is a rational organisation — like a factory — which can be managed and improved by rational management procedure. Indeed, much of the collective effort of policymakers, researchers and administrators is aimed at making school reality conform to the rational model. We then bemoan the fact that the schools fail to conform to the model. It just may be that we need a new paradigm (p.57).

If we want to understand the nature of schools, and how to lead, manage, inspire and change them, we need to view them less as organisations and more as communities. Drucker (1995) explained the difference:

> Unlike communities, societies, or families, organisations are purposefully designed and always specialised. Communities and societies are defined by the bonds that hold their members together, whether they be language, culture, history, or locality. An organisation is defined by its task … Indeed, an organisation is effective only if it concentrates on one task (p.76).

Teachers and school leaders are often bemused at the number of society's expectations that are foisted on schools. Whether bullying, violence, binge drinking, discourtesy, lack of parenting skills, unemployment, economic difficulties … the finger is pointed at schools for allowing this to happen.

Perhaps it's to ease the community conscience; perhaps it is an expression of frustration at not having any other community institution to turn to. Whatever the reason, Drucker's notion of confining an organisation to specialisation in one task seems to be a poor fit. This is notwithstanding our argument in this book that schools ought to focus on their core business of student learning and wellbeing. Perhaps the notion of referring to this less as 'core business' and more as 'moral purpose' moves us away from the school as organisation to the school as community. Despite the move for businesses to be more socially aware and sensitive and to seek to 'do good' for their communities, business executives do not tend to speak of the business's moral purpose. This is not a criticism of the business perspective, but an argument that schools do not fit the model.

While schools clearly display some organisational features, the community bonds referred to by Drucker are a prominent feature of schools. Definitions of community suggest the dominance of relationships, an emphasis missing from definitions of organisations.

The business of schools takes place within relationships between teachers and students. The motivation and purpose for much of the work of schools emerges from those relationships. Teachers' major motivation is found in their relationships with students, their care for them, and the reward of seeing them succeed. Similarly, most students are motivated to learn by teachers and their relationships with them, not by the innate joy of the subject matter itself. Organisation theory is inadequate to explain an enterprise structured and powered by these forces. It is important to better understand the nature of schools if we are to develop appropriate assumptions, expectations, structures and processes for them.

What is a community?

'Community' is a fashionable word. It is a romantic concept, embodying an aura of 'goodness' which implies that anything it is attached to is favourable, right and good. To challenge its use is almost to question the fundamental values of society. Hence, the word is found in an amazing array of literature, both academic and popular. It is evident in many school mission statements, newsletters and other documents.

However, community seems to be such a warm and friendly word that it seduces people into its employ without really offering anything in return. It promotes a warm glow in the listener and elevates the speaker to the high moral ground. To challenge someone who argues a school issue on the basis of 'community' is almost like educational blasphemy.

Yet there is a difference between being *in a community*, and being *in community*. 'Community' is used as a generic term for a group of people who typically share some common ideas, purpose or location. The problem with this understanding is that it suggests that the guests in a hotel, or the spectators at a football match — groups of people in the same place at the same time for a similar purpose — would be communities. And the difficulty with this is that the word community implies so much more.

When people speak of community, they often mean that the members are somehow more than an aggregation of fellow travellers, enjoying in addition strong bonds of purpose, commitment and relationship, representing a strong sense of community, the feeling of being *in community*, and not simply in *a* community. Yet a community really only exists when people have a sense of community, 'a feeling members have of belonging, a feeling that members matter to one another and to the group, and a shared faith that members' needs will be met through their commitment to be together' (McMillan & Chavis, 1986, p.9).

Many schools describe themselves as communities. Whether the members of the school community experience a sense of community is a different matter. Sergiovanni (1994) explained it this way:

> Authentic community requires us to do more than pepper our language with the word 'community', label ourselves as a community in our mission statement, and organise teachers into teams and schools into families. It requires us to think community, believe in community, and practice community — to change the basic metaphor for the school itself to community. We are into authentic community when community becomes embodied in the school's policy structure itself, when community values are at the centre of our thinking (p. xiii).

Writing of schools, Schaps & Lewis (1998) described a sense of community as 'a student's experience of being a valued, influential, contributing participant in a group whose members are committed to each other's learning, growth and welfare'. The authors go on to argue that 'the sense of community which students feel has two major components: (1) their sense of influence or 'say' in the classroom, and (2) their experience of the classroom and school as supportive' (p.24). More recently, Osterman (2023) described it as student experiences of belonging, feeling comfortable, supported and able to connect with their peers and where the teacher respected and worked 'with' students. While these are helpful descriptions of a student's experience of community, it highlights a key issue for educators: that we tend to believe our own rhetoric, to assume that because we speak about community and, from our vantage point, see examples of community, then community is present pervasively and for all. It may not be so.

Typically, education writers imply that if a sense of community is evident among one group of stakeholders in the school community (in the above quote, students, but more often, teachers), then it is experienced by all — students, all staff and parents. Yet a school cannot be accurately described as a community if teachers feel the bonds of community but other groups do not: if, for example, parents are excluded, since they represent a significant part of the community, numerically and functionally; or if a significant number of students do not feel part of the community. A school can only be described as a community if all stakeholders — or, at least, some large but realistic percentage of them — experience a sense of community within the school.

Realistically, a member of a school community cannot be expected to feel the same way towards every member of the school community. Their sense of community may be experienced within a friendship group, a class group, a faculty group, a parent group, or some other group. People do not experience a sense of community *with* the community, but *within* the community.

Is your school a community?

Given these descriptors, then, is your school a community? Do all stakeholders feel a sense of community? How can you know?

There are some difficulties in the description above, because a school is a functional community: people drawn together to perform the function of education, rather than people choosing to be together because they necessarily share a passion.

Some educators might argue that the problem in developing a school community is the range of perspectives which different people bring to it. That is a misunderstanding of the notion of 'common' values or directions. People belong to multiple communities (for example, a school, a sports club, a church, a workplace, and so on.) Although the members of the school community share a common locality or some common values and ideas, they do not think, and do not need to think, the same way in all things. However, communities are inclusive. The members of community retain their individuality within the community, which is concerned for individual and minority views.

The challenge for school leaders is to create unity *within* diversity, rather than unity *from* diversity. The latter implies a forced homogeneity, whereas communities of difference find unity without eliminating their diversity. However, it is not the differences that are a problem in community, but how people handle them. Whereas educators seem to like to speak of 'tolerating' difference, which implies 'to put up with' (Moloney et al, 2023), we prefer to speak of accepting differences, which requires an ethics (that word again!) of care to be manifested by leaders. Ryu et al (2022) go further, advancing the concept of 'caring leadership' as 'leadership that generates a culture of connectedness and mutual support through ... dense social relationships within the school, and creating conditions that enable caring' (p.587).

A common word people use to describe their experience of community is *belonging*. Those who feel a sense of community within a school (or other group) feel that they belong (Osterman, 2023). Another common word, increasingly in use in online communities, is *connection*. Royal & Rossi (1996) defined three sets of dimensions that contribute to a sense of community:

- mutual obligation and support — the 'heart' of community — comprising trust, respect, caring and recognition
- interdependence and inclusiveness — the 'hands' of community — comprising communication, participation, teamwork and incorporation of diversity
- shared direction and purpose — the 'head' of community — comprising shared vision, shared purpose and shared values.

The challenge for leaders is to build a sense of community, to help each member of the school community to feel that they belong. What evidence will you see to indicate the sense of community which is experienced within the school?

- It will be heard in the language. People speak of *us* and *we* and *our school*. It will be seen in the relationships. People exhibit trust in one another; demonstrate respect for everyone, irrespective of their role in the school; recognise and acknowledge the contributions and abilities of others, not just the 'high flyers' or 'serious contributors'; and relate to others with care, concern and compassion.
- It will be observed in the behaviours of members. Communication is authentic, honest and reliable, so that people do not feel excluded or manipulated, and so that trust is engendered; members participate willingly in the life of the school; members exhibit teamwork as they collaborate in various projects and activities; and diversity is accepted (not just tolerated), so that all feel included and all feel that they can belong.
- It will be evident in a shared sense of purpose, direction and values. Although people do not all agree on issues, the threads that hold them together are greater than those threads which pull in another direction; so they are able to bind together, sharing some common understandings, expectations and norms.

Build community

To build community in a school is not to force people into a common mould, but to enhance the experience of community for all members of the school community. Rossi's elements of a sense of community, summarised above, are a useful focus. To what degree to people exhibit and feel trust, respect, recognition and care? To what degree is there open and effective communication, active participation in the life of the school, effective teamwork, an incorporation of diversity? To what degree do people feel that, despite their different thinking, they share a common sense of direction and purpose, and a common core of values? The answers may be different for students, staff and parents, and even for sub-groups of these larger groups. If you identify areas where you feel growth is needed, how will you go about that?

The nature of contemporary schools, which are simply a microcosm of the wider society, makes this a particularly challenging task. Much of the interaction between students or colleagues has been replaced by interaction with a digital device. Having been exposed to online learning, many students eschew the structure and restrictions of the classroom for home-based learning. Many teachers are keen to do the same. It is not yet clear where the balance will life in the future. How does a school leader create a sense of community among people who share minimal contact?

It is almost obligatory these days for schools to describe themselves as student-centred, and for teachers to claim that their teaching is student-centred. Unfortunately, this is another concept which has almost as many meanings as the people who use it. It is also worth challenging. Should schooling be centred on individuals per se, or on individuals in the context of community? Schools are very emphatic about developing individuals, but not so emphatic about developing community. Teachers speak often about developing independence (although this often really means compliance — the ability to get on with work without needing attention and without disrupting others); yet speak far less about developing interdependence.

Why a sense of community?

Creating a sense of community in schools is important for a number of reasons. A sense of community contributes to academic learning. In schools in which students experience a strong sense of community, students are more likely to be academically motivated, enjoy school more, have higher educational aspirations and be less prone to disruptive and problem behaviours, allowing more effective learning. In such schools, there are opportunities for all students to develop a sense of community with adults and peers within the school, and students feel that they have a voice, enabling them to contribute to and influence daily life in the school.

A sense of community is critical to individual and societal health. Connection and belonging are essential to the mental and emotional health of our children and youth. When students feel alienated and are unable to find a sense of community within the school and within their wider community, tragedy can ensue.

Community may be the key purpose of schools in the future, with technology threatening the traditional structure of schools, paralleling a breakdown in traditional community structures. Our youth need to grow and learn within the secure, caring, value-rich context of a community, where meaningful relationships provide a vehicle for encouragement, coaching and discipline (Ridden 2003a).

Learning communities

Many schools are adopting the term 'learning community', some using it to replace the word 'school'.

Sergiovanni & Green (2015) offered this description:

> At the point where communities of practice bubble up and collaborative cultures trickle down, learning communities emerge. They learn from both successes and failures. They are good at continuous learning and at dispersing what they know to places where it is most needed. Learning communities have faith in the craft knowledge and wisdom of those closest to the classroom. They believe in collaboration and view learning as a professional obligation (p.130).

While schools are places of learning, and while collaboration is a feature of learning communities, the preceding discussion poses the challenge to consider whether the school is a community, a place of belonging, not just for staff, but for all.

It is certainly a goal to pursue.

CASE STUDY: BUILDING COMMUNITY AT WALLES LAKE SCHOOL

Walles Lake School is known as 'a great place to work' by teachers and 'a really tight community' by its parents. Teachers and parents attribute this positive community atmosphere to the principal, Mary Field.

The recent school review included a survey about school climate, and the responses from students, parents and staff were largely positive.

According to one student, 'The teachers really seem to support one another. It's like they're friends, on the same wavelength or something, they all seem to get along okay. Mrs Field is very nice to them. I often see her having a laugh with teachers.'

A parent wrote, 'Mary is the glue that holds this school together, I think. She is always reaching out to people. She's always approachable and has time for our kids and us. She seems to remember who we are, which is amazing in a school of 500-odd students, and always asks us what we are up to. I know she has helped a few families with problems as well.'

One of the teachers commented, 'I've never worked in a school where everyone is so supported. Mary and all members of the executive team take time out to help us whenever we need it. They've given me assistance every time I've needed it with the challenging students I have this year. I personally feel trusted in the classroom and feel that communication among staff is fairly open. Everyone looks after each other.'

Mary believes that support is the key to the school's community atmosphere. She knows that people feel they belong if they are supported and isolated out if they are not. She prioritises supporting people, and sees that her support has a positive effect on the way people relate to each other.

MAKE IT PERSONAL

The challenge for school leaders is to create authentic community, an environment in which people can feel a sense of belonging.

Ask yourself:

- To what degree do staff, students and parents feel that they belong, that this is 'their' school, and that this is real community. What evidence do I have?
- To what degree do I foster the sense of belonging? How?
- How might we enhance the sense of community experienced by members of our school community?

FURTHER INVESTIGATION

Sense of community

Seminal works by Tönnies (1887/1955) and Bellah et al (1985) have been influential in shaping theories around the notion of community, and are valuable reading. Writers such as Peck (1987), Sergiovanni (1994), Etzioni (1993), Rossi & Hanson (2002) and Sergiovanni & Green (2015) each bring a different perspective to the concept of community. It may be interesting to compare these orientations.

People are well able to describe their understandings of a sense of community, although their words may not match the language used by the theorists listed above; for example, they might describe caring as supporting each other, kindness, love or loving, unselfishness, thoughtfulness or consideration. Recognition might be described with words like praise, affirmation or encouragement.

Listen to the dialogue within your school community — among staff, students and parents — to identify words which seem to indicate that people feel a sense of community within the school.

It may be useful to collect prospectuses or newsletters from a number of schools, and look for the word community. If its use is prolific, it may be even more helpful to question the principal about the experience of community within the school.

Belonging

People who experience a sense of community within a school (or other community) feel they belong. Many researchers are concerned about a global decline in belonging, especially for young people. A lack of belonging in schools is associated with mental illness, wellbeing and academic outcomes. It is related to inclusion, a concept which society has revised dramatically in recent years (Boyle & Allen, 2022, Allen & Boyle, 2020).

Explore the degree to which students experience a sense of belonging in your school.

9

Certainty, uncertainty and coherence

From certainty to uncertainty

Wisdom consists of the anticipation of consequences (Cousins, 1978).

REFLECT

- How confident do you feel about your decisions?
- What situations or decisions recently have left you feeling uncertain about your response?
- What situations have you had to deal with which required you to decide between two 'right' choices or two 'wrong' choices? How did you choose? What were the consequences of the decision?

SHIFT THE FOCUS

Past generations of school leaders seemed more certain of their decisions. Their choices appeared to be more clearly between right and wrong, potentially successful or potentially disastrous, compassionate or uncaring. When the leader managed to discern the right, the potentially successful, and the compassionate, their actions were determined by their moral courage, their personal confidence and their relational values. They acted, or seemed to act, with confidence and certainty in their judgements and decisions, and in the consequences of them.

Leaders were also confident in what they knew. They knew how things should be done, and how things should be managed.

The focus has shifted. So often now school leaders are choosing uncertain pathways with uncertain outcomes. They are aware of the inadequacy of their knowledge. The school community is also aware of the inadequacy of any one person's knowledge and prepared to challenge it.

In the past, for example, the consequences for a disobedient student were clear, and a principal's actions in dealing with such a student would be understood, anticipated and generally accepted. Now, in dealing with a student's disobedience, we are seeking to teach about consequences and change the student's long-term behaviour, but the ways to achieve that are idiosyncratic and therefore uncertain, and there is also uncertainty about how the student's parents will respond to the consequences.

Similarly, the expectations of principals by the governing authority, and the procedures to be followed in prescribed and familiar situations, were clear. Now, while there are legal and regulatory parameters in place, more is expected of leaders' judgement, which enables decisions and actions to be more appropriate to the particular situation and people involved. Principals are also aware that their actions may well be challenged by their superordinates, colleagues, parents — even the media.

Increasingly, school leaders work in an environment in which their knowledge and the expectations of others are uncertain. Leaders need to accept uncertainty, be change-ready, and learn to apply existing skills to new situations.

Reactive or responsive

It is easy as a principal to be reactive; that is, to deal with a conflict based on our immediate thoughts and feelings. Admittedly, when our judgement is challenged, when a decision is questioned, when we are asked to justify a choice made in the course of a busy and sometimes stressful day, our first thoughts and feelings may be to feel hurt, indignant, offended, angry or irritated. To react is understandable — but not necessarily helpful.

Leaders need to be responsive; that is, to deal with the situation with consideration, beyond the initial reactive emotions. In practice, it helps to:

- Take time. The old advice to 'take three deep breaths' or 'count to 10' is useful. Avoid responding instinctively. It may mean explaining to someone that you will get back to them about a matter, or to be honest about asking them to wait while you think about this or consult with someone else. Few people will criticise your desire to ensure you make the best decision.
- Respond with consideration. Consider more than your instinctive action. Entertain some other options. Look ahead, and evaluate the options not just in terms of their immediate consequences, but their longer-term implications.

- Consult. Ask a colleague what they would do, or invite their considered response to your intentions. Explain your thinking, and encourage them to identify any flaws in your thinking.
- Act calmly. When the action is determined, convey it with calm assertion, so that others can see that you are not acting impulsively, but have made a considered decision.
- Be open to correcting errors. Sometimes even a well-considered decision proves to be wrong. Perhaps further information becomes available, perhaps someone responds in an unexpected way, which causes other consequences. If this is so, be open about changing your decision, explaining why you have done so.

Of course, the steps you take, and how long you take with each step, will depend upon the perceived importance and impact of the decision. During the course of a day, school leaders make many decisions which have consequences for other people. Many of these decisions need to be made on the spot; some require short consideration; others may be considered for several days, or even longer. Part of the skill of a leader is in discerning how much consideration is needed for a given decision. The key challenge is to be conscious of responding, rather than reacting.

Even experienced leaders make decisions they regret. What marks them as skilled leaders is their ability to recognise a decision which has led to unexpected consequences, their honesty in admitting and addressing it, and the skill with which they are able to move from one course of action to another, without leaving people traumatised and frustrated.

Visionary and strategic

When we are certain about the future and believe that the future is simply a better version of the present, then our focus is on conformity, maintenance, and effectively replicating past practices. When the future is uncertain, and we know it will not be like the present, then replicating past practices is not enough. Preparing for an uncertain future requires visionary and strategic thinking.

The school's vision should be an imaginative picture of how the school should look in several years' time (Caldwell, 2003). It is most powerful if it touches not just the head, but the heart (Fullan, 2019). Therefore it is best if it evokes images, sensations or feelings. A good vision is real, easily communicated, shared, inclusive of mission and values, and challenges the status quo (Bruford, 2008; Leithwood et al, 2020).

Leaders need the ability to construct a future which is creative, optimistic and innovative. They need to be network leaders — non-linear, transformational, values- and purpose-driven.

Strategy follows vision. Strategy without vision is anarchy, but vision without strategy is just a dream. So the implementation of vision relies upon planned and strategic action.

Accepting paradox

Many leaders feel that the most difficult challenges present themselves as dilemmas, paradoxes and tensions. These tensions are usually people-centred, and involve competing values or ethical contradictions (Duignan, 2003).

Dilemmas and tensions abound in schools and the education system. For example:

- Educators are constantly bombarded by the need to support students to cope with their emotional and social issues, to minimise the incidence of mental health issues and self-harming behaviours. Simultaneously, governments introduce national academic testing, placing pressure on teachers (and sometimes on students) to spend more time teaching and learning 'the basics'.
- At a time when we have never had better and easier access to knowledge, restrictive curricula and high stakes testing threaten to impose limitations on what knowledge should be taught or learnt.
- Schools increasingly partner with other schools for their mutual benefit and to support the health of their local community, while the Australian government's My School website publicises the performance of schools in national testing, inciting completion between schools for status and enrolments.
- One of the most frequent and difficult dilemmas for principals is dealing with staff underperformance. While principals may wish to support colleagues, some of whom may have given long service to the school, principals must also ensure that teachers have the skills and attitude to effectively meet the needs of students.
- Removal of a troublesome student from a class raises a similar dilemma, in which the long-term welfare of the individual student and the needs of other students may appear to be in conflict.
- The allocation of resources, including staff, often poses ethical dilemmas.

It is choosing the 'high moral ground' and weighing competing values that keep principals awake at night (Belardi, 2010). Handy (1995) suggested how to respond to these tensions:

> Paradox I now see to be inevitable, endemic and perpetual ... We can, therefore, and should, reduce the starkness of some of the contradictions, minimise the inconsistencies, understand the puzzles in the paradoxes, but we cannot make them disappear, nor solve them completely, nor escape from them, until that new order becomes established. Paradoxes are like the weather, something to be lived with, not solved, the worst aspects mitigated, the best enjoyed and used as clues to the way forward. Paradox has to be *accepted*, coped with and made sense of, in life, in work, in community and among the nations (p.17–18).

Duignan (2012) suggested that in attempting to make sense of dilemmas or paradoxes, we shouldn't take an 'either/or' approach, choosing one side over another. Rather, the most effective decisions will involve a 'both/and' approach, reflecting concerns for all people and all values involved. He cited research by English (1995), who argued that leaders should analyse paradoxical situations, not in terms of contradiction, polarity and either/or frames, but in terms of a relationship that encompasses both competition and complementarity. By describing situations as a double-headed arrow, instead of being mutually exclusive, the opposites are 'in tension'. When the various tensions in the situation are identified, a profile of the tensions emerges. While this does not identify an 'answer' to the dilemma, it enables leaders to see more clearly the various tensions, and to be therefore better able to make a balanced decision, and to satisfy more of the competing values and expectations.

While dealing with tensions has always been part of a leader's role, increasingly the choices to be made by leaders are not about right and wrong, nor about 'good' and 'poor' choices, but about two or more 'good' alternatives. That means that decisions require discernment, the ability to evaluate short- and long-term implications, to balance competing needs and priorities, to consider the impact of decisions on people's feelings and relationships, to find ways to meet the needs of the school and sub-groups or individuals within it.

Dealing with discontinuity and reinvention

A related issue is that of discontinuity. For most of us, most of the time, the future is seen simply as an extension of the present — better or worse, different in a number of ways, but essentially similar. As a result, we change little, simply adapting our thinking or behaviour in minor ways as circumstances demand. However, Caldwell & Loader (2009) point out that momentous events in history cause discontinuities, which 'interrupt people's lives and profoundly disturb their thinking. "The known" turns out to be not as "known" as had been assumed' (p.32). The authors suggest that discontinuous thinking, as distinct from incremental thinking, holds a key to addressing problems which we struggle to change. They suggest beginning by questioning values and their expression, and accepted practices. They also argue that dreaming is important: 'Whether it is about addressing inequality or some other curriculum, pedagogical or structural change, it all begins with a dream. One sees in one's mind's eye a new possibility, a new way that has the potential to lead to a better solution to the problem being addressed (p.35).

Similar to the difficulty of discontinuity is the concept of reinvention. Degenhardt & Duignan explain that, in a reinvention process, people have to let go of comfortable old habits, methods and mindsets, and embrace a new, often uncomfortable process of cognitive restructuring, in order to make a new beginning. This is often defined as a learning culture. The authors explain the paradox of a learning culture, as identified by Schein (2010):

> On the one hand, culture is by definition a stabilising, conservative process. But on the other hand, a learning culture attempts to institutionalise and stabilise innovation and change. The paradox inherent in the concept of a learning organisation is at the heart of the challenges faced by a reinventing school (p.34–35).

Anticipating the future

While it is obvious that the future is uncertain, insightful thinkers can observe signs and anticipate future outcomes. In Chapter 6, we described some guidelines for recognising 'the next big thing'. But disruptive events and innovations, which cannot be anticipated, will continue to bring change. The challenge for leaders is to be courageously flexible and adaptable, and to prepare their schools to be the same.

CASE STUDY: A NEW DISCIPLINE POLICY AT DUNCAN PRIMARY SCHOOL

For some time there has been some confusion about what to do with challenging students at Duncan Primary School. There is a behaviour management policy, but this was created two principals ago and is more a set of principles than actual procedure.

Mike took up the principalship at Duncan this year and became aware of people's lack of knowledge of policy and procedures regarding behaviour problems. He found the current policy unclear. What the school needed was a new policy, but first the school needed a vision of how school discipline should be managed.

Early in Term 2 he asked for volunteers to form a steering committee, the aim of which was to develop a 'vision' for behaviour management in the school. This committee would be required to survey staff about current practice and survey literature about effective practice. By the end of term the steering committee had produced a document that outlined basic principles for behaviour management.

During Term 3, staff, parent and student representatives formed a working party to draft a whole-school behaviour management policy, based on the steering committee's report.

The draft policy was then distributed for comment and input among staff, parents and students, and a problem emerged. At a meeting of the school's parents and friends' association, set to discuss the new policy, a group of parents representing about 10 families protested against the policy, declaring it was a 'namby-pamby soft-touch policy' and that if it was implemented they would take their kids out of the school. Keeping his composure, Mike responded that, given the opposition, it would be appropriate to put the policy to a vote.

Walking away from that meeting Mike became momentarily unsure of whether he had done the right thing about the vote. He still felt strongly that the policy was in the right direction. But *was* he right? What if it turned out more people are against the policy? The vote would be lost, leading to an embarrassing situation that would be difficult to resolve.

At the next staff meeting he asked for comment, really honest comment, about the policy. There was no evidence of opposition there, only some suggestions for changes in wording here and there. So Mike went ahead and organised the vote, a little more confident that he was 'on the money'. Parents were given a hard copy of the draft policy and a voting ballot with an envelope, which requested parents to vote to accept or reject the policy. Of the 224 distributed 184 votes were returned. The verdict: 95 per cent of respondents voted to accept the new policy.

At a recent professional development course for aspiring leaders, Mike shared this story to illustrate how leaders can make a decision even though they may not be 100 per cent certain it's the right one.

'If you have a vision, and you know it's right for the school, you have communicated it, and had your people involved in it too, don't lose heart when others put it down,' Mike said. 'Persist, believe in it and follow it through, because good ideas have a way of trumping the bad ones.'

MAKE IT PERSONAL

The challenge for school leaders is to operate in an environment in which paradoxes are common, in which decision are often between competing 'rights' rather than 'right and wrong', and in which decisions are subject to scrutiny and challenge by all members of the school community.

Ask yourself, to what degree do I:
- cope with uncertainty and paradox?
- seek to understand each point of view in difficult conflicts?
- achieve resolutions of conflicts that leave all parties feeling heard, satisfied and reconciled?

FURTHER INVESTIGATION

Uncertainty

An orientation that allows one to deal with uncertainty, and to assist others to do the same, requires a change to people's mental models. A number of authors describe theories of change that assist in understanding this process. These include Schein (2004), Argyris (1999), and Bridges (1995), along with earlier work by Hall and his colleagues (1974). A comparison of models of change will provide insight into managing people's responses to uncertainty.

Beyond uncertainty to coherence

The need to clarify values becomes important when one needs to be clear about intent and purposes (Begley, 1999, p.318).

REFLECT

- How do you make decisions in a time of uncertainty?
- What criteria or values do you use?
- When did you last articulate the values you were applying to a situation?

SHIFT THE FOCUS

Uncertainty and paradox are here to stay. Leaders must adapt to making decisions when the 'right' choice is unclear.

The key to doing this is to be clear about your purpose and the various values at play. When the consequences are clear, then the relative merit of these helps to determine appropriate action; but when consequences are unclear, or when the consequences are clear, but not easy to adjudicate, then leaders must apply an analysis of values. However, a leader who applies values at random to justify a decision lacks credibility. Leaders must act transparently in identifying and applying values to a particular situation. There should be neither surprise nor manipulation in the selection of values. We have called this acting with 'coherence'.

Various types of decisions

So often, in difficult situations, leaders seek safety in rules. By citing an inflexible set of rules and procedures, they see the resolution as resistant to challenge. While there are clearly situations in which rules and procedures matter, this is not always a helpful way to resolve dilemmas.

In his *Six Action Shoes*, de Bono (1992) identifies six bases for decision-making: the application of routines or formal procedures; exploration, investigation and evidence-gathering; pragmatism and flexibility; consideration of safety issues; prioritising of people's feelings; and recourse to authority, with action determined by the responsibilities of the role.

While de Bono's framework is very helpful in many situations, in times of uncertainty there is a need to resort to a careful consideration of purpose and an evaluation of the values which impact upon the situation and people involved or affected by it.

Coherence

We suggest the application of 'coherence'. When ideas are coherent, they are clear, the various parts connect together ('cohere') logically and consistently, they have a natural agreement.

Torralba et al (2011) describe coherence as agreement between thought and word, a transparency between what we think and say. The writers cite Weber's argument that coherence requires conviction and responsibility: conviction to state and defend our norms and responsibility to accept their consequences. In ethical terms, coherence requires us to identify a credo, and have a willingness to follow it. It means being loyal to our ideas. It also means being willing to be self-critical, to ensure that we recognise our own lack of coherence and endeavour to correct this.

We extend this concept to describe a source of moral authority for decision-making in schools in times of uncertainty. Coherence is values-based leadership. It is the transparent relationship between the beliefs and values which apply to a situation and the decision or action which results. In times of uncertainty and paradoxical situations, leaders demonstrate coherence when they clearly articulate the relevant school values, and, if appropriate, their own values and those of others involved, and explain logically how their decision or action reflects these values. This does not mean that a given decision will be completely acceptable to everyone. Others may hold differing values. However, it does mean that the basis upon which the decision is made is clear and justifiable in terms of core values.

Torralba, et al (2011) suggest that coherence is good for organisations and for the individuals within it:

> A person who acts professionally from a standpoint of coherence is a guarantee for an organisation, and, in this respect, a source of confidence, since their decisions and actions are foreseeable within the framework of the organisation … The member of an organisation knows what to hold onto, knows what mechanisms are in play … When a person is located within an organisation that esteems and values coherence, they can anticipate processes and situations (p.161).

Identifying purpose

The basis for decision-making is not always to focus on who should make the decision or how the decision should be made. It may be necessary to review the purposes of the school, and how these might influence the decision. Without purpose, it is easy to lose perspective.

Questions are often framed in terms of consequences: What will happen if we choose this course or that course? Decisions can then get caught in the mire of things that possibly won't work or might not be popular. A focus on purpose reframes the question in terms of what the school is trying to achieve. The best choice is the one that is most consistent with that purpose. In schools purpose is defined most clearly in terms of learning and wellbeing. However, there are many nuances of emphasis between schools in the articulation of their purpose.

Identifying values

A school's core purpose is created upon its core values. Most schools are able to identify a set of perhaps four to six core values. If used appropriately, these will often form the basis for decision-making. Individuals also have their own core values, and these, too, will influence their actions. For example, suppose a school facing a politically tricky situation is uncertain whether to keep the matter secret or make it public within the school community. If the school declares *honesty* to be one of its core values, or if the principal consistently states that 'honesty is the best policy', then this would suggest that the information should be disclosed. However, if the principal personally values compassion, and respect for the growth of students, even if these are not stated as school goals, he may decide that the matter ought to be kept confidential.

In another example, our own experience has been that school leaders often face dilemmas in providing errant students with appropriate consequences for their actions in a manner which protects their privacy and dignity, yet allowing other students to see that consequences have resulted, that 'justice has been served'.

In any situation, several values may compete. Again, de Bono is helpful in providing a framework for identifying and evaluating the relative importance of competing values. In *The Six Value Medals* (de Bono, 2005), he suggests a way to identify and evaluate in a particular situation the relative merit of six different types of values: human values; the values of the organisation; quality values, which impact on the intended direction or purpose of the product, service or function; the value of innovation, simplicity and creativity; the impact on the environment, meaning all those people and things not directly involved; and the value of how things appear, are perceived or are interpreted.

Competence and capability

Leaders need the capability to make such judgements. Duignan (2003) cited Stephenson's argument that capability is not the same as competency:

> Competency is about delivering the present based on past performance; capability is about imaging the future and bringing it about. Competency is about control; capability is about learning and development. Competency is about fitness for (usually other people's) purpose; capability is about judging fitness of the purpose itself (p.18).

Stephenson (2000) defined capability as 'an all-round human quality, an *integration* of knowledge, skills, personal qualities and understanding *used appropriately and effectively* — not just in familiar and highly focused specialist contexts but in response to *new and changing* circumstances' (p.2). It requires creative, intuitive frameworks based on in-depth understanding of human nature and of the ethical, moral, even spiritual dimensions inherent in human interaction and choice. Duignan (1994) drew on the work of Bogue in suggesting that:

> Capable leaders tend to be people with 'character' shaped by a value-set fine-tuned through the warp and weft of life's experiences. The often have 'spiritual scars and calluses on their characters' from having battled with the complex perplexing dilemmas and tensions of life and work. They are morally courageous, unafraid to question unfair and unjust processes and practices when conformity would be the easier path (p.22).

Hence, to lead in a time of uncertainty and in the presence of dilemmas and value conflicts, leaders require a strong sense of purpose and a clear values stance. This enables them to make decisions in changing circumstances, by evaluating action and consequences in terms of the impact on purpose and values.

The problem of trained dependency

In such a context, there is no place for the trained dependency, as discussed in Chapter 7, of schools and leaders on the central authority for decisions and resources. In large systems, in particular, regulations are prolific and proliferating. Some provide an important and helpful framework for acting; others seem to attempt to provide answers for every conceivable situation. In some schools and systems, there appears to be an expectation that leaders will check 'higher up' for answers to unspecified situations. To be fair, sometimes the expectation is in the eyes of the school leaders, not in the understandings of the system or board.

However it is perceived, the reality is that there are many dilemmas faced by school leaders for which a solution cannot be prescribed, and for which the person best equipped to determine the answer is the leader 'on the ground'. Leaders in schools must have the courage to make decisions, and to defend their choices, without appealing to a supervising authority. Exercising such authority may itself present a dilemma for a school leader. How can one act with any confidence in such a situation? Some guidelines are necessary.

Be aware of legal and regulatory requirements

No leader can know all such requirements any more, let alone interpret with confidence the application of these in a particular context. However, leaders need to know the essence of relevant legislation and regulations, and to have access to those who know more. Where a situation bristles with legal barbs, seek advice from someone who understands the requirements better than you.

Know the compliance standards of your context

Canny leaders are aware of the particular emphases of those to whom they are accountable, of what 'rattles their cage'. One may be passionate about student welfare, another may be overly-sensitive to parent complaints, yet another may be nervous about occupational health and safety. By knowing your particular politics, you will know when to risk and when to check.

Assess the risk. Some decisions have serious consequences; other don't. Leaders make many decisions during the course of a day in which the consequences pose minimal risk. Even experienced leaders make errors of judgement. However, they have finely attuned risk detectors, so that they know whether a decision requires serious consideration or quick judgement. They are able to recognise when a decision has gone wrong and when the consequences of that decision are unacceptable; they are willing to acknowledge that a review is necessary; and they have strategies to change a decision and implement another without causing a loss of confidence or serious fallout.

Act

Procrastination is sometimes a useful tool for leaders: some situations go away if left alone! In other situations, delay aggravates a situation, and action of some sort is called for. The skilled leader is able to determine what action to take and when.

Monitor the decision

Some situations are resolved when the decision is made and enacted. Others require monitoring, to ensure that the consequences are as predicted, or, at least, acceptable. Sometimes conscious action is needed to implement the decision. This may involve talking with a number of people, perhaps assisting them to do what the decision requires them to do. In these situations it may be a matter of making the decision, then making the decision work.

Be clear about the basis for your decision.

In times of uncertainty, people will perceive a situation differently, and will value the various options differently. You will not please everyone. What is important is that you can clearly articulate the reason for your decision, the relative value you ascribed to the various options. You do not then defend your decision; you defend the values which you considered.

Autonomy

Coherence brings with it a confident autonomy. Historically, school leaders tended to avoid risk, for fear of failure, and fear of discipline or reprimand. But contemporary school leaders need to be entrepreneurs, always seeking new opportunities and new ways. That means mapping and walking your own path, even if it means walking in a different direction from systemic or political power. How can you do this without being cavalier or reckless?

Be critical

An OECD report identified 'tensions between classroom-based formative assessments, and high visibility summative tests to hold schools accountable for student achievement, and a lack of connection between systemic, school and classroom approaches to assessment and evaluation' (Pont et al, 2008, p.1). The critical leader is aware of contradictions between what is and what should be, between what is expected and what is right, between what reflects the values or expedience of governments and authorities and what reflects sound educational practice.

Further, the leader is articulate about these contradictions and seeks ways to address them The Western Australian Primary Principals Association commissioned a position paper which sought to respond to the concern that 'the use of NAPLAN data to evaluate the performance of educators has resulted in an over-reliance by teachers, principals and system leaders (even an obsession with) standardised tests; a decline in teachers' confidence in using their own assessments; and a desire by teachers and principals to justify their performance with numerical data, no matter how inappropriately devised or analysed.' (WAPPA, 2016, p.11). Its recommendations did not suggest rebelling against authorities, but finding ways to enhance the confident and skilful use of classroom formative assessment strategies.

Be discerning

There is an abundance of educational research available. It is reported in national and international conferences and a range of regular journals published by professional associations. There is so much that it is sometimes difficult to discern what is worth responding to. Every speaker and writer attempts to make their research and insights sound irresistible.

The discerning leader is able to sift through the noise and fanfare to identify research which is credible and potentially valuable in achieving their own or the school's development.

The key purpose of this book is to identify those ideas which contemporary leaders ought not to dismiss, but should incorporate into their practice — or at least consider doing so.

Be receptive

Schools have been criticised in the past for failing to learn from research and experience. Prior to the technological revolution precipitated by the computer, classrooms, and the behaviours of teachers and students, were remarkably similar to those of a century earlier. The receptive leader is listening, reading and exploring, always on the lookout for new thinking and strategies that could improve student learning in their school.

Practical strategies, which are relevant to your school, need not come from international research papers, but may come from those who are in the front line day after day. Encourage colleagues to think, to share their ideas, and to give things a try. When a colleague comes to you with an idea, be willing to say 'Yes', but explore the idea with them. Ask questions, not to destroy the idea, but to refine it. Ensure they have thought about how and with whom it will be trialled; how and when it will be communicated to parents and colleagues; how success will be defined; how the outcomes will be monitored and assessed; what difficulties can be anticipated and how they will be handled. Be adventurous about innovation, allowing time and support for an idea to be thoroughly tested.

Be flexible and agile.

Businesses speak of being agile, able to move to a new position quickly. Turning some schools to a new direction is like turning a massive container ship in a narrow channel. It is slow, laborious, and carries significant risk of disaster. Schools need to be flexible in their structures and procedures so that change can be implemented quickly and effectively.

During the recent pandemic, schools were forced to change their curricula, methodology, procedures, and other arrangements quickly. There was no opportunity for a twelve month transition. And the changes kept on coming, with schools having to adapt repeatedly to new circumstances.

Create a culture of autonomy within the school, a set of values, attitudes, procedures and communication channels which allow the school to be critical, discerning and receptive.

Create your own identity.

While it is important to listen and watch for ideas which others are exploring, and while there is nothing wrong with adopting — or adapting — an idea developed by someone else, be prepared to create your own identity — as a leader and as a school. Be prepared to stand alone.

Contemporary school leaders need to be entrepreneurs, always seeking new opportunities and new ways. Rather than subversion, the challenge for school leaders is to walk the path they know to be right, while meeting the expectations of authorities, and working with others to change those expectations.

CASE STUDY: THE ENROLMENT DECISION

It is enrolment time at Marsford South Public School and interviews are underway. The principal, Helen, and her deputy, Alastair, are troubled by one particular application for enrolment. Jasmine, a bright and bubbly young girl, is hemiplegic. While her parents could have enrolled her at neighbouring Marsford East, which caters for students with disabilities and is fully funded, they have heard great things about this school and want to enrol Jasmine here, which concerns Helen and Alastair greatly as their school does not have any of the accommodations that would be needed for Jasmine to be properly mobile and safe. At the interview Helen made an on-the-spot decision, advising the parents that she would consult her staff and the education department before going ahead with the enrolment. However, immediately after saying this, she felt nervous. What if it went to staff and they said no?

She convened a quick meeting of the leadership team, explained things and asked what they thought. The leadership team was unanimous about going ahead with the enrolment subject to a staff vote. The response from the department was less than enthusiastic. The neighbouring school was suggested and Helen had to explain the parents' choice. The department representative left it in Helen's hands, but warned that if the enrolment went ahead, the school would have to foot the bill for most of the necessary modifications such as ramps and lower stair railings.

At a staff meeting Helen presented Jasmine's case, explaining the pros and cons, but expressing her feeling that the school should enrol her. However, the staff vote resulted in a no, by one vote.

Helen went back to her office deeply troubled. She thought the staff decision would make things easier, but things were now far more complicated. She realised that she had wanted to let Jasmine enrol from the start and had let her fears about funding, care of the child and staff support overwhelm her. Perhaps she had made an error in asking the staff to vote.

After thinking about it for a while, she decided to accept the enrolment.

MAKE IT PERSONAL

In making decisions in complex situations, the challenge for school leaders is to balance personal values with rules, regulations and the needs of others. This can be a source of considerable internal conflict, and conflict with others. The values which leaders apply may not be congruent with the values of others.

Ask yourself, to what degree do I:

- consciously apply my personal values when making decisions?
- allow the beliefs and values of others to influence my decision-making?
- articulate a values stance in seeking to resolve difficult issues?
- act coherently?

FURTHER INVESTIGATION

Coherence

Begley (1999) has written about values-based leadership, which acknowledges the importance of the personal values of leaders, and that focuses on the issues that occur when institutional and community values also need to be considered. Research into the connection between moral purpose and shared leadership in school posits that a shared sense of values is fundamental for effective education (Bezzina, 2012; Conway & Andrews, 2016).

Personal values will influence how leaders act, and community values may predict the response, but conflicts often occur. What issues do you understand about the application of values-focused leadership? How might you see the concept of coherence developing and being applied?

10

The top, the centre and the heart and soul

From the top to the centre

A good listener is not only popular everywhere, but after a while he gets to know something (Mizner, 2022).

REFLECT

- How do you define yourself as leader?
- Has your definition or understanding of leadership changed while reading this book?
- If you were to draw a diagram to represent every person in your school, where would you place yourself?

SHIFT THE FOCUS

Many school leaders see themselves at the 'top' of the school. Some love to draw accountability structures that show the principal at the top, with everyone else at various levels below. Traditionally, school leaders received their authority and power from their position. The employer reinforced it; the principal was the conduit through which directives flowed from the employer to staff. Their responsibility was to ensure that these directives were implemented, and this was often achieved by using authoritative and coercive strategies.

However, this book began with a focus on leadership as the exercise of influence. While a hierarchical diagram may be useful to define accountabilities, it does not define influence. Influence is exercised from the *centre* of the networks, rather than the *top*. It is lonely at the top, and from there, influence can only be achieved by loud noise, heavy footsteps and grand gestures. There needs to be a shift to leadership from the centre. At the centre, leaders influence by listening, communicating strategically and personally, connecting people with others, seeding conversations, suggesting explorations, involving others in decisions, and so on.

These activities require relational skills. At the centre of the school, the leader relies less on position, authority, power and responsibility, and acts as consultant, linker, communicator and advocate, drawing together the disparate agenda and perceptions of the school community into a process for planning, deciding and acting which reflects a shared vision.

The centre of influence

Leadership is influence. There are many people and factors acting to influence the staff, students and parents of a school. Some of those influences are overt, some covert. Some are predictable, some unpredictable. Some are consistent with the leader's goals and the school's purpose; some are not.

It is critical that leaders are at the centre of influence. That means influencing the understanding of educational issues in the school, the focus of the discourse, the evolving directions and priorities, and the dreams and hopes of the people involved in the school. It means ensuring that those influences which are consistent with the school's goals are endorsed and encouraged; and those influences which offer a contrary view are identified and modified. It means ensuring that the leader's influence is not simply part of the background noise, but is clearly heard above the babble.

The centre of culture

Everyone who is a part of the school community experiences the culture of the school. Not only is the culture a reflection of the dominant and accepted thinking and behaviours of the members of the school community, it also influences the community's thinking and behaviour. For the school, and for individuals, it is a reciprocal process of influencing and being influenced by. The influential school leader is at the centre of the culture, monitoring it, articulating it, maintaining it, nudging it in new directions or towards new emphases if appropriate. This is Sergiovanni's notion of the 'cultural leader', at the apex of the five dimensions of leadership he identified, leading the school community by defining, strengthening and articulating values and beliefs that give the school its unique identity over time (Sergiovanni & Green, 2015).

The centre of learning

Principals are also at the centre of learning. That does not mean that they must teach a lot of classes. Some principals believe that such action gives them credibility with their colleagues, helps them to connect with students, and keeps them aware of the 'real' issues faced by teachers every day, but others argue that this restricts their outlook to the classroom instead of the school.

The more critical role is in influencing the teaching–learning discourse, the quality and focus of discussions about teaching and learning. Dempster (2009) described these conversations as 'disciplined dialogue' (p.5), scaffolded dialogue which is disciplined in two ways. The first is that it is focused on the moral purpose of schools; that is, improvement in student learning and performance. The second is that it is informed by qualitative and quantitative data, which is scrutinised using three questions: What do we see here? Why are we seeing what we are seeing? What should we be doing about it?

It is at the centre of these conversations that the school leader can move the discussion beyond complaints about individual student effort, the lack of home support, the lack of resources, and the like, to a fruitful dialogue about how learning might be improved for each student, and what each teacher's role is in that process.

The centre of networks

The nature of communication has a significant effect on the culture of the school. Communication which is open, honest, timely, encouraging and uplifting reflects and enhances a positive environment.

At the centre of communication, the principal is able to monitor the nature of conversation, and influence it. What does this mean in practice? It does not mean that all communication must be directed through the principal, nor that there is any attempt to prevent people talking together! It means being connected with the key communication pathways and networks of the school.

At the centre of the networks, the leader can identify those who are influential, supportive, oppositional, creative and so on. It is at the centre that the leader can influence the conversations, using the already active networks. At the centre, the leader can also create new networks, bringing together people with the expertise, drive, vision and influence to create an influential group, able to draw others into the vision and the reality.

Knowing how to identify, create and influence networks is a critical skill for the school leader. It is wrong to assume that the most effective networks are the formal ones; that is, the curriculum team, the leadership team, or similar. While some of these formal networks may need to be part of any planned change in the school, they are not necessarily the most influential, and may not be focused appropriately. The principal can spend a long time, with limited success, trying to convince such a group of the need for change. However, members of the group may have their own agenda, some of which may be strongly focused on maintaining the status quo, continuing patterns that have worked for them in the past, with which they are comfortable, and in which they have credibility. New ideas may be threatening.

It may be more effective to work with a separate group of staff that understands and connects with the principal's vision. One or two supportive members of the relevant 'formal' network may be enlisted to be part of the new group. As the new group begins to influence thinking and practice, and as staff see the value in the new vision, the groundswell may influence the formal network more quickly and effectively than the leader alone was able to.

To successfully influence the professional conversations within the school, the leader needs to be at the centre of the networks.

The centre of teams

An extension of this is that school leaders are at the centre of teams. School leaders belong to a multitude of formal teams or groups. Each team does public work, meeting, discussing issues and deciding on actions. It then dissipates to implement these decisions, or to influence the professional dialogue with colleagues.

However, there can be a lot of politics in teams, not all of which is helpful. Some members may say little in the meetings. Is it because they don't understand the issues; do they disagree with the decisions, but not want to say so; are they opposed to the dominant thinking, but fear being ostracised by their colleagues if they speak out? The school leader needs to spend time talking privately with these colleagues, encouraging their participation or talking through issues with them. Some members may dominate the discussion. Again, it is important for the principal or leader to identify why that is so, and to work with that situation.

Some people are supportive or acquiescent in meetings, but undermine decisions afterwards. Again, the principal needs to identify this, and spend time working with this staff member to understand why they act in this way, and to coach them in more open, honest and respectful interactions.

These things can be addressed only when the principal is at the centre of the team, interacting not just as a chairperson of meetings, but working with people outside the meetings to influence people's thinking.

The centre of alignment

In effective schools, the 'stars line up'! The values of individuals are aligned with (though not necessarily identical with) the core values of the school. The strategic priorities, policies, procedures and practices are aligned with the core values of the school. The allocation of resources, including staffing and the professional learning focus, are aligned with the strategic priorities.

Alignment adds impact. So often in schools there are competing priorities, the priorities adopted from time to time have little connection to the declared strategic directions, purpose or mission. The allocation of resources reflects traditional or accepted arrangements, or satisfies political pressures, rather than relating to the priorities. When these things align, there is a multiplier effect.

Critical concepts

This book has suggested a number of concepts that school leaders need to have at the centre of their thinking. These include:
- influence, the essence of leadership
- achievement, a measure of the success of the school's efforts
- alignment, the impact achieved when all of the school's efforts are focused towards goals
- partnership and collaboration, working with others to achieve more than each individual alone can achieve
- globalism, an awareness of the impact that distant events and thinking have on our local context
- succession, growing leaders to replace us
- community, the context in which people find a sense of belonging
- coherence, the articulation of consistent values as a basis for dealing with paradox and dilemma.

And, later in this chapter we will discuss heart and soul leadership, which involves the coming together of values, purpose, commitment and passion. Along the way, we explored notions of transformation, change, empowerment, relationship, ethical leadership, service, negotiation, teams and uncertainty.

Many of these concepts are not new, but our purpose has been to bring them together in one place, and to place them before you. These do not stand alone. They work together.

CASE STUDY: THE BOUNDARY RIDER

Paul is very different from the previous principal of Hastings Community School in the way he relates to the school community. The previous principal was the office-bound type, friendly and obliging with parents, but rarely mingling. It was the same with staff. Paul, however, is everywhere, especially in the mornings. You will often find him walking around the playground shaking hands and engaging in conversations with parents before the morning bell. He will also talk to students on the playground and is even seen playing handball with them. During breaks he always makes sure he is in the staffroom and he sits in a different place each time, talking to different teachers. One habit that some teachers find peculiar is his tendency to roam around the school in the middle of the school day when he has time, occasionally coming into classes and talking with the students about what they are learning.

Once during an executive team meeting one of the teachers commented on this roaming around the school and asked Paul why he felt the need to. His response was quick and matter-of-fact: 'I am boundary riding. You know how farmers get on their horses and ride around the farm checking all the animals and equipment, making sure everything's okay? I am doing essentially the same thing.'

He went on to explain how he was finding out all sorts of things about how the parents think and that he now has a really good idea of the grapevine network that exists and where the information hubs are. He knows what is going on in the school and what is being learnt. He knows the kids. When he wants to change things, he has a fair idea who will be for and against his ideas, as he has gained a sense of what people value — parents and teachers especially.

He has managed to get a few initiatives started with minimal fuss, like the school harmony garden and the new behaviour reward system. He obviously uses his boundary riding as some sort of influence. But how?

If you ask him, he just says he has a way with people. This is true, but it understates his real intentions. Paul has gained influence by deliberately establishing networks with people. Parents see him as someone genuinely interested in the life of the school rather than as an administrator. Students see him as someone who is interested in them, rather than a distant power figure. Staff members see Paul as 'different' to previous bosses, but, as one staff member put it, 'He knows everyone and everything. He's the heart and soul of the place.'

MAKE IT PERSONAL

The challenge for school executive staff is to lead from the centre to involve the school community in building a school culture that will improve student outcomes.

Ask yourself, to what degree do I:
- play a central role in influencing the thinking of staff, students and parents?
- understand, use and create formal and informal networks of the school?
- work at aligning the key elements and influences within the school?

FURTHER INVESTIGATION

Democratic leadership

Democratic leadership has increasingly become both a function and feature of school leadership over the last two decades. This has been as a result of the devolution of authority for some areas of decision-making from system to school level and the trend in staff member participation in decision-making that has been experienced across many occupations (Seibold & Shea, 2001).

Among the many positive outcomes of democratic leadership are increased teacher empowerment, which can lead to teachers taking greater risks with new techniques to improve their teaching (Amanchukwu et al, 2015; Woods & Roberts, 2016); school effectiveness, ability to adapt to challenges, transformation of schools into learning organisations (Kools & Stoll, 2016); teacher job satisfaction, commitment and overall staff morale (De Nobile & Bilgin, 2022; De Nobile & McCormick, 2008). Explore these and other effects of this style of leadership. Consider personal stories of educators as well as research studies.

Beyond the centre to the heart and soul

The responsibility we have as leaders is to discover our own enlivening 'breath' so that we can awaken and remind those we work with, of theirs (Hurley, 2011)

REFLECT

- Why do you do this job? What do you bring to it? What do you contribute?
- When you welcome a new cohort of students to the school, what do you hope for them during their time at the school? When you farewell graduating students, what difference do you feel the school has made to them?
- How does your leadership make a difference?

SHIFT THE FOCUS

Leaders may be at the top of the hierarchy of accountability, but at the centre of the relationships, networks and culture of the school.

However, leaders are not just at the centre of what happens, but at the heart of what matters, and in the soul of what defines the school.

There is a need to integrate the head intelligence and heart intelligence in a process which enables the leader and the individual to move forward. The key to moving people through a difficult issue lies in navigating a balance between the two kinds of intelligence (Wiggins, 2017). Many a disaster has ensued for 'feeling where we ought to think, and thinking where we ought to feel' (Collins, 2024).

Understand the heart and soul

Leadership is, at times, an intellectual activity, in that effective leaders think leadership. Their minds are attuned to what needs to be done to encourage, motivate, direct, focus, organise, communicate, network, support, grow, improve and influence their people, organisation, relationships, reputation, product or service.

Leadership is also an emotional activity. Leaders influence people more through the heart than through the mind. They are most effective when they can connect with people's hearts, through their passions and emotions; and when they assist other people to connect with their own hearts.

Leadership is also a spiritual activity. If we want people to be exceptional in what they do, then we must find a way to make it matter to them, and we must show that it matters to us; and it must matter not because of coercion or fear of consequences, but because it means something. Successful leaders bring meaning to people's work and activity. They take the mundane tasks of life or employment and imbue them with meaning and purpose. They connect with the soul.

So the heart and soul of leadership is leadership that connects with the heart and soul. It refers to the way leaders nurture relationships, connecting with people at every level.

Heart and soul leadership requires passion and conviction, being clear and consistent in the reasons for why things are done, the values which underpin them and the purpose behind everything. It is evident in leaders' integrity, the consistency between their words and actions, and in honesty, which generates trust and confidence. It is also evident when leaders make clear to all that their work is not just a job, but a calling, work that matters. It is expressed when leaders move beyond the professional to a place of genuine compassion and care for the wellbeing of members of the school community.

Communication is essential to this type of leadership. This includes effective listening, which enables the leader to hear other people's hearts and souls, their true feelings, their desire for meaning, including that which is not expressed; and clear speaking or writing, which reinforces the core messages of values, purpose and meaning.

Good leaders 'should have a cool brain, a warm heart and a clean hand' — rational in their thinking, caring in their relationships, and honest and principled in their behaviour (Sarros, 2002, p.11).

Find and nurture the heart and soul of the school

The heart and soul of the school is seen in the school culture. This is the expression of the school's core values, which determine what is expected of all members of the school community, the way things are done, the basis on which success is measured. It is the essence or spirit of the school. While culture may change over time, it is reflected in the life of the school wherever the school exists (including when students are on a camp, tour or excursion); whatever the school's circumstances (for example, even if the school buildings are destroyed by fire); and whoever enters or leaves the school community (including when staff change, or a cohort of students is replaced by a new cohort).

In his influential work in the 1980s that still holds true today, Sergiovanni & Green (2015) described a hierarchy of 'leadership forces' available to school leaders:

- technical — derived from sound management techniques
- human — derived from harnessing available social and interpersonal resources
- educational — derived from expert knowledge about matters of education and schooling
- symbolic — derived from focusing the attention of others on matters of importance to the school
- cultural — derived from building a unique school culture.

Sergiovanni argued that the most effective leaders are those who have the skills to understand, evaluate, maintain and influence the school's culture. They focus the attention of the entire school community on a shared vision, and gain commitment to the goals and values of the school from students, staff and parents by their words and actions, and through appropriate symbols and ceremonies.

Because 'Culture shapes the school and the people in it' (Ridden, 2018b, p.37), school leaders must build, maintain or shape the culture of the school.

The kinds of ideas leaders may communicate about school culture include values, beliefs and assumptions about how things should work and best practice, mission, goals and aspirations for the future. Examples of cultural leadership might include:

- selecting staff who will contribute appropriately to the culture
- modelling the culture in interactions with colleagues, students, parents and others
- teaching the culture at every opportunity
- acculturating new staff members and new families, overseeing and involving them in induction programs, mentoring new staff, and informing new community members of what is valued, what is expected and how things are done
- affirming or reviewing school mission and vision, and articulating and confirming existing values and beliefs
- ensuring that the behaviours and relationships of all students, staff and parents, and that the school's policies and procedures, are consistent with the school's values
- explaining the purpose and meaning of rituals, traditions and celebrations, in terms of culture
- sharing narratives of past and present heroes, incidents and events that make the culture real

- rewarding members of the school whose actions or character embody the culture
- challenging unacceptable behaviours by focusing on values and explaining how they negatively impact culture
- using values as a basis for decision making
- using conflict to clarify and build the culture
- changing the culture to achieve school improvement and renewal (Ridden, 2018b).

Find your own heart and soul

The soul of leadership must also include some reference to spiritual leadership. Spiritual leadership is not about how we journey, but rather about where we journey and, even more deeply, why we journey. While leaders need to guide others to find meaning in their work through answers to these questions, they first must find answers to the questions for themselves. The answers tap into our beliefs about the meaning of life.

They matter because leaders bring their own values and sense of meaning to their work, so it is important to see where that matches and mismatches with the school. Our values represent the lens through which we view life, and our view of life affects the way we live our life. If our values are significantly different from those of the school, or school community, then there is a risk of serious conflict with others or within ourselves.

Values determine how we interpret events, establish priorities, make choices and reach decisions. They guide our actions by orienting us in particular ways towards social and political problems; predisposing us towards certain beliefs; guiding our evaluations of others and ourselves; and offering the means by which we rationalise our behaviour. Within an organisation, values provide a context for action; a sense of order without excessive rules; reduced ambiguity without detailed plans; and focus and cohesion for the organisation, while allowing for individual self-determination (Barker & Coy, 2002; Gruenert & Whitaker, 2015; Schein, 2017).

The authors argue that it is critically important that leaders come to terms with their own core values. Since leadership with soul is about integrity, leaders must then make sense of their personal values in the work context. And when we find those answers, we must use them as a touchstone, a 'place' to which to return to review our actions, our motives, our visions, our hopes and our dreams, and to help others do the same.

The heart and soul of leadership, then, involves:

- acting with integrity, character and consistency
- acting with conviction and clarity about values and purpose
- acting with empathy, care and compassion
- helping others to find their heart and soul, and to express this within their work
- imbuing people's work with meaning and purpose.

Be the heart and the soul to the school

Barker and Coy (2003, p. ix) suggest that 'healthy, positive and aligned organisations are shaped by leaders who are seen by their followers as being virtuous … It's about discovering what really matters to *you*; being brave enough to acknowledge it; and then finding a way to live, work and lead that is congruent.' Elsewhere they write that 'leadership (whether good or bad, successful or ineffective) is a reflection or consequence of the values and beliefs of the leader (for better or worse) and so must have a personal dimension.' (Barker & Coy, 2002, p. viii).

The challenge for school leaders is to express their own heart and soul and that of the school in such a way as to *be* that heart and soul. When that is visible to others, they are inspired to mirror it, because passion and commitment are contagious.

Or even 'exhilarating'! Caldwell (2006) used this word in his report on research into the way principals perceive their work. The participants identified aspects of their work which they found exhilarating, and those they found dispiriting. Yet when asked how to make the work more exhilarating, one third identified factors which lie to a large extent in the hands of the leaders themselves — achieving a better life balance, finding time to have fun, becoming more tolerant and sensitive, improving delegation and relationships, and so on.

Exhilaration in leadership is a wonderful concept. It is akin to passion, a source of unlimited energy from your soul (or spirit or heart) that enables you to produce extraordinary results (Kovess, 2002).

According to Hurley (2011), it is the heart, not the head, that inspires greatness. Good leaders inspire others to have confidence in them; great leaders inspire others to have confidence in themselves.

This confidence is empowering. It gives people purpose; focuses their attention on the 'big' issues rather than the trivial detail; and provides a framework of values and purpose within which to think differently and act creatively about their work.

Your inner leader

This book has been written for those who lead our schools, and those who aspire to do so. This includes those with a leadership title and designated role *and* those who lead because they see a need and have a conviction to meet that need.

We have said that leaders are people who lead when a leader is needed. However, this is not about ego or hubris. It is about leadership which connects with the heart as well as the head. It is servant leadership, which, as discussed in Chapter 8, is characterised by service to others. Servant leaders help others — those who are served — to grow as persons, become more knowledgeable, more autonomous and willing to become servants themselves. Greenleaf (1977) comments on this passionately:

> The real enemy is fuzzy thinking on the part of good, intelligent, vital people, and their failure to lead, and to follow servants as leaders. Too many settle for being critics and experts. There is too much intellectual wheel spinning, too much retreating into 'research', too little preparation for and willingness to undertake the hard and high risks of building better institutions in an imperfect world, too little disposition to see 'the problem' as residing *in here* and not *out there*.
>
> In short, the enemy is strong natural servants who have the potential to lead but do not lead, or who choose to follow a non-servant. They suffer. Society suffers. And so it may be in the future (p.45. Italics in original text).

So if you are reading this book, but have no formal leadership role, what's stopping you from leading? Sharma's (2010) words are challenging:

The CEO gets buried next to the street cleaner. And on your last day, all that truly matters is whether you got to know your inner leader, and if you did, whether you had the bravery to allow it to offer its gifts to the world around you (p.33. Italics in original text.)

So lead, with heart and soul.

CASE STUDY: THE CULTURAL LEADER

Since Wei started as principal at St John's School three years ago the change has been amazing. One of the things that concerned her when she arrived was how students seemed 'invisible' in the school in terms of its mission and vision; indeed the word 'students' was not even in the vision statement, which focused on curriculum. The classrooms and the curriculum seemed to be centred around teachers or be teacher-focused. The students did not seem to have a voice in the school, even at assemblies.

Wei made it clear that there was a new culture being developed at St John's soon after arriving. She would use phrases like 'student centred', 'striving for excellence', and 'doing the best you can' whenever she could. Wei's mission to place students at the centre of the school's culture is certainly evident. A parent recently commented, 'You really get a sense that this school is all about the kids' learning, striving for excellence and giving everything a go.'

Some of the changes she initiated with the help of the leadership team included:

- establishing a student representative council to deal with student concerns that could be raised at staff meetings or parents and friends gatherings
- creating a new school crest, designed by students, which is now included in the school letterhead and signage
- developing a school song which was written in a workshop with a local musician, and which incorporated student and school values such as belonging, working together and doing the best you can, and which is now sung at all assemblies and most liturgical celebrations
- ensuring that students, mostly members of the student council, lead assemblies.

You get the feeling that, if Wei were to retire tomorrow, this new ethos of 'students at the centre' would live on. As one teacher commented, 'This place has come to life since Wei arrived. People feel good about coming here and the students really love coming to school. I think what we are doing here is really special, really important.'

MAKE IT PERSONAL

The challenge for school leaders is to nurture the heart and soul of the school.

Ask yourself, to what degree do I:

- understand my own heart and soul?
- articulate the heart and soul of my school?
- nurture the heart and soul in the life of the school and those within the school community?
- know the school's culture, articulate it, influence it and reinforce it, and in other ways focus the attention of others on it?

FURTHER INVESTIGATION

Cultural leadership communication

The heart and soul of a school is its culture. Developing and maintaining a school culture requires that leaders be cultural communicators. This means being able to articulate key values, act on them and set an example for expected behaviour. Building on the work of other scholars, De Nobile (2007) identified cultural communication as a key skill for school leaders. Hargreaves (1995), Deal & Peterson (1999, 2016), Sergiovanni & Green (2015), Gruenert & Whitaker (2015) and Brion (2021) also provide perspectives. Explore the literature on the communication of culture, and consider how this applies to your school.

Drawing on his research on communication in schools, De Nobile (2021a) identified three main types of cultural communication that leaders engage in. Leaders who engage in *visional cultural communication* are explicitly sharing their views (and perhaps, but not always, a collective view) of the overarching vision, mission or goals. *Operational cultural communication* refers to information that shows staff members how things should be done in the school. Senior and (increasingly) middle leaders often do this through induction processes and mentoring. *Historical cultural communication* concerns the sharing of stories and other information from the past.

Cultural intelligence (sometimes referred to as cultural quotient or CQ) has become a concept of increasing importance to the study of organisations. It refers to one's ability to operate effectively in different cultural settings and work successfully with people from other cultural backgrounds (Earley & Ang, 2003; Sternberg et al, 2022). The increased prominence of CQ has no doubt emerged from an increasingly globalized workforce and education has become increasingly 'cross-cultural' enterprise with, for example increased numbers of students from other countries studying in Australia. However, the same considerations apply to leaders who are moving schools or who are leading staff who are changing employment from different schools or (again increasingly apparent) leaders who oversee multiple campuses. In each of these cases the research suggests that when dealing with behaviours that might seem unusual or 'out of synch' with the prevailing school culture leaders should suspend judgement and consider where those behaviours are coming from before responding to them (Alifuddin & Widodo, 2022; Livermore, 2009; Triandis, 2006).

We encourage you to explore the literature on organisational/school culture, and cultural intelligence and consider how this applies to your school.

11
THE CRITICALLY REFLECTIVE LEADER

By three methods we may learn wisdom: First, by reflection, which is noblest; Second, by imitation, which is easiest; and third by experience, which is the bitterest (Confucius)

REFLECT

- How often do you actually reflect on your work and its impact on the school?
- If you do engage in reflection, what are you focusing on and does it help your practice?
- What skills do you have that could be stretched to a higher level? In what aspects of your work would you like to become more proficient? How could you enable this?

SHIFT THE FOCUS

An old adage says that we learn from experience. It's not necessarily true. Whether we learn and what we learn depends on how we reflect on our experience. In this book you have been asked to reflect on numerous occasions, sometimes about your understanding of concepts, but also on how you think about things, and what you do. There needs to be a shift towards embedding regular critical reflection as an integral part of leadership practice.

Reflective practice

Reflective practice provides leaders with an opportunity to think about how their actions might be impacting on others, as well as how various factors might be impacting on them. Schon (1983) provides two valuable tools for reflection. They are applied to leadership here.

Reflection *in* action is the process of thinking while acting. The decisions made or actions taken reflect the emotions felt at the time, and learning from past experience. Emotional intelligence can be important here because control over emotions will lead to better, more balanced decisions.

This can be difficult, especially when 'heart' and 'head' are in tension. Leaders are often required to make prompt decisions:

> Much reflection-in-action hinges on the experience of surprise. When intuitive, spontaneous performance yields nothing more than the results expected for it then we tend not to think about it. But when intuitive performance leads to surprises, pleasing and promising, or unwanted, we may respond by reflecting in action (Schon, 1983, p.56).

Reflection *on* action occurs when one thinks about their decisions and actions after the situation has occurred and has the opportunity to analyse what happened and why. Schon (1983) proposed that this process can provide the bank of 'know-how' that can inform better reflection *in* action. He advises:

> Practitioners do reflect on their knowing-in-practice. Sometimes in the relative tranquillity of a post-mortem they think back on a project they have undertaken, a situation they have lived through, and they explore the understandings they have brought to their handling of the case. They may do this in a mood of idle speculation or in a deliberate effort to prepare themselves for future cases (p.61).

Over subsequent years scholars have attempted to refine or update this model of professional reflection. The aim of such work has been to better align reflective practice to the work people in various occupations do to ensure their effectiveness.

Reflection *for* action happens when one is intentionally planning for an event or situation ahead of time. Described as a reflective strategy for teaching practices (Grushka et al, 2005), it can apply to leadership as well. Reflection *for* action is a more deliberate reflective process that requires leaders to anticipate what will occur, as well as ponder their past experiences, before the anticipated time, in order to perform better when the times comes.

Reflective practice is a cyclical process of thinking, acting and thinking and might be described as experiential learning; that is, the process of creating meaning from our experiences. Kolb's (2015) well known model can help us to understand how we learn from experiences. Firstly, we have the experiences themselves, often concrete, lived experiences. Sometimes, these force us to reflect on what happened, so, secondly, we review and reflect on the experience we just had. Thirdly, we form conclusions about the experience, which can include decisions about future actions. Finally, we indulge in active experimentation, trying out what we have learned in a new or subsequent situation.

Critically reflective practice

Critically reflective practice goes a step further, requiring us to critically examine the assumptions that underlie our actions as well as the possible explanations for why situations occur. Being a critically reflective practitioner does not mean being negative about ourselves or others, but rather questioning what might seem obvious through systemic investigation. We will often make assumptions about why people do things and how things work, but are we just adopting conventional wisdom and knowledge? Is there new knowledge that could show us how people could do things better or how things work more efficiently? Are there perspectives that we have not considered about an issue, about ourselves and about our actions?

Other perspectives are a vital input to critically reflective practice. They help us to see things in ways we might not have otherwise. In relation to teaching, Brookfield offers four useful perspective 'lenses' through which teachers can understand what they do, why they teach the way they do and the outcomes:

- The autobiographical lens is the teacher's own experiences as a learner and teacher. This is, in essence, self-reflection.
- The student lens is student feedback and results. Here, teachers stop and think about what these sources of data are saying to them.
- The colleague lens is feedback, advice and guidance from peers. Peer reviews and mentoring are examples, along with informal feedback.
- The literature lens is the use of theory and other scholarship to inform teaching. It helps us to name and explain current practice as well as desired practice (Brookfield, 1995).

The ideas can be extended to school leaders, who can reflect on their work through the lenses of self, data (about the school, student achievement and their own performance gathered from students, staff and students), colleagues (both on-site and off-site peers, and professional mentors) and literature. Other sources of information include performance reviews, which might provide 360-degree feedback, and the school review process, which provides insights with the help of the community 'lens'. Whatever the process, the critically reflective leader seeks feedback from a range of perspectives, including co-leaders, teachers, support staff, parents, students, mentors, critical friends, superordinates and others.

The other aspect of critically reflective practice is dealing with critical incidents. These are not the dramatic, possibly harmful, events that we may think of as critical incidents, but occurrences or realisations that challenge our assumptions and knowledge of how things should work (Bruster & Petersen, 2013; McGarr, 2021). Some examples might include:

- you accept that students do not appreciate your use of humour
- a respected peer disagrees with a leadership strategy you have long employed
- you realise that your assumption about how you are perceived by parents is wrong.

How we deal with critical incidents has a significant influence on how our practice develops. There are usually two choices: ignore the issue and hope that it will go away, which means we are unlikely to reap benefits in the long term; or use the feedback and thinking from reflective practice to plan a change of direction, which is likely to make us more effective leaders.

There are many models for reflecting on critical incidents, some complex, some as simple as asking: What? So what? Now what?

One model, based on a series of questions, is Cox's (2005) critical incident process, which involves identifying:

- the critical incident, through a brief description of how you see the situation
- its effects on you, including the emotional, cognitive and other immediate effects of the critical incident
- any problem or dilemma faced as a result of the critical incident
- the choices or alternative solutions to the problems, based on feedback and other sources
- the way forward, which necessitates a decision from the choices listed in the previous step, and involves justifying the choice and outlining its implementation

- the results, including monitoring the success of the implemented change, seeing if whether further work is needed, and acting on new opportunities created by the change.

Critically reflective practice assists educators to continually improve their practice so that it is aligned with student needs and school vision. Critically reflective leadership has the potential for school principals and other leaders to become more responsive to the needs of the school community.

There are so many aspects of leadership to reflect on that school leaders might find themselves wondering what they should be looking at and how. Duignan (2006) suggested the following:

- reflection on leadership experience and achievements
- reflection on aspects of leadership expected by the school and the system
- reflection on experiences of best practice
- reflection and critical review of professional development needs in relation to the previous points.

The critically reflective leader applies the process describes above to their own thinking and practice, reflecting on their work and issues from several perspectives. They are open, responsive and willing to deal with challenges to assumptions and long-held beliefs — and that might hurt a little. Critically reflective leaders:

- welcome perspectives on their leadership practices from various sources
- are open to challenges to values, beliefs and preferred practices
- change their attitudes and behaviour based on systemic examination
- accept critical incidents as opportunities for learning and growth
- learn as they do things and do things they learn
- have a genuine desire to be the best they can be s seek to be effective leaders.

Are you critically reflective? While we have highlighted a process of critical reflection in this chapter, we have encouraged reflection throughout this book. There is good reason.

This book was not written to show our knowledge; we can identify more issues *not* included in the book than issues we included. We realise that school leaders have limited time for professional reading, and this forced us to be selective. Rather, this book was written to challenge the thinking of school leaders. No doubt you were familiar with some of these concepts, but, hopefully, there were also many ideas here that have challenged your thinking and encouraged you to examine your practice.

We encourage you to respond to the book by continuing to question your leadership and that of your colleagues — not just those who carry titles, but all those who offer leadership or could do so. Share some of the ideas with them. Ask for their feedback on your leadership. Create some individual intentions, and some intentions to aspire to together. Challenge one another to grow as leaders.

Why? Because your work matters; your leadership matters; those you lead matter. Improve your practice in ways that will help your colleagues to become more capable leaders, your students more effective learners, your parents more involved partners, and all members of the school community more connected.

We will be delighted to hear stories of how you get on.

CASE STUDY: 360-DEGREE VIEW AT PATERSON BRIDGE SCHOOL

Jason has been the Year 10 coordinator at Paterson Bridge School for three years. After reading about 360-degree feedback in a journal he decides to conduct the process himself. He wants to learn more about his leadership, and while he knows it might dent his ego a little bit, he is keen to use input from others to develop his skills. He decides on areas that he wants to look at closely. These include approachability, decision-making, organisation, and treatment of students.

Jason decides that he want feedback from his Year 10 teacher peers, students, and parents of students with whom he has had significant interventions.

He then devises open-ended surveys requiring respondents to answer questions about the four areas he identified for review. There is a different survey for students, parents and teachers, but the questions ask for information from the same areas. The survey is delivered via email attachment to staff and students and by mail to parents. All returned surveys are to be sealed in an envelope provided, with no names; he wants it to be anonymous.

The surveys went out more than two weeks ago, were due back last Monday, and he has received about 30 responses. Jason is feeling both excited and nervous. What has he learned so far?

Jason arranged the comments under themes. His strengths appear to be that he is well organised, professional and has good rapport with the students. Two areas of concern have emerged so far. One is that some staff members perceive him to be a poor listener who does not always take on board suggestions. The other, raised by parents, is that he takes too long to resolve behaviour issues among students, especially reports of bullying.

While both of these revelations are somewhat surprising to him, he has decided to set these two areas as his focus points for professional development and annual performance review, in consultation with his supervisor.

Jason knows he has some work to do, and some challenges, but is happy to have a focus for his development as a leader, knowing that he has received good, honest feedback that will improve his capabilities in the long-term.

MAKE IT PERSONAL

The challenge for school leaders is to be critically reflective, to seek to continually grow in their insights into leadership and their skill in leading.

Ask yourself, to what degree do I:
- seek honest feedback from others, including those whose perspectives I might not particularly want to hear?
- have conversations with others about 'who I am' as a leader?
- listen to and reflect on feedback provided?
- allow feedback to influence the way I do my work?

FURTHER INVESTIGATION

Critically reflexive leadership

The concept of critically reflexive practice has philosophical similarities to critical theories. There are many scholars in this area who have influenced thinking in education, including Habermas, Foucault and Derrida. Explore how their perspectives might add to understanding of critical reflection, or offer another way of thinking that challenges your own.

From an educational perspective, critically reflexive practice has been described as moving beyond simply thinking about our experiences and actions, to explore the underlying values and assumptions that guided our perceptions of experiences and our actions. Such thinking should lead to more informed practice and, importantly, new ways of doing things (Cavanagh & Prescott, 2022).

Critically reflexive leadership, therefore, demands that we think about what we do and how we feel about things, primarily via a process of self-questioning (Cunliffe, 2016; Willis, 2019). We can engage in critically reflexive leadership in a variety of ways, including thinking about the way we judge people and situations; considering alternatives to the ways we respond to critical incidents; adopting a view of leadership actions as neither good nor bad, but influenced by context; finding out how others see our leadership behaviours; and comparing how we behave to our espoused values and beliefs. You can read more about reflexive practices in works by writers such as Cunliffe (2009; 2016), Alvesson et al (2017), and Evans (2021).

References

Abrahamsen, HN & Aas, M (2023). Deputy heads: Leadership and power in change? *International Journal of Leadership in Education*. DOI: 10.1080/13603124.2023.2258108

ABS (Australian Bureau of Statistics) (2022). Accessed 7 February 2024, https://www.abs.gov.au/statistics/people/education/schools/latest-release

ACEL (Australian Council for Educational Leaders) (2023). The ACEL Leadership Capability Framework. Accessed 13 November 2023, https://www.acel.org.au/ACEL/ACELWEB/Leadership_Academy/The_ACEL_Leadership_Capability_Framework.aspx

Admiraal, W, Schenke, W, De Jong, L, Emmelot, Y, & Sligte, H (2021). Schools as professional learning communities: what can schools do to support professional development of their teachers? *Professional Development in Education, 47*(4), 684-698.

AITSL (Australian Institute for Teaching and School Leadership) (2014). *Australian Professional Standard for Principals and the Leadership Profiles*. AITSL.

Alifuddin, M & Widodo, W (2022). How is Cultural Intelligence related to human behaviour? *Journal of Intelligence 10(3)*. https://doi.org/10.3390/jintelligence10010003

Allen, K-A & Boyle, C (Eds.) (2018). *Pathways to belonging: Contemporary research in school belonging*. Brill.

Alvesson, M, Blom, M, & Sveningsson, S (2017). *Reflexive Leadership: Organising in an Imperfect World*. Sage.

Amanchukwu, RN, Stanley, GJ, & Ololube, NP (2015). A review of leadership theories, principles and styles and their relevance to educational management. *Management, 5(1)*, 6–14.

Anderson M & Cawsey, C (2008). *Learning for leadership*. ACER Press.

Antoniou, P, Myburgh-Louw, J & Gronn, P (2016). School self-evaluation for school improvement: Examining the measuring properties of the LEAD surveys. *Australian Journal of Education, 60*(3), 191-210.

APAPDC (Australian Principals Associations Professional Development Council: now Principals Australia) (2003). Leaders lead: Major contemporary challenges. In APAPDC, *Leaders lead: Beyond the lost sandshoe*, 105–114. Commonwealth of Australia.

APAPDC (Australian Principals Associations Professional Development Council) (2007). *A school review checklist,* APAPDC.

Aparicio, J, Lopez-Torres, L, & Santín, D (2019). Economic crisis and public education. A productivity analysis using a Hicks-Moorsteen index. *Economic Modelling, 71,* 34-44.

ARG (Assessment Reform Group) (2002). *Research-based principles of assessment to guide classroom practice.* Accessed 7 February 2024, http://assessmentreformgroup.files.wordpress.com/2012/01/10principles_english.pdf

Argyris, C (1999). *On Organizational Learning (2e).* Wiley-Blackwell.

Arlestig, H (2007). Principals' communication inside schools: A contribution to school improvement? *The Educational Forum, 71,* 262–273.

Banks, GC, Fischer, T, Gooty, J, & Stock, G (2021). Ethical leadership: Mapping the terrain for concept cleanup and a future research agenda. *The Leadership Quarterly, 32.* DOI: https://doi.org/10.1016/j.leaqua.2020.101471

Barcan, A (1995). The state and education in Australia. *Educational Research Perspectives, 22(1),* 27–41.

Barker C & Coy, R (Eds), *The heart and soul of leadership.* AIM/McGraw Hill.

Barker, L (2002). Power, influence and action: making leadership work. In C Barker & R Coy (Eds), op. cit., 17–18.

Bass, BM (1990). From transactional to transformational leadership: learning to share the vision. *Organizational Dynamics, 13,* 26-40.

Begley, PT (1999). Values and Educational Leadership: An agenda for the future. In PT Begley (Ed.) *Values and Educational Leadership.* SUNY Press, 315-323.

Belardi, L (2010). Conflicts, conundrums and the greater moral good. *Education Review,* November, 16–17.

Belbin, RM (2010). *Management Teams: Why They Succeed or Fail (3e).* Butterworth Heinemann.

Bellah, RN, Madsen, RD, Sullivan, WM Swindler, A, & Tipton, SM (1985). *Habits of the heart.* University of California Press.

Berkovich, I & Eyal, O (2021) Transformational leadership, transactional leadership, and moral reasoning. *Leadership and Policy in Schools, 20(2),* 131-148.

Bezzina, M (2007). Moral purpose and shared leadership: The leaders transforming learning and learners pilot study. *The leadership challenge: improving learning in schools,* Proceedings of the 2007 Australian Council for Educational Research Conference. Accessed 22 September 2011, http://research.acer.edu.au/research_conference_2007/14.

Bezzina, M (2012). Paying attention to moral purpose in leading learning: Lessons from the Leaders Transforming Learning and Learners project. *Educational Management Administration & Leadership, 40(2)*, 248–271.

Blanchard, K & Shula, D (1995). Everyone's a coach: five business secrets for high-performance coaching. HarperCollins.

Bowler, WM (2006). Organizational goals versus the dominant coalition: a critical view of organizational citizenship behavior. *Journal of Behavioral and Applied Management, 5(3)*. Accessed 7 September 2011, http://www.ibam.com/pubs/jbam/articles/vol7/no3/jbam_7_3_2_organizational_%20goals.pdf

Boyd, S (2012). Key messages about change in schools: A literature scan for Sport New Zealand. New Zealand Council for Educational Research.

Boyle, C & Allen, K-A (2022). *Research for inclusive quality education: Leveraging belonging, inclusion, and equity.* Springer.

Breakspear, S, Sheahan P & Thurbon, D (2009). Talent magnets: attracting and retaining young teachers through courageous leadership and inspiring cultures, The Centre for Skills Development.

Bredeson, PV (1987). Principally speaking: An analysis of the interpersonal communications of school principals. *Journal of Educational Administration, 25*, 55–71.

Bridges, W (1995). Managing transitions: Making the Most of Change. Nicholas Brealey.

Brion, C (2021). Creating intentionally inviting school cultures during crisis. *Journal of Interdisciplinary Studies in Education, 10(1)*. DOI: https://ecommons.udayton.edu/eda_fac_pub/258

Brookfield, SD (1995). Becoming a Critically Reflective Teacher. Jossey-Bass.

Bruford, R (2008). Vision and leadership. *The Australian Educational Leader, 30(2)*, 25-27.

Bruster, BG & Peterson, BR (2013). Using critical incidents in teaching to promote reflective practice. *Reflective Practice, 14(2)*, 170–182.

Buchanan, DA & Badham, R (2003). Power, politics, and organizational change: winning the turf game. Sage Publications.

Buckingham, M & Clifton, DO (2020). *Now, Discover Your Strengths*. Gallup Press.

Bywaters, L, Parkinson M, & Hurley, J (2007). *Learn: Lead: Succeed — A resource to support the building of leadership in Australian schools.* APAPDC.

Caldwell, B (2006). *Re-imagining educational leadership,* ACER Press.

Caldwell, BJ (2023). Reimagining Schools and School Systems. Tellwell.

Caldwell, BJ & Harris, J (2008). *Why not the best schools?* ACER Press.

Caldwell, BJ & Loader, DN (2010). *Our school our future: Shaping the future of Australian schools.* Education Services Australia.

Caldwell, BJ & Spinks, JM (2008). *Raising the stakes: from improvement to transformation in the reform of schools.* Routledge.

Cavanagh, M & Prescott, A (2022). *Your Professional Experience Handbook (2e).* Pearson.

Center for Comprehensive School Reform and Improvement (2009). *School review process guide.* Learning Point Associates.

Cieminski, AB (2018). Practices that support leadership succession and principal retention. *ICPEL Education Leadership Review,19(1)*, 21–41.

Cliffe, J, Fuller, K, & Moorosi, P (2018). Secondary school leadership preparation and development: Experiences and aspirations of members of senior leadership teams. *Management in Education, 32(2)*, 85–91.

Cole, K (2019). Leadership & Management: Theory & Practice (7e). Cengage.

Collard, J (1990). The communication of principals. In J McMahon, H Neidhart, J Chapman, & L Angus (Eds), *Leadership in Catholic Education,* Spectrum Publications, 166–182.

Collins, JC (2024). BrainyQuote.com. Accessed February 7 2024, https://www.brainyquote.com/quotes/john_churton_collins_158489

Confucius, cited in the *Analects,* Book 16, 475–221 BCE.

Conway, J & Andrews, D (2016). A school wide approach to leading pedagogical enhancement: An Australian perspective. *Journal of Educational Change, 17(1)*, 115–139.

Cousins, N (1978). Editor's odyssey: Gleanings from articles and editorials by NC. In S. Schiefelbein (Ed), *Saturday Review,* 15 April.

Cox, E (2005). Adult learners learning from experience: Using a reflective practice model to support work based learning. *Reflective Practice, 6(4)*, 459–472.

Cranston, N (2000). A system level approach to school review and development. *The Clearing House, 62(1)*, 32–35.

Cranston, N & Ehrich, L (2009). Senior management teams in schools: Understanding their dynamics, enhancing their effectiveness. *Leading & Managing, 15(1)*, 14-25.

Cranston, N, Tromans, C, & Reugebrink, M (2004). Forgotten leaders: what do we know about the deputy principalship in secondary schools? *International Journal of Leadership in Education, 7(3)*, 225-242.

Cross, D (2021). The William Walker Oration 2021: Improving equity and excellence through school leadership, school culture and student wellbeing, Monograph No. 61. Australian Council for Educational Leaders.

Cunliffe, AL (2009). The philosopher leader: On relationalism, ethics and reflexivity – A critical perspective to teaching leadership. *Management Learning, 40,* 87–101.

Cunliffe, AL (2016). "On becoming a critically reflexive practitioner" redux: What does it mean to be reflexive? *Journal of Management Education, 40(6)* 740–746.

d'Arbon, T, Duignan, P & Duncan, D (2002). Planning for future leadership of schools: an Australian study. *Journal of Educational Administration, 40(5),* 468–485.

Day, C & Gurr, D (Eds) (2014). Leading schools successfully: Stories from the field. Routledge.

de Bono, E (1992). *Six Action Shoes*. Fontana.

de Bono, E (2005). *The Six Value Medals*. Random House.

De Nobile, J (2007). Cultural communication in Catholic primary schools, Paper presented at New Imagery for Schools and Schooling: Challenging, Creating and Connecting, the 2007 International Conference of the Australian Council or Educational Leaders, 10–12 October, Sydney.

De Nobile, J (2008). Democratic Communication in Catholic Primary Schools. Proceedings of the 2007 Annual Australian Association for Research in Education International Conference, Fremantle, November 25-29. Melbourne: AARE. http://www.aare.edu.au/07pap/den07070.pdf

De Nobile, J (2009). Supportive Communication in Catholic Primary Schools. Proceedings of the 2008 Annual Australian Association for Research in Education International Conference, Brisbane, November 30–December 4. Melbourne: AARE. http://www.aare.edu.au/08pap/den08791.pdf

De Nobile, J (2013). Upward supportive communication for school principals. *Leading & Managing, 19(2),* 34–53.

De Nobile, J (2015). The directive communication of Australian primary school principals. *International Journal of Leadership in Education, 18(2),* 239–258.

De Nobile, J (2018). Towards a theoretical model of middle leadership in schools. *School Leadership & Management, 38(4),* 395–416.

De Nobile, J (2021a). Leadership communication in Australian primary schools: The story so far. *Leading & Managing, 27(2),* 50–60.

De Nobile, J (2021b). Researching middle leadership in schools: The state of the art. *International Studies in Educational Administration, 49(2),* 3–27.

De Nobile, J (2023a). Neither senior, nor middle, but leading just the same: The case for first level leadership. *Leading & Managing, 29(1),* 9–20.

De Nobile, J (2023b). The search for first level leadership: Initial evidence from Australian secondary schools. Paper presented at the Annual International

Conference of the Australian Association for Research in Education, Melbourne, 26–30 November.

De Nobile, J & Bilgin, A (2022). A structural model to explain influences of organisational communication on the organisational commitment of primary school staff. *Education Sciences, 12(6)*, 395. DOI: 10.3390/educsci12060395.

De Nobile, J & McCormick, J (2008). Organizational Communication and Job Satisfaction in Australian Catholic Primary Schools. *Educational Management Administration and Leadership, 36(1)*, 101-122.

Deal, TE & Peterson, KD (2016). Shaping school culture: the heart of leadership (3e). Jossey-Bass.

Degenhardt, L & Duignan, P (2010). Dancing on a Shifting Carpet: Reinventing Traditional Schooling for the 21st Century. ACER Press.

Delaware School Leadership Taskforce (2001). Building successful school leaders in times of great change: report of the Delaware School Leadership Taskforce. Delaware Department of Education and University of Delaware.

Dempster, N (2009). Leadership for learning: a framework synthesising recent research. Griffith University, 6. Accessed 7 February 2024, https://research-repository.griffith.edu.au/bitstream/handle/10072/28012/57815_1.pdf?sequence =1

Dinham, S (2016). *Leading Learning and Teaching*. ACER Press.

DISC Profile (2023). *What is DiSC?* Personality Profile Solutions. Accessed 11 January, 2024, https://www.discprofile.com/what-is-disc

Drucker, PF (1995). *Managing in a time of great change*. Butterworth-Heinemann.

Drysdale, L & Gurr, D (2011) Theory and practice of successful school leadership in Australia. *School Leadership & Management, 31(4)*, 355–368.

Duignan, P (1994). Formation of capable, influential and authentic leaders for times of uncertainty.

Duignan, P (2003). Formation of capable, influential and authentic leaders for times of uncertainty. Paper presented at Australian Primary Principals' Association National Conference, Adelaide, September.

Duignan, P (2006). Educational Leadership: Key Challenges and Ethical Tensions. Cambridge University Press.

Duignan, P (2010). Influential leaders building deep, rich, engaging learning environments in schools. *Perspectives in Educational Leadership, 8*, 1–2.

Duignan, P (2012). *Educational Leadership (2e)*. Cambridge University Press.

Duignan, P (Chief Investigator) (2003). Contemporary challenges and implications for leaders in frontline human service organisations. ACU National.

Earley, PC & Ang, S (2003). *Cultural Intelligence: Individual interactions Across Cultures.* Stanford University Press.

Eden, D (2001). Who controls the teachers? Overt and covert control in schools. *Educational Management and Administration, 29,* 97–111.

Education Council (2019). *Alice Springs (Mparntwe) Education Declaration.* Education Services Australia. Accessed 7 February 2014, https://www.education.gov.au/alice-springs-mparntwe-education-declaration/resources/alice-springs-mparntwe-education-declaration

Ehrich, LC & English F (2024). Re-Imagining leadership roles beyond the shadow of bureaucracy. *Education Sciences.* In Press.

Ehrich, LC, Harris, J, Klenowski, V, Smeed, J, & Ainscow, M (2015). Ethical leadership in a time of increasing accountability. *Leading & Managing, 21(1),* 22–35.

Ellyard, P (1998). *Ideas for the new millennium,* Melbourne University Press.

English, AW (1995). *The double-headed arrow: Australian managers in the context of Asia.* Unpublished doctoral thesis, University of New England.

Etzioni, A (1993). *The Spirit of Communit.,* Touchstone.

Evans, P (2021). Reflexive Leadership in Context. Routledge.

Fitzpatrick, JL, Sanders JR & Worthen, BR (2004). *Program evaluation: alternative approaches and practical guidelines (3e).* Allyn & Bacon.

Forster, M (2009). Informative assessment: understanding and guiding learning. Proceedings of the ACER Research Conference — Assessment and student learning: Collecting, interpreting and using data to inform teaching. Perth. Accessed 7 February 2024, https://research.acer.edu.au/cgi/viewcontent.cgi?article=1040&context=research_conference

Freedman, I, & Somech, A (2021). Translating teamwork into school effectiveness: A systematic review of two decades of research. *European Journal of Educational Management, 4(2),* 109–127.

Fullan, M (1997). *What's worth fighting for in the principalship: strategies for taking charge in the principalship (2e).* Ontario Primary School Teachers' Federation.

Fullan, M (2010). Motion leadership: The Skinny on Becoming Change Savvy. Corwin Press.

Fullan, M (2013). *Motion Leadership in Action.* Hawker-Brownlow Education.

Fullan, M (2019). Nuance: Why Some Leaders Succeed and Others Fail. Corwin.

Gadman, L & C Cooper, C (2009). *Open source leadership.* Palgrave Macmillan.

Garfield, C (1986). Peak performers: The new heroes of American business. William Morrow and Company.

Goksoy, S (2016). Analysis of the relationship between shared leadership and distributed leadership. *Eurasian Journal of Educational Research, 65*, 295–312.

Goldsmith, M (2009). *Succession: Are You Ready?* Harvard Business Press.

Goleman, D (1995). Emotional Intelligence: Why it can matter more than IQ. Bloomsbury.

Greenleaf, RK (1977). Servant Leadership: A Journey into the Nature of Legitimate Power and Greatness. Paulist Press.

Grootenboer, P (2018). The Practices of School Middle Leadership: Leading Professional Learning. Springer.

Gross, MS, Haines, SJ, Hill, C, Francis, GL, Blue-Banning, M, & Turnbull, AP (2015). Strong School–Community Partnerships in Inclusive Schools Are "Part of the Fabric of the School....We Count on Them". *School Community Journal, 25(2)*, 9–34.

Gruenert, S & Whitaker, T (2015). School Culture Rewired: How to Define, Assess and Transform it. ASCD.

Grushka, K, McLeod, JH, & Reynolds, R (2005). Reflecting upon reflection: theory and practice in one Australian University teacher education program. *Reflective Practice, 6(2)*, 239–246.

Gurr, D (2010). Thinking about leadership for learning. *The Australian Educational Leader, 32(4)*, 15–20.

Gurr, D, Acquaro, D, & Drysdale, L (2022). The Australian context: National, state and school-level efforts to improve schools in Australia. In RM Ylimaki & LA Brunderman (eds), Evidence-Based School Development in Changing Demographic Contexts. Studies in Educational Leadership 24. Springer. (pp. 133-157).

Gurr, D (2015). A Model of Successful School Leadership from the International Successful School Principalship Project. *Societies, 5*, 136–150. DOI:10.3390/soc5010136

Gurr, D & Drysdale, L (2020). School leadership that matters. *Leading & Managing, 26(1)*, 54–62.

Guthrie, JW & Koppich, JE (1993). Ready, AIM, reform: Building a model of education reform and 'high politics'. In H Beare and WL Boyd (Eds), *Restructuring Schools: An International Perspective on the Movement to Transform the Control and Performance of Schools,* Falmer, 26–45.

Hall, GE (1974). The concerns-based adoption model: developmental conceptualization of the adoption process within educational institutions. Research and Development Centre for Teacher Education, University of Texas.

Hallinger, P & Hosseingholizadeh, R (2020). Exploring instructional leadership in Iran: A mixed methods study of high- and low-performing principals. *Educational Management Administration & Leadership, 48*(4), 595-616.

Handy, C (1995). The empty raincoat: Making sense pf the future. Arrow Business Books.

Hardy, I (2021). School Reform in an Era of Standardization. Routledge.

Hargreaves A & Fink, D (2006). *Sustainable leadership*. Jossey-Bass.

Hargreaves, A & Fullan, M, (1998). *What's worth fighting for out there?* Ontario Public School Teachers' Federation.

Hargreaves, A & Shirley D (2009). *The Fourth Way*. Corwin.

Hargreaves, D (1995). School culture, school effectiveness and school improvement'. *School Effectiveness and School Improvement, 6(1),* 23–46.

Harris, A (2009). Distributed school leadership: Developing tomorrow's leaders. Routledge/Farmer Press.

Harris, A (2014). Distributed Leadership Matters: Perspectives, Practicalities, and Potential. Corwin.

Heldsinger, S (2012). Using a measurement paradigm to guide classroom assessment processes. In CF Webber & JL Lupart, (Eds.), *Leading student assessment*, 241–261.

Hesketh, I, & Cooper, C (2019). *Wellbeing at Work*. Kogan Page.

Highfield, C & Rubie-Davies, C (2022). Middle leadership practices in secondary schools associated with improved student outcomes. *School Leadership & Management, 42(5)*, 543–564.

Hogan, J, Carr, D, & Down, B (2020). Transforming schools: All of the design, all of the time, all of the way through: The implementation of Big Picture Education in five schools. Murdoch University.

Holmes, JA (1927). *Wisdom in small doses*. University Publishing Company.

Hoy, WK & Miskel, CG (2013). Educational administration: theory, research and practice (9e). McGraw-Hill.

Hunjan, R & Keophilavong, S (2010). *Power and Making Change Happen*. Carnegie UK Trust.

Hurley, J (2011). Inspiring leadership; being and doing (even at a Wednesday afternoon staff meeting). Paper presented at Leadership on the Edge 2011 Senior Staff Conference, Association of Heads of Independent Schools Australia (AHISA), Perth, 18 April.

Jensen, UT, Andersen, LB, Bro, LL, Bollingtoft, A, Eriksen, TLM, et al (2019). Conceptualizing and measuring Transformational and Transactional Leadership. *Administration & Society, 51(1)* 3–33.

Johnson, LB (1964). The President's News Conference at the LBJ Ranch (28 November 1964). The American Presidency Project. Accessed January 10 2024, https://www.presidency.ucsb.edu/documents/the-presidents-news-conference-the-lbj-ranch-1

Karan, B & Angadi, GR (2024). Potential risks of artificial intelligence integration into school education: A systematic review. *Bulletin of Science, Technology & Society, 43(3-4),* 67–85.

Kolb, DA (2015). *Experiential Learning: Experience as the Source of Learning and Development (2e)*. Pearson.

Kools, M & Stoll, L (2016). *What Makes a School a Learning Organisation?* OECD Education Working Papers, No. 137, OECD Publishing.

Kovess, CB (2002). Passion. In C Barker & R Coy (eds), *The seven heavenly virtues of leadership,* AIM/McGraw Hill, 137–166.

Leaf, A & Odhiambo, G (2017). The deputy principal instructional leadership role and professional learning: Perceptions of secondary principals, deputies and teachers. *Journal of Educational Administration, 55(1),* 33–48.

Leithwood, K & Jantzi, D (2006). Transformational school leadership for large-scale reform: effects on students, teachers and their classroom practices. *School Effectiveness and School Improvement, 17(2).*

Leithwood, K, Sun, J, & Schumacker, R (2020). How school leadership influences student learning: A test of "The Four Paths Model". *Educational Administration Quarterly 56(4),* 570–599.

Levin, B (2010). 20 minutes to change a life?. *Australian Educational Leader, 32(1),* 22–23.

Lingard, B, Thompson, G, & Sellar, S (2016). National testing from an Australian perspective. In B Lingard, G Thompson & S Sellar (Eds), *National testing in Schools: An Australian assessment.* Routledge, 1–17.

Lipscombe, K, Tindall-Ford, S, & Lamanna, J (2023). School middle leadership: A systematic review. *Educational Management Administration & Leadership, 51(2),* 270–288.

Livermore, DA (2009). *Cultural Intelligence.* Baker Academic.

Loader, D (2003). "Mentor Partners" for principals—a step forward. In APAPDC, *Leaders lead: Beyond the lost sandshoe.* Commonwealth of Australia, 28–30.

Long, C & Writer, S (2023). Standardized testing is still failing students. NEA Today, 30 March. Accessed 18 January 2024, https://www.nea.org/nea-today/all-news-articles/standardized-testing-still-failing-students#:~:text=Key

Majors, MS (2012). The Majors Personality Type Inventory (Majors PTI) & Majors PT-Elements. ACER Press.

Marginson, S (1997). *Educating Australia: Government, economy and citizens since 1960*. Cambridge University Press.

Marsh, S, Waniganayake, M & De Nobile, J (2016). Leading with intent: cultivating community conversation to create shared understanding. *School Effectiveness and School Improvement, 27*(4), 580-593.

Maxwell, JC (2007). *The 21 irrefutable laws of leadership workbook: Follow them and people will follow you*. Thomas Nelson.

McGarr, O (2021). The use of virtual simulations in teacher education to develop pre-service teachers' behaviour and classroom management skills: Implications for reflective practice. *Journal of Education for Teaching, 47(2)*, 274–286.

McMillan, DW & Chavis, DM (1986). Sense of community: a definition and a theory', *Journal of Community Psychology, 14*, 6–23.

Miles, RE (1978). The origin and meaning of Miles' Law. *Public Administration Review, 38(5)*, 399–403.

MCEETYA (Ministerial Council on Education, Employment, Training and Youth Affairs) (1999). *The Adelaide Declaration on National Goals for Schooling in the Twenty-first Century*. MCEETYA.

MCEETYA (Ministerial Council on Education, Employment, Training and Youth Affairs) (2008). *Melbourne Declaration on Educational Goals for Young Australians*. MCEETYA.

Mizner, W (2022). The Institute for Habits of the Mind. Accessed 7 February 2024, https://www.habitsofmindinstitute.org/resources/hom-quotes/3-listening-understanding-empathy/

Moloney, R, Lobystyna, M, & De Nobile, J (2023). *Interculturality in schools: Practice and research*. Routledge.

Morgan, G (2006). *Images of Organization*. Sage Publications.

N MacNeill, N, Cavanagh, R & Silcox, S (2003). Beyond instructional leadership: towards pedagogic leadership, Paper submitted for presentation at the annual conference for the Australian Association for Research in Education, Auckland. Accessed 3 September 2011, http://www.aare.edu.au/03pap/mac03415.pdf

Neuschel, RP (2005). *The servant leader: unleashing the power of your people*. Northwestern University Press.

Nexus Strategic Solutions (2009). *The performance management and development of teachers in Australian schools: report to the teacher quality steering group*. Ministerial Council for Education, Early Childhood Development and Youth Affairs, Canberra.

Organ, DW (2018). Organizational citizenship behavior: Recent trends and developments. *Annual Review of Organizational Psychology and Organizational Behavior, 80*, 295-306.

Osterman, KF (2023). Teacher practice and students' sense of belonging. In T Lovat et al (Eds.), *Second international research handbook on values education and student wellbeing.* Springer, 971–992.

Owen, J (2006). *Program evaluation: forms and approaches (3e).* Guildford Press.

Owens, RG & Valesky, TC (2022). Organizational behavior in education: Leadership and school reform (12e). Pearson.

Patterson, K, Grenny, J, Maxfield, D, McMillan, D, & Switzler, A (2008). *Influencer: The power to change anything.* McGraw-Hill.

Peck, MS (1987). *The different drum,* Rider.

Peshawaria, R (2017). Open source leadership: Reinventing management when there's no more business as usual. McGraw-Hill.

Pont, B, Nusche, D, & Moorman, H (2008). Improving school leadership: Volume 1 – Policy and practice. OECD.

Pritchard, A (2003). Issues concerning succession planning for the principalship in Western Australian Catholic, state and independent schools, Australian Principals Association Professional Development Council, Adelaide.

Reid, A (2019). *Changing Australian education.* Allen & Unwin.

Richards, DJ (2010). What is organizational development?' Accessed 29 December 2010, http://www.odportal.com/ OD/whatisod.htm

Ridden, P (1992). *School management: A team approach.* Ashton Scholastic.

Ridden, P (2003a). *Sense of community in schools.* Unpublished doctoral thesis, Graduate School of Education, University of Western Australia.

Ridden, P (2003b). Foreword. In A Pritchard, op. cit.

Ridden, P (2011). *For Those Who Teach.* ACER Press.

Ridden, P (2018a). Reclaiming teacher assessment. *Australian Educational Leader, 40(1),* 49–51.

Ridden, P (2018b). Shaping culture. *Australian Educational leader, 40(4),* 36–39.

Ridden, P & Heldsinger, S (2014). What teachers need to know about assessment and reporting. ACER Press.

Rimfeld, K, Malanchini, M, Hannigan, LJ, Dale, PS, Allen, R, Hart, SA, & Plomin, R (2019). Teacher assessments during compulsory education are as reliable, stable and heritable as standardized test scores. *Journal of Child Psychology and Psychiatry 60,* 1278–1288.

Ritchie, M (2020). Succession planning for successful leadership: Why we need to talk about succession planning! *Management in Education, 34(1)*, 33–37.

Robertson, J (2016). Coaching Leadership: Building educational leadership capacity through partnership (2e). NZCER Press.

Robinson, V, Hohepa, M & Lloyd, C (2009). School Leadership and Student Outcomes: Best Evidence Synthesis Iteration [BES]. New Zealand Ministry of Education.

Rodwell, G (2020). The Australian Government muscling in on school education: A history (1901–2018). Routledge.

Rogers, W (2011). Cited in http://www.cmgww.com/historic/rogers/about/life_human_ nature.html, Accessed 1 July 2011.

Rossi, RJ & Hanson, KA (2002). *Community in the neighbourhood*, Centre for Community Research, American Institutes for Research.

Royal, MA & Rossi, RJ (1996). Individual-level correlates of sense of community: Findings from workplace and school. *Journal of Community Psychology, 24*, 395–416.

Ryan, J, Koelher, N, Cruickshank, D, Rogers, SL, & Stanley, M (2023). Teachers are the guinea pigs: Teacher perspectives on a sudden reopening of schools during the COVID-19 Pandemic. *The Australian Educational Researcher*. DOI: 10.1007/s13384-022-00577-6

Ryu, J, Walls, J, & Seashore Louis, K (2022). Caring leadership: The role of principals in producing caring school cultures. *Leadership and Policy in Schools, 21(3)*, 585–602.

Sachs, J (2003). *The Activist Teaching Profession*. Open University Press.

Sackson, E (2011). I'm Building a Cathedral … What Ed Said. June 23, 2011. Accessed 18 January 2024, https://whatedsaid.wordpress.com/2011/06/23/im-building-a-cathedral/

Sahlberg, P (2018). FinnishED Leadership: Four big inexpensive ideas to transform education. Corwin.

Sarros, J (2002). The heart and soul of leadership: the personal journey. In C Barker & R Coy, *The heart and soul of leadership*. AIM/McGraw-Hill.

Schaps E & Lewis, CC (1998). Breeding citizenship through community in school, *Education Digest, 64(1)*, 23–27.

Schaps, E (2003). How to build partnerships that work, *APPA Gold Matters, 4(1)*, February.

Schein, EH (2017). Organisational Culture and Leadership (5e). Jossey-Bass.

Schermerhorn, JR, Davidson, P, Woods, P, Factor, A, Junaid, F & McBarron, E (2020). *Management (7th Asia-Pacific Edition)*. Wiley.

Schon, DA (1983). The reflective practitioner: how professionals think in action. Basic Books.

Scoular, C, Duckworth, D, Heard, J & Ramalingam, D (2020). *Collaboration: Definition and structure*. Australian Council for Educational Research.

Seibold, DR & Shea, BC (2001). Participation and decision making. In FM Jablin & LL Putnam (Eds), *The new handbook of organizational communication: advances in theory, research and methods*, Sage Publications, 664–703.

Seligman, M (2011). *Flourish*. Random House.

Senge, PM (2006). The fifth discipline: the art and practice of the learning organization. Random House.

Sergiovanni, TJ (1984). Leadership and excellence in schooling, *Educational Leadership*, February, 5–13.

Sergiovanni, TJ (1994). *Building community in schools*. Jossey-Bass.

Sergiovanni, TJ (1996). Moral leadership: getting to the heart of school improvement. Jossey-Bass.

Sergiovanni, TJ & Green, RL (2015). The principalship: A reflective practice perspective (7e). Pearson.

Sharma, R (2010). *The leader who had no title*. Simon & Schuster.

Sharratt, L (2019). Clarity: What matters most in learning, teaching and leading. Corwin.

Shaw, EE (1978). Minutes of the 92nd Meeting, May 4–5, Nashville Tennessee, Association of Research Libraries.

Sheehan, P (2007) Flip: how counter-intuitive thinking is changing everything – from branding and strategy to technology and talent. Random House.

Smith L & Riley, D (2010). *The business of school leadership: a practical guide for managing the business dimension of schools*, ACER Press.

Spillane, JP (2006). *Distributed leadership*. Jossey-Bass.

Spillane, JP & Diamond, JB (2007). Taking a distributed leadership perspective. In JP Spillane and JB Diamond (Eds.) *Distributed leadership in practice*, 1–15. Teachers College Press.

Starratt, RJ (2004). *Ethical leadership*. Jossey-Bass.

Stephenson, J (2000). Corporate capability: implications for the style and direction of workbased learning. Working Paper 99–14, University Technology Sydney, Research Centre for Vocational Education and Training.

Stephenson, J (2003). Cited in P Duignan, Formation of capable, influential and authentic leaders for times of uncertainty, Paper presented at Australian Primary Principals' Association National Conference, Adelaide, September.

Sternberg, RJ, Siriner, I, Oh, J, & Wong, CH (2022). Cultural Intelligence: What is it and how can it effectively be measured? *Journal of Intelligence 10,* 54. DOI: https://doi.org/10.3390/jintelligence10030054

Stone, AG, Russell, RF, & Patterson, K (2003). Transformational versus servant leadership – a difference in leader focus. Servant Leadership Research Roundtable, October. Accessed 3 August 2011, http://www.regent.edu/acad/global/publications/sl_proceedings/2003/stone_transformation_versus.pdf

Symes, C & Gulson, KN (2008). Faith in education: The politics of state funding and the "new" Christian schooling in Australia'. *Educational Policy, 22(2),* 231–249.

Tang, J, Bryant, DA, & Walker, AD (2022). School middle leaders as instructional leaders: building the knowledge base of instruction-oriented middle leadership. *Journal of Educational Administration, 60(5),* 511–526.

Taylor, LA (2019). Negotiating discourses of curriculum and time: Tensions of humanizing and dehumanizing discourses in an urban elementary school. *Equity & Excellence in Education, 52(2–3),* 312–326.

Teo, I, Mitchell, P, van der Kleij, F, & Dabrowski, A (2022). Schools as community hubs: Literature review. *Australian Council for Educational Research.* https://doi.org/10.37517/978-1-74286-684-0

Tönnies, F (1887/1955). *Community and association (Gemeinschaft und Gesellschaft).* Translated and supplemented by CP Loomis, Routledge.

Torralba, F, Palazzi, C, & Seguro, M (2011). Coherence, the foundation of authority within organisations. *Ramon Llull Journal of Applied Ethics, 1(2),* 151–162.

Triandis, HC (2006). Cultural Intelligence in organizations. *Group & Organization Management, 31(1),* 20–26.

Tuckman, BW (1965). Developmental sequence in small groups. *Psychological Bulletin, 63,* 384–399.

University of New Hampshire (1999). *Community Profile Project.*

Vaida, S & Serban, D (2021). Group development stages: A brief comparative analysis of various models. *Studia Universitatis Babeş-Bolyai Psychologia-Paedagogia, 66(1),* 91–110.

Victorian Department of Education (2020). Performance and Development for Education Support Class Employees. Accessed on 1 February, 2024 from https://www2.education.vic.gov.au/pal/performance-development-education-support/print-all.

WAPPA (Western Australian Primary Principals Association) (2016). *Informative assessment, a position paper: An examination of research and response to the concerns of Western Australian school leaders.* WAPPA.

Washington, BT (1990). Cited in RA Hill (Ed.), *The Marcus Garvey and Universal Negro Improvement Association papers,* Marcus Garvey, Universal Negro Improvement Association, University of California Press.

Wattam, C (2021). Understanding the role of the middle level leader in New South Wales (NSW) Catholic secondary schools. *Leading & Managing, 27(2),* 39–49.

Wellington, P (2000). Instant Kaizen: what it is and how it works. In M Colenso (Ed.), *Kaizen strategies for improving team performance, 3–22.* Prentice-Hall.

Willis, P (2019). Retroduction, reflexivity and leadership learning: Insights from a critical realist study of empowerment. *Management Learning, 50(4),* 449–464.

Wise, AE (1977). Why educational policies often fail: the hyperrationalization process. *Journal of Community Psychology, 9,* 43–57.

Wooden, J (2004). Cited in ESPN staff, 'The wizard's wisdom: Woodenisms', June 4. Accessed 26 August 2011, http://sports.espn.go.com/ncb/news/story?id=5249709

Woods, PA & Roberts, A (2016). Distributed leadership and social justice: images and meanings from across the school landscape. *International Journal of Leadership in Education, 19(2),* 138–156.

Woolfolk Hoy, A & Hoy, WK (2008). *Instructional leadership: a research based guide to learning in schools,* Pearson.

Youngs, H (2017) A critical exploration of collaborative and distributed leadership in higher education: developing an alternative ontology through leadership as practice, *Journal of Higher Education Policy and Management, 39(2),* 140–154.

www.ingramcontent.com/pod-product-compliance
Lightning Source LLC
Chambersburg PA
CBHW062046290426
44109CB00027B/2752